Pelican Book A287
Byzantine Art

David Talbot Rice was born in 1903, and educated at Eton and Oxford. In 1925 he joined the staff of the Oxford–Field-Museum expedition to Kish, Mesopotamia, the next year excavated in Cyprus, and in 1927 became field director of the British Academy excavations in Constantinople. In the following years he travelled extensively in the Near East, including a journey to Mount Athos with Robert Byron, the results of which were published in their joint book, *The Birth of Western Painting*. At the end of 1927 he married Tamara Abelson, the author of another Pelican, *Russian Art*. Together they made journeys to the Near East almost every year until the Second World War, the results of their investigations being published in numerous articles, and in two books, *Byzantine Painting at Trebizond* (in collaboration with Professor Gabriel Millet) and *The Icons of Cyprus*. Mr Talbot Rice was lecturer on Byzantine and Near Eastern art at the Courtauld Institute from 1932, and in 1934 was appointed Watson-Gordon Professor of the History of Art at Edinburgh University, at the early age of thirty-one. He became a D.Litt. in 1938. He served in the Intelligence Corps throughout the Second World War, being awarded the M.B.E. in 1942. In 1946 he returned to Edinburgh, and has since made three expeditions to excavate at Constantinople on behalf of the Walker Trust of St Andrews, and has directed an expedition to clean some fine thirteenth-century wall paintings in Hagia Sophia at Trebizond for the Russell Trust. He organized the famous exhibition of Byzantine Art in 1958. He is the author of numerous books on Byzantine and Near Eastern art. In 1967 he was appointed Vice-Principal of Edinburgh University.

Byzantine Art

D. Talbot Rice

Penguin Books

Penguin Books Ltd, Harmondsworth, Middlesex, England
Penguin Books Inc., 3300 Clipper Mill Road, Baltimore, Md 21211, U.S.A.
Penguin Books Australia Ltd, Ringwood, Victoria, Australia

First published by the Oxford University Press 1935
Revised edition first published in Pelican Books 1954
Reprinted with revisions 1962
Revised and expanded 1968
Copyright © D. Talbot Rice, 1935, 1954, 1962, 1968
Illustrations copyright © Prestel-Verlag, Munich, 1964

Made and printed in Great Britain by
Jarrold & Sons Ltd, Norwich
Set in Monotype Times

Contents

List of Colour Plates

Frontispiece: Bargello, Florence. Ivory. The Empress Ariadne. *c.* 500

List of Maps

Preface to the Revised Edition

When the first edition of this book appeared in 1935 the student of Byzantine art was still working at something of a disadvantage. The spirit of Gibbon's thesis – Decline and Fall – still dominated historical thinking in England, if not on the Continent; the older school of Classical archaeologists were loath to recognize the Byzantine world or to accept its art as a valid field for study; the storm raised by the publication of Strzygowski's epoch-making work, *Orient oder Rom*, in 1901 was still raging, so that scholars were at variance if not actually at war, while the general public, nurtured in a taste for the Classical, and in the West in one for the Renaissance also, was hardly ready to accept the conventions of Byzantine art as a viable stylistic formula. True, the artistic quality of the works of the earlier phases had perhaps been accorded acceptance, but the originality and significance of the so-called Second Golden Age was still far from truly recognized, while even as recently as 1926 such ardent admirers of Byzantine art as Peirce and Tyler still only recognized the earlier phases and even wrote in their otherwise admirable little book, *Byzantine Art*, that 'The manner grows dry and hard before the twelfth century is half over and although a few new ideas are seen stirring in the XIII and XIV centuries, the story of Byzantine art really ends with the sack of Constantinople by the Franks in 1204' (p. 15). Such a view represented not only a singular lack of understanding of the nature and quality of Byzantine art, but also failed to recognize the validity of the life-work of one of the greatest scholars of the period, Gabriel Millet, to whose astonishing energy and zeal the recognition of the importance of the last phase of Byzantine art was principally due.

Early in the 1930s, however, the attitude both of scholars and of the art-loving public began to change. The Byzantine world had already been accorded a prominent place in historical study; the importance of the East Christian world, whether of Syria and Palestine, where the Christian faith was born, or of Asia Minor or the Caucasus, whence so many ideas in architecture have emerged, was beginning to be recognized; most of all the true quality of Byzantine art in the narrower sense, including that of the later ages, was beginning to be appreciated. Further, thanks to excavations and even more to the progress of cleaning and conservation, the field of study has been immensely enlarged. Few who have seen Kariye Camii at Constantinople, now that the mosaics have been cleaned and the paintings of the Pareccleseion uncovered, would not be prepared to class its decoration as a work of art able to stand beside Giotto's Arena Chapel at Padua – frescoed at almost exactly the same date. The paintings of Yugoslavia, especially those at Mileševa and Sopoćani, must take a primary place among the major relics of the thirteenth century; there is good work of the fourteenth century there and in Greece, and the paintings of Mistra are outstanding.

The role that this little book may hope to play in 1968 is thus rather different from that of more than thirty years ago. Then the author sought to launch a crusade, to convince an audience of the value of Byzantine art and of the joy to be acquired in its study. Now its aim is rather to serve those who seek for up-to-date information in a convenient form. This change of purpose was already recognized when a new English edition was prepared in 1953; it had become even more apparent when a third edition was issued in 1962 and a German one in 1964, with a large number of additional plates. Now in revising the text for a more lavishly illustrated English edition, a few further changes have been made, with a view to incorporating the results of recent research. Discoveries have moved rapidly since 1934, and they are continuing apace, so that this new edition will in its turn soon be out of date. But it is hoped that it may prove of interest to a new body of English readers and be of real use, in its new form, to a wide body of students.

Penguin Books wish to thank Prestel-Verlag, Munich, for allowing them to include the black-and-white and colour illustrations, as well as the maps by Alfred Beron, that were first used in the German edition, 1964.

1 Byzantium: the Historical Background

Byzantium, in the narrowest sense of the word, is no more than the ancient name of the Greek city-state which was founded at the junction of the Golden Horn and the Sea of Marmara in the seventh century B.C. The state survived until the year A.D. 330, when Constantine selected the site for the capital of the Christian world, in succession to pagan Rome. The new capital was called after its founder, but the old name has been retained by scholars to describe the Christian culture which was subsequently developed, and it now usually serves as a general term to designate all that was done and produced in the Byzantine Empire as a whole between 330 and the arrival of the Turks at the middle of the fifteenth century. Not all writers, however, agree as to its exact connotation. Thus Peirce and Tyler, in their books, use the term Byzantine to describe the works of the earlier centuries only, and regard anything subsequent to the thirteenth century as hardly worthy of the name, while modern Greek and Russian scholars stress the significance of all that was done after the ninth century, and hardly accept anything earlier than the sixth century as truly Byzantine. And in addition to these restrictions as to time, there are others as to place. Some scholars thus restrict the term to the art products of Constantinople and of such regions as were in close contact with the capital, while others use it more loosely, to describe works produced in Italy on the one hand or in Syria or even Armenia on the other. Such loose use of the term, however, only creates confusion, and a definite distinction must be made in early times between the products of Syria and Armenia, and even perhaps of Anatolia, on the one hand, and those of Constantinople and the associated areas on the other.

As far as date is concerned, it is probably best to restrict the term Byzantine to describe works of a distinctive type, wherein a fusion of the Classical and Oriental styles has already taken place; in some cases such a fusion was complete by the fourth or fifth century, in others not until the sixth or seventh. Indeed, it was this fusion that was the very essence of the Byzantine, elements from Rome, from the Hellenistic world, and from the East being welded together and tempered by the directing influence of the new Christian faith. From the sixth century onward the new art reigned supreme in the region of Constantinople, and its influence was spread very far afield, thanks to the dominating role of the capital. As long as Byzantine rule lasted, the art flourished. Sometimes there were long periods of conservative production during which little was done that was new or experimental; sometimes there were periods of more rapid progress; but in general the age was quite definitely not one of prolonged decline and decadence such as Gibbon described. Indeed, modern research has shown that there were a number of revivals, each a Renaissance on its own, which gave new life and spirit to art; each of them was, in its own way, no less experimental than the great Renaissance in Italy, which took place after the Byzantine Empire had come to an end. It may thus be confidently stated that there was a Renaissance in the sixth century, another at the end of the ninth, marked not only by a turning back to the models of the Classical world but also by the birth of a new spirit of adventure and experiment. There was a similar Renaissance in the twelfth century, coincident with the birth of the new art in the West which we know as Romanesque, and there was a third Renaissance in the fourteenth century, which took place quite independently of what was being done in Italy. And even after the fall of Greece, the Balkans, and Constantinople itself to the Turks around 1450, Byzantine art persisted, and even if it ceased to be a great style, some very delightful work in the old manner still continued to be produced by the subject peoples of the Balkans. In Russia, which retained its independence, art of an essentially Byzantine type survived until the reforms of Peter the Great in the late seventeenth century brought in new ideas from the West. The story of Russian art, indeed, really constitutes the last chapter in that of the Byzantine.

The exact nature of Byzantine art can really be properly appreciated only when the art itself has been fully examined; it can be more easily defined at the conclusion of a book on the subject than at the outset. In general, however, it may be understood to include all the work produced in the area which was ruled over by the Byzantine emperors when once the fusion of Classical and Eastern elements had been brought about by the governing action of Christianity. The fusion was gradual. In the fifth century it was achieved in individual instances only. By the sixth it had progressed further, and it was wellnigh completed by the middle of the century as the result of the encouragement of Justinian (527–65), perhaps the greatest individual patron in the whole story of art. The climax of the new style was reached in his great Cathedral of Sancta Sophia, which was to become not only the principal church of Christianity, but also the very centre of the cultured universe. It has survived to this day, though it was converted to the service of Islam soon after the Turkish conquest of Constantinople (1453). It is still not only the greatest monument of Byzantine art, but perhaps also the greatest monument of Christian art. Justinian, when he entered it, on its completion, exclaimed in awe, 'Glory be to God, who has found me worthy to finish so great a work, and to excel thee, O Solomon.' Solomon's temple has not survived. But no other faith, no other benefactor, has ever been responsible for a structure that can in beauty, in spatial conception, or in its religious atmosphere surpass the Church of the Holy Wisdom at Constantinople. But like the Faith to which it was dedicated, Sancta Sophia is not very easy of comprehension; it does not attract through superficial charm; it is not picturesque; it does not at first sight overawe by vastness of proportions. Only when one knows it intimately does one begin to appreciate its true character; only when one takes into account every balancing curve does one begin to appreciate the subtlety of its architecture; only when one has stood in its galleries for a considerable time does one begin to appreciate the immensity of the space that it encloses. If it does not attract at first, the building lingers in the memory, and its appeal is infinite and eternal. In this search for infinity lies the great distinction between Sancta Sophia and the Parthenon, between Byzantine and Classical architecture. The Parthenon represents the apex of finite perfection. Like all Byzantine art, Sancta Sophia has something indefinite, something unrealizable about it; it seeks for the infinite rather than the finite. It is perhaps this characteristic above any other that constitutes the hall-mark of Byzantine art, and it is that rather indefinite quality that it will be my aim to try to express and describe in the course of this book.

It was, then, to the old Byzantium that Constantine transferred the seat of the imperial court and government in 330. He did this in much the same way as the Turks transferred the capital to Ankara shortly after the First World War and adopted an entirely new policy of judicious Westernization. And just as Ankara, a typically Turkish hill town in the middle of Anatolia, served as an ideal centre for the development of a national policy, so was Constantinople in the fourth century an ideal capital for an empire which comprised within its bounds most of the civilized Nearer East, which took as its religion a faith which was at that date more firmly established in Syria and Asia Minor than it was in Italy or the West, and which, in the spheres of economics and politics, was more closely concerned with Arabia, Persia, and the lands north of the Danube than with the West.

Together with the imperial court and the paraphernalia of government, the imperial art of Rome was brought to the new capital, and during the next two hundred years this art was developed and transformed to suit the demands of the changing conditions and of a refounded state. The manners and customs of Rome were, indeed, on the whole more to the fore than those of Greece or the Hellenistic world. Latin was still retained as the language of officialdom, though Greek was the tongue of the street. Constructions in massive stonework of Roman type were used in architecture. Portrait statues were set up as in Rome, and ivory carvings and metal work remained closely akin to what had been done hitherto. Roman law and Roman statecraft dominated the scene. The city of Rome itself remained well-nigh as important as in the previous age,[1] and it was definitely more influential than the great Hellenistic cities of the eastern coastlands of the Mediterranean with Alexandria and Antioch foremost among them. Athens, though still a centre of philosophical study and thought, had ceased to be of any direct importance. The age which extended roughly from the time of Constantine to that of Anastasius I (d. 518) was thus predominantly Roman. Art and culture were not at this time Byzantine, though it was during these two centuries that the great fusion that was to produce Byzantine art was slowly progressing.

The most important personality of this age was probably Theodosios I, the Great (379–95), an administrator of ability, and a builder who did much to improve the capital. It was during his reign that the Olympic games were held at Constantinople (393), a number of antique monuments being brought to adorn the capital in honour of the occasion; they remained there as part of its permanent decoration. Under his successor Arcadius there was a renewal of friendly relations with Sasanian Persia, for the Emperor appointed the

Sasanian king Yasdegird I as the guardian of his successor Theodosios II.[2] This probably indicated artistic links with the East at the same time. The rule of Theodosios was enlightened; a university was established at Constantinople in 425, teaching being conducted both in Latin and in Greek; new walls were built for the protection of the city,[3] and other important buildings were founded. Slightly later, under Zeno (474–91) the most outstanding event was probably a squabble between the ecclesiastical authorities in Rome and Constantinople, the first signs of a dispute which was to rack Christendom for many centuries to come, and which was finally to result in the separation of the Western or Roman from the Eastern or Orthodox Churches. It was during the reign of the same emperor that the Bulgars, who in later days played so important a part in Byzantine history, first established themselves in the Balkans. The age was brought to a close with the death of Anastasius I in 518.

The second main period of Byzantine history, and the first age of purely Byzantine art, opened with the accession of Justin I, who founded a new dynasty in the same year. The first period had in Constantinople been one of formation, in Italy one of decline, during which the Goths harried the countryside and looted the towns. Now a return of prosperity came to the West, but it came to a great extent as the result of the progress made at Constantinople. Some two hundred years earlier Byzantium had been no more than the child of Italy. Now the role was reversed, the new capital had become the supreme centre of civilization, and it was from Constantinople that there emanated the power that could set her tottering parent on a sure footing. The role of Italy as a major creative influence in art and culture had come to an end almost with the age of Constantine, and in reality it was not so much the old heritage of Rome as the inspiration of Constantinople that was responsible for the superb buildings and mosaics set up in Rome and Ravenna during the fifth and sixth centuries. The very fact that the principal building form remained the timber-roofed basilica in both these cities is proof of this. However important the role of Rome may have been in developing the use of vault, arch, and dome in imperial days, the initiative had passed from Italy by the fifth century, and it was in Asia Minor and Constantinople that the vaulted basilica and the domed structure saw their full development as Christian buildings.

In the military and political spheres the age of Justinian (527–65) was a remarkably prosperous one. Italy, Dalmatia, and Sicily, taken by the Goths in the first age, were all restored to the Empire by 554; north Africa was conquered, and in 550 Justinian founded a province in what is now Andalusia, which remained under the control of Constantinople for the next seventy years.[4] In the East the Persians were driven out of Asia Minor, and the bounds of the Empire were established as widely as they had ever been in the days of imperial Rome. In the cultural sphere success was even more marked; the code of Justinian was brought into force, and it has ever since remained one of the world's most famous legal systems; Sancta Sophia was erected as the Cathedral of Christendom, and it has ever since remained one of the world's most important buildings; an essentially Byzantine architectural style was established, and a great deal was done both in the way of secular and religious construction; the first purely Byzantine mosaic decorations were set up, not only in Constantinople, but over the whole sphere of the Empire, from Sinai to Italy; they remain among the finest ever executed. Trade flourished, and embraced an amazingly wide field; long journeys of exploration were undertaken – the account of one of them, that of Cosmas Indicopleustes, who navigated to India, has since come to be recognized as one of the most important literary products of the period;[5] the age was one of exploration and adventure in every sphere. All the resources of a seemingly limitless treasury were, in fact, expended on this expansion, on the development of the Empire, and on the adornment of Christian shrines and imperial palaces in the capital and principal cities.

The brilliance and the vast expenditure of Justinian's day left a difficult situation to his successors. It was a task beyond the abilities of most of them, and it was made even more difficult by the rising power and energy of the Lombards and Franks in the West and of the Sasanian Persians, and later of the Arabs, in the East. In 570 the Lombards invaded Italy; soon after Slavs began to penetrate into the Balkans and Greece, and the physical type of many of the inhabitants of Greece today serves as proof of the depths to which this penetration reached. In 611 the Persians conquered Syria and took the True Cross away with them to Ctesiphon. These losses were soon afterwards made good to a greater or lesser extent, and Heraclius, founder of the Heraclean dynasty (610–717), not only freed Constantinople from the fear of a joint attack by Persians from the East and barbarians, headed by the Avars, from the North in 626, but also reconquered all the territories that had been lost in Asia

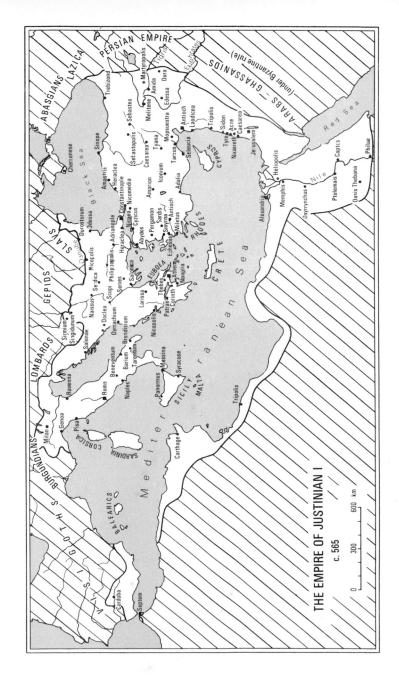

THE EMPIRE OF JUSTINIAN I

c. 565

0   300   600 km

PERSIAN EMPIRE

ARABS – GHASSANIDS
(under Byzantine rule)

ABASGIANS

LAZICA

Euphrates

Tigris

Martyropolis
Trebizond
Amida
Edessa
Melitene
Dura
Sebastea
Setastopolis
Caesarea
Tyana
Mopsuestra
Antioch
Laodicea
Tripolis
Sidon
Tyre   Acre
Nazareth   Caesarea
Jerusalem
Seleucia
Adalia
Heliopolis

Chersonese
Sinope
Amastris
Heraclea
Nicomedia
Constantinople
Nicaea
Cyzicus
Abydos
Amorion
Pergamon
Sardis
Iconium
Tarsus
Antioch
Smyrna
Ephesus
Miletus
Naupia

Black Sea

CYPRUS

RHODES

Red Sea

Nile

Memphis
Alexandria
Oxyrrynchus
Ptolemais
Oasis Thebana
Philae
Captis
Thebana

SLAVS

GEPIDS

LOMBARDS

Danube
Durostorum
Idessa
Adrianople
Philippopolis
Micopolis
Sergica
Scupi
Naissus
Serres
Salonica
Doclea
Dyrrachium
Larissa
Thebes
Athens
Patras   Corinth
Nicopolis
EUBOEA

Sirmium
Singidunum
Salonae
Brundisium
Tarentum
Barium
Beneventum
Naples
Messina
Syracuse
Panormus

BURGUNDIANS
Milan
Genoa   Pisa
Ravenna
Rome

SICILY

MALTA

Mediter   ranéan Sea

CRETE

Tripolis

CORSICA

SARDINIA

BALEARICS

Carthage

VISIGOTHS

Cordoba
Septem

19

Minor. A more serious foe, however, soon nullified his victories, for the Arabs, spurred on by the militant faith of Islam, conquered first the Persians and then the Byzantine provinces of Syria, Palestine, and Egypt. The first Islamic capital was established at Damascus in 634.[6]

About a century later the dynasty which had supported all these reverses bravely, if not gloriously, came to an end, and with the death of Theodosios III in 717 an age which was one of the most eventful of all Byzantine history was brought to a close. It is an age which is probably most familiar through its wars; in the sphere of culture and art it is less clearly distinguished from that of Justinian. Yet craftsmen and artists of the very first rank were still to be found, and the superb mosaics in St Demetrius at Salonica, in the Dome of the Rock at Jerusalem and in the Great Mosque at Damascus, though in the two latter cases executed for Islamic patrons, may be classed as Byzantine monuments, attesting the importance of the age in the world of art.

For the next century and a half the Empire was under the control first of the Isaurian, then of the Amorian, dynasties. It was a period of considerable interest in religious history, for the rulers of these dynasties forbade the inclusion of any figural works of art in the decoration of churches, and from 726 until 843 mosaics and paintings, anyhow in the capital, were restricted to formal compositions or symbols like the cross.[7] Numerous earlier monuments which depicted Christ, the Virgin, saints, or religious scenes were destroyed, while any new church decoration was strictly confined to non-representational subject-matter. In secular art, on the other hand, representation of the human form was still permitted, and it has been suggested that artists who would normally have worked for the Church turned rather to secular work, in any case at the beginning of the period, and that what they did in the decoration of houses and palaces played an important part in keeping alive the old Hellenistic and Classical traditions. There is, however, little evidence to support this theory. It would seem, rather, that many of the artists fled to the West, where they were employed on paintings and mosaics at Rome and elsewhere, and that the rebirth of the Hellenistic spirit after the close of Iconoclasm was due to a conscious revival of the old themes and ideas, rather than to the fact that they had been kept alive in secular art in the intermediate period. There is, in fact, little evidence to show that figural art in the secular sphere was any more important during the Iconoclast age than in the religious, though we do know that decorations of an oriental taste were in favour, and it was an Iconoclast emperor, Theophilus (829–42), who set up in the Great Palace the famous throne, supported by metal lions which roared and a metal tree with birds on its branches which sang.

The ideas directly underlying the Iconoclast movement have been variously interpreted by different authorities. Some regard the movement as directed primarily against the growing power of the monasteries, and the attack on the images as intended to screen an attempt at their dissolution. Others, most notably Bréhier, distinguish two main aspects of the movement, the question of image worship, which had undoubtedly become a danger owing to the tremendous reverence accorded to the painted representation of the divine or saintly form, and that of the legitimacy of religious art, which had been brought to the fore by the teaching of Islam. According to an old Eastern legend, which had been adopted by Islam, the artist would be required to give life at the day of judgement to the figures he had painted on earth, and it is likely that this idea had penetrated to the Byzantine world at this time along with a good many other Eastern ideas. Indeed, perhaps the most important characteristic of the movement, from the point of view of art, is its Eastern character, the Iconoclast emperors all being of Eastern origin, while the army, on which they depended for support, was principally drawn from the eastern provinces. When we remember the purely non-representational character which the religious art of Islam assumed at much the same period, the strength of the movement in the Byzantine world need hardly surprise us, and there seems every reason to attribute it to an underlying feeling which was both powerful and universal all over Hither Asia at the time.

In the political sphere the early days of Isaurian rule were marked by wars with the Arabs. In 718 Leo III succeeded in driving them out of Asia Minor – even from the very walls of Constantinople – and though frontier skirmishes continued, the Moslems were left powerless to undertake any very serious attack for a century or more. Soon after the commencement of Amorian rule (820), however, these skirmishes began to assume a more imposing character, and the attacks of the Arabs met with some success, especially at sea. In the reign of Michael II (820–9) the Byzantines thus lost Crete, and Sicily fell soon after. Nearer home the most serious threat was from a different source, for the Slavs moved against Byzantium, and in 813 the Bulgar king Krum penetrated right to the walls of Constantinople. But his successor concluded a thirty years' peace, and in 864 Boris, king of the Bulgars, was baptized and Christianity became the official religion of his country. More formidable than the Bulgars, however, were the Slavs of Russia, who made a first advance in 860. Yet here again Christianity triumphed, and slightly more than a hundred years later the Orthodox faith was adopted as the state religion by Vladimir, and Kiev became one of the most important outposts of Byzantine art and culture. Until the revolution of 1917, religious art in Russia remained faithful to the Byzantine tradition, and even today, in spite of the absence of political support, the Byzantine heritage still lives.

This age, which saw such wide-sweeping events along the eastern fringes of the Mediterranean and in the area to the north, experienced wellnigh equally important developments in the West. Most significant was the rise of a new culture in northern France and western Germany, the Carolingian, marked by the coronation at Rome of Charlemagne as Emperor of the West in 800. Though at a later age this event became clearly marked as a breaking point in the history of the Western world as a whole, its effect at the time was probably not very considerable, and it no doubt left the trend of life and thought at Constantinople but little affected. In the political sphere the Empire had been set on a sure basis by the strategical skill of the Isaurian rulers; in the realm of art the West was to look to the East, rather than vice versa, and for many years to come France, Germany, and even Italy were to borrow from Byzantium, even if their rulers were independent and their bishops accepted allegiance to Rome rather than to the Patriarch at Constantinople.

The period from the end of Iconoclasm (843) until the Latin conquest of Constantinople (1204) may, from the point of view of the history of art, be regarded as a single unit, for though there was naturally a vast deal of change and evolution in these 360 years, the period was marked by no sudden variation. It is usually known as the Second Golden Age, though some authorities prefer to restrict this term to the later ninth, the tenth, and the eleventh centuries only. Historically, however, the age may be subdivided into two main periods, those of the Macedonian dynasty (867–1056) and the Comnene dynasty (1081–1185). The whole age was one of considerable internal prosperity. Vast riches were at the disposal of the rulers; life was lived at a level of high luxury; palaces were built and

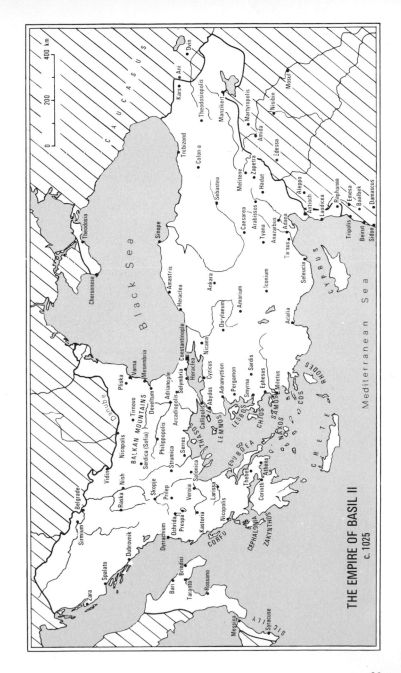

THE EMPIRE OF BASIL II
c. 1025

400 km
200
0

Dvin
Ani
Kars
Theodosiopolis
Manzikert
Martyropolis
Nisibin
Mosul
Colon a
Trebizond
Amida
Edessa
Sebastea
Melitene
Zapetra
Hadat
Aleppo
Raphanea
Emesa
Caesarea
Arabissus
Laodicea
Baalbek
Damascus
Tyana
Anazarbus
Antioch
Tarsus
Adana
Tripolis
Berut
Sidon
Seleucia
CYPRUS
Iconium
Ankara
Amorum
Amastris
Sinope
Atalia
Heraclea
Dorylaeum
Mediterranean Sea
Chersonese
Black Sea
Nicaea
Constantinople
RHODES
Heraclea
Cyzicus
Selymbria
Adramytion
Pergamon
Sardis
Smyrna
Ephesus
Miletus
SAMOS
COS
CRETE
Theodosia
Varna
Mesembria
Pliska
Adrianople
Abydos
Develtum
Arcadiopolis
Callipolis
LEMNOS
CHIOS
LESBOS
Tirnovo
BALKAN MOUNTAINS
Serdica (Sofia)
Philippopolis
Serres
Strumica
THASOS
NAXOS
EUBOEA
Nicopolis
Vidin
Nish
Skopje
Prilep
Veroia
Salonica
Larissa
Thebes
Athens
AEGEA
D.
Corinth
Nicopolis
Belgrade
Raska
Ochrida
Prespa
Kastoria
CEPHALONIA
ZAKYNTHOS
Danube
Sirmium
Dubrovnik
Dyrrachium
CORFU
Spalato
Zara
Bari
Brindisi
Taranto
Rossano
SICILY
Messina
Syracuse

CAUCASUS

decorated with the finest materials; churches were endowed with the richest of treasures. The most superb textiles, the most delicately carved ivories, the finest enamels, the most sumptuous metal work, the brightest and most exquisite mosaics, both on a large and on a minute scale, were produced. It is to this age that we owe nearly all the finest decorations and individual works of art that have come down to us, and which serve to illustrate for us the most typical specimens of Byzantine art.

The Macedonian rulers were, however, not only great art patrons. During their rule the bounds of the Empire were extended very considerably over the whole Near East. Thus during the reign of Romanos II (959–63) Crete and Cyprus were recaptured; in 969 Antioch was retaken from the Moslems; under Basil II (976–1025) Armenia and parts of the Caucasus were conquered, thus bringing the Empire into close touch with Persia and the East. But the main activities of this remarkable emperor were concentrated on suppressing the growing power of the Bulgarians, a task which he accomplished with such energy that he was given the nickname of Bulgaroctonos or Bulgar-slayer. The first Bulgarian Empire, which had been founded about 680, was brought to an end by Basil's victories in 1018. A Christian power since 864, Bulgaria had naturally learnt a great deal from Byzantium, and her culture was necessarily an offshoot of that of Constantinople. After Basil's victories this link became even more secure, for the land became a Byzantine province, and Constantinopolitan culture penetrated with renewed vigour. Bulgarian art was in fact more closely affected by Constantinople than was the art of many of the numerous portions of the Empire which never enjoyed national independence, such as Anatolia.

With the death of Basil II the period of territorial expansion came to an end, and reverses were suffered in the East owing to the arrival on the field of a new power in the form of the Seljuk Turks. The Seljuks, a tribe of central Asian origin, established their rule in Persia in the eleventh century and conquered Armenia about the same time. In 1071 their leader, Alp Arslan, secured a decisive victory over the Byzantines at Manzikert, and from that time onwards their power increased in western Asia; by the twelfth century Asia Minor was partitioned between them and the Byzantines. In the West, again in spite of an increase in Byzantine influence in south Italy,[8] the eleventh century was in the main marked by reverses. The republic of St Mark had by now established its independence at Venice, and the Normans, who had adopted the local Byzantine culture of Calabria and Sicily, had already become so powerful that the Byzantine emperor had to seek the aid of Venice against them, which was granted in return for commercial privileges. In 1130 the Norman, Roger II, was crowned at Palermo as king of Sicily and southern Italy. He shortly afterwards seized an opportunity to attack Greece, an event of some importance in the history of art, for he took back with him weavers, and established the silk-weaving industry in Sicily on a large scale. The products of the Sicilian looms remained definitely Byzantine in type, and it is today by no means easy to distinguish them from works which were produced at Constantinople or elsewhere in the Byzantine area. Though the Normans of Sicily were frequently at war with Byzantium, peaceable relations also existed, and it was to Constantinople that they turned for help in the decoration of the great churches that they founded at Cefalù, Palermo, and Monreale, the mosaics of which were to a great extent the work of Greek masters hired from Constantinople.

With central and northern Italy temporal relations were on the whole less strained, in that the area was not at war with the Byzantine world, but at the same time cultural relations were less close, for art there had begun to develop along distinctive lines of its own, and there was less desire to turn to the Byzantine world for inspiration and technical assistance. The absence of contact was also probably accentuated by the state of affairs in the religious sphere, for in 1054 the final separation of the Eastern and Western Churches took place, and it was actually from this date that the Orthodox and Roman Catholic faiths developed along diverse paths, though in actual fact the separation had been immanent for some centuries.

With France and Germany there were still important contacts, and the whole basis of Ottonian art owed a great debt to Byzantine influence, as did that of Saxon England farther to the West. Relationships with the West were especially close under the Comnenes, and Western travellers visited the East in small numbers as pilgrims and in larger bodies as members of crusading expeditions. From the Byzantine point of view the Crusades were almost as much of a menace as the Islamic enemy himself, but Alexios I (1081–1118) dealt with the menace of the First Crusade with considerable diplomatic skill, and he took advantage of crusading victories to increase his own dominions without subjecting the Byzantine troops to any great risks. But the crusaders regarded him as little less than an open enemy, and it was only with difficulty that friendly relations were maintained. The most serious bone of contention was without doubt the city of Antioch, a prize sought by the Western warriors, by the Byzantines, and by the Moslems alike.

This hostile attitude towards the Byzantines was not forgotten, and with the Second Crusade the cupidity of the Greeks was worked up as a war-cry to mask the greater cupidity of the French. The failure of the Crusade was ascribed to the treachery of the Emperor Manuel I, and Roger II, the Norman king of Sicily, attempted to exploit Western exasperation to abet his own designs on Greece and the Balkans. He planned a European coalition headed by France and the Papacy, at a time when both Hungary and Serbia were at war with Byzantium. Fortunately for Manuel, Conrad III the emperor of Germany remained aloof. Had he too thrown in his support, it is possible that the Latin conquest of Constantinople would have taken place half a century earlier than it did. Roger's daring design, however, came to nothing, and Byzantium, though not out of danger, was reprieved for a time, since failure had a discouraging effect on crusading enthusiasm.

Encouraged perhaps by the absence of Western armies Manuel I (1143–80) thought himself strong enough to attempt expansion on his own; he took Antioch in 1159. But in 1176 his army was routed by the Seljuks at Myriocephalum, and, in the opinion of Vasiliev, Manuel's failures at this juncture set in train the decline which even the zealous reforms of his successor Andronicos I were not able to check. Manuel was equally unsuccessful in the West, for Frederick Barbarossa proved a most serious enemy, and succeeded in checking Manuel's efforts to regain influence in Italy. Again in the Balkans the Byzantines were unsuccessful, for shortly after Manuel's death the Bulgars succeeded in establishing in 1187 a second independent Bulgarian Empire, with a capital at Tirnovo. In the same year Salonica was looted by the Normans of Sicily. Yet in spite of all these reverses in the political sphere, Byzantine art continued to flourish; the twelfth century was a period of great productive energy, and at the same time, of expansion, and one need do no more than mention the mosaics of Sicily, Venice, or Kiev to indicate the missionary character and the quality of the art.

But still, events were moving fast towards a climax. In 1187 Saladin defeated the army of the Latin kingdom in Palestine and retook

Jerusalem, thus occasioning a popular outcry in the West which was responsible for the launching of the Third Crusade. There was little to show in the Holy Land for the fierce battles and heavy losses of three years' campaigning, till Richard I of England seized the Byzantine province of Cyprus; in 1192 the Lusignan kingdom was founded there. If the failure to retake Jerusalem incited the religious to further effort, Richard's conquest of Cyprus served to encourage more material desires; it showed in fact that Byzantine territories offered a far more acceptable prey than the Moslem lands, and the Fourth Crusade, leaving the sacred cities of Palestine to the protection of fate, turned all its energies and resources to the conquest of Constantinople. In 1204 the blow fell, and the richest city in the world was subjected to one of the most extensive sacks of history. A Latin dynasty set up its rule in the city; Salonica became a second but minor Latin kingdom, and the members of the Greek ruling house established themselves as best they could in Epirus, at Trebizond, and at Nicaea.

Of the three minor Greek empires that were founded as a result of the Latin conquest of Constantinople that of Epirus was short-lived; that of Trebizond survived in full independence till 1461, though it was of purely local significance; that of Nicaea showed in the most striking manner those remarkable powers of recovery so characteristic of the Greeks. Theodore Lascaris, the first emperor of Nicaea, was a man of the strongest character, and he established his Empire on a sure and sound footing. His work was carried on by his successor, John III Vatatzes, who was able to reconquer much of Macedonia, including Salonica, which fell to him in 1246. In 1254 Michael Palaeologos assumed control, and was crowned in 1259. Entering into a treaty with the Genoese, who had by now challenged the Venetians as the principal trading power in the Mediterranean, he captured Constantinople in 1261, and reinstated the Empire, at the same time doing all that was in his power as the head of a somewhat restricted empire to patronize art, literature, and culture. These had been zealously maintained on the old basis throughout the period of exile at Nicaea. There is, indeed, reason to believe that the Nicaean age was important in the history of art, for few of the finer traditions of the great middle period of Byzantine art seem to have been lost, while certain new elements were introduced which served to revivify culture. Most notable of these was the introduction in literature in such new forms as fiction and lyric poetry.

The history in the Palaeologue age at Constantinople (1261–1453) is sad, but extremely romantic. The Empire was reduced to little more than Constantinople, Salonica, and the lands immediately bordering the Marmora, together with a few islands in the Aegean; towards the end the once proud capital was ruling little more territory than could be seen from its own walls. The days of the great emperors had passed; the imperial palaces were either in ruins or little better furnished than the poorer houses of the past; the lavish imperial patrons, with an immensely rich treasury behind them, were no more. Religious edifices were now the property of the people as much as of the Emperor, and the finest of them were set up in the smaller towns and villages rather than in the capital. The sumptuous treasures of Macedonian and Comnene times had mostly been destroyed or carried off as loot by the Latins, and the state was too impoverished to attempt to replace them. Such things had to depend on individual generosity rather than imperial patronage. Pottery supplanted vessels of gold and silver, painted decorations to a great extent replaced mosaics on the walls, panel paintings served instead of precious enamels; works of art, in fact, had to depend on their own intrinsic merits, without the added enhancement of fine or precious material. Yet the old ceremony, the old grandeur, survived, and records exist which show that the vast proportions of the court were to a great extent retained. The Emperor, though impoverished, was unable to live on an economic scale, and seemed incapable of reducing an expenditure which he was no longer in a position to maintain.

Historically the most important feature of this age was the gradual advance of the Turks from the East. The advance had begun at least two centuries before, but it was now accelerated, firstly by the westward pressure exerted on the Turks themselves by the Mongols, who were pushing outwards from central Asia (Hulagu sacked Baghdad in 1258), and secondly by the rise to power of a young and energetic tribe, the Ottoman, which gradually supplanted the older Seljuk dynasties in Asia Minor. The advance of the Turks was also assisted by the state of affairs in the Balkans, where Byzantine power was again threatened. Under the leadership of Stephen Nemanja (1168–96) the Serbians had succeeded in establishing an independent state, which reached the height of its prosperity under Stephen Dushan (1331–55). Dushan, after conquering all the western parts of the Balkans, even set out to try to capture Constantinople, but he died before reaching the city, and with his death the Serbian Empire crumbled. But its rise had considerably weakened the Byzantines, and with its fall a strong bulwark, which might have helped to resist the Moslems, was itself removed. This enabled the Ottoman sultan Murad to establish his capital at Adrianople, and in 1389 he and his son Bayazid utterly routed what remained of the Serbian power at the battle of Kossovo. Thus the greater part of Macedonia fell to the Turks. In 1393 Bulgaria experienced the same fate, for first Tirnovo fell, and then the rest of the country. In 1396 the Turks also defeated at the battle of Nicopolis a Franko-Hungarian crusade which had been assembled to resist the menace of their advance. In 1422 they laid seige to Constantinople. Serbia, Bulgaria, and other states had fallen before these new invaders from the East, but the Byzantine was still a sterner foe, and the first Moslem attack was repulsed.

But in 1430 Salonica was captured, and great advances were made westwards, a Christian league of defence, with Hungary as the leading power, being defeated at Varna in 1444. Practically all the Balkans were now in Turkish hands, with the exception of the great bastion of Constantinople. Mohammad II, who had by now succeeded to the Sultanate, was consequently able to concentrate all his energies on the capture of that great prize. For ten years the preparations went forward, till finally the great attack was launched in 1453, and the city fell after a defence which is one of the epics of history. With it the great Empire which had ruled Eastern Christendom for more than a thousand years came to an end. Athens fell in 1456, Trebizond in 1461, and all Greece soon after. Only in Rumania and in the powerful Slavonic state of Russia was Orthodox Christianity left as the official religion of an independent state. Yet the Christian faith of the minorities in Turkish lands remained, and it was an important factor which upheld Byzantine culture wellnigh down to the present day. Though it may be that little great art was produced after the last quarter of the fifteenth century, a great deal of minor work of definite quality must nevertheless be assigned to the Christian minorities throughout the Balkans. And the very considerable debts that the Turks themselves were soon to owe to their Byzantine predecessors must also not be forgotten. Just as, at the very outset of Islamic history, the Omayyads of Syria had founded their art and culture on that of an old Byzantine province, so the Turks, at the apogee of Islamic power, culled a very great deal from the Palaeologan heritage.

So ends the history. Yet in the story of art this last age is little less glorious than the epic of Constantinople's defence. The Byzantine Renaissance of the fourteenth and fifteenth centuries is a fact which can no longer be disputed, and modern research has shown that the revival that painting experienced at that time was paralleled to some extent in literature and philosophy, and, though the Greek world of this age never produced a Dante, it has been suggested that the writers might have progressed wellnigh as far had not the Moslem conquest put a stop to their work.[9] That they did produce the equivalents of a Giotto or a Duccio is, however, shown by a number of painted churches in Macedonia, at Mistra in the Peloponnese, and at Constantinople itself, where the lovely decoration of Kariye Camii was being set up at much the same time as Giotto was working in the Arena Chapel at Padua. Indeed, the importance of the revival in painting can hardly be exaggerated, and it is with the wall paintings of the fourteenth century and the panels of the fifteenth and sixteenth that the studies of many writers on Byzantine art have in recent years primarily been occupied. Yet the character of these paintings is still little known, for something of the old prejudice against later Byzantine art still lingers, and the erroneous belief that it was no more than a pale reflection, at second hand, of what was being done in Italy, is still to some extent prevalent.

2 The Geographical Basis of Byzantine Culture

The importance of Constantinople, first in the development, and subsequently as the main centre of Byzantine art, cannot be exaggerated, and this importance is to be attributed not only to the fact that Constantinople was the capital, but also to its geographical situation. A glance at a map will serve to throw this into perspective. The city stands on a promontory, at the very eastern extremity of Europe, and on the only direct sea route between Russia and the Black Sea to the north and Greece, Syria, Italy, Egypt, and all the rich and powerful area of the Mediterranean to the south. To the west stretches a broad peninsula of low hills, which present no very considerable barriers until the high mountains of Bulgaria are reached; and even here the valley of the Maritsa offers a clear route inland from the Mediterranean for some two hundred miles. Nowadays this is a somewhat desolate region, mainly as a result of the political situation; in Byzantine times it was a good deal more prosperous, as the ruins and sites testify; at a still earlier date it was even more intensively inhabited, if the numerous burial mounds of the last centuries before Christ that dot the area can be taken as an indication.

More important than the land from the point of view of communication, however, were probably the sea routes, to the south by way of the Marmora and its various ports and cities, to Salonica and Greece, and to the north by way of the coast of the Black Sea to Burgas and the maritime provinces of Bulgaria. These two regions, so far as art is concerned, appear to have been more closely linked with Constantinople than any other area. The links will be discussed as they arise; here it may be noted that Salonica was, throughout the Byzantine period, the second city of the Empire, and that her art was wellnigh identical with that of the capital, while in Bulgaria, both in the interior and on the coast, we find a series of very important buildings and wall paintings which are closely allied to those of Constantinople; and it may be noted that Constantinople on the one hand and the Bulgarian towns of Patleina, Preslav, and elsewhere have been the main centres of discovery of the finest types of Byzantine pottery.

To the east, Constantinople is closely linked with the coastal fringe of Asia Minor, the city being in reality as much a part of Asia as of Europe. But the links are here again closest with the coastal fringe rather than with the interior, for once more communication by sea played a more vital role than communication by land. Indeed, it is essential, so far as art is concerned, to make a distinction between the coastal belt of Asia Minor, where stand the ruins of the great Greek and Hellenistic cities like Troy, Pergamon, Priene, or Ephesus, and the upland of Anatolia, a vast plateau which gradually rises eastwards, until the mountains of Armenia are reached. And this is the highest and most severe region of western Asia, the passes to north and east being under snow for a good eight months of every year, while even those to the south are not easily practicable in winter. Thus trade between Constantinople and the lands of the east, notably Persia and Mesopotamia, was probably more easily carried on by way of the sea route to Syria and the river valley of the Euphrates than it was along the more direct route across Asia Minor. An alternative route, by way of the southern coast of the Black Sea to Trebizond, and thence overland, was used, however, for trade with Persia. The coastal fringe of the Black Sea, though generally speaking narrow, was again cut off from the hinterland, and its natural links were by sea with Constantinople on the one hand and Trebizond on the other, rather than with the Anatolian plateau to the south.

Thus, though the artistic influence of Constantinople was quite extensive along the coastal fringes of the Black Sea and the Aegean, it was not much exercised on the central plateau of Anatolia. Here the current seems to have run rather in an opposite direction, the plateau being shaped rather like a funnel, with its narrow end at Constantinople, and its wider end extended along the frontiers of Persia and Mesopotamia. Anything introduced into the open end tended to converge on the Constantinopolitan corner, and in Byzantine, just as in Classical and pre-Classical times, a continuous pressure was exercised in this way. Early waves of migration, driven forward by some impulse from Asia, pressed across Anatolia, crossed

St George, Salonica. Mosaic. Head of Onesphiros, the martyr. *c.* 400

either by the Bosphorus or the Hellespont, and exercised a wide-sweeping effect on Macedonia; later waves, though bottled up for a time in Anatolia by the concentration of Byzantine power at Constantinople, eventually crossed in just the same way. And in the sphere of art a great deal of influence apparently travelled along the same route, though like the later waves of invaders, Constantinople for a time afforded a bastion, and the stream was deflected by it, so that Greece in the south and the Balkans farther to the north were more closely linked with Anatolia than was Constantinople itself. Gabriel Millet has shown how important these links between Greece and Anatolia were in the sphere of architecture,[1] but the Anatolian contribution to the development of other arts in the Byzantine world as a whole and in Greece in particular yet remains to be studied.

In the last centuries before Christ the focus of culture was moving gradually westwards and northwards. Greece had supplanted Mesopotamia, Persia, and Egypt; Rome had supplanted Greece, and a new and more clement continent, Europe, was, from early Christian times, to supplant the old continent of Asia as a centre of the development of culture. Yet the old Eastern world had by no means lost all its importance. Antioch, Alexandria, and the other fine cities of the Aegean were still of great size and wealth, and were vital centres of art and culture, which could not be disregarded. If it was inevitable, as a result of the unwritten laws of cultural change, that some new centre had to supplant Rome, it was still essential, as a result of the more tangible laws of economics and sociology, that this new centre should remain in contact with these great east Mediterranean cities. And Constantinople, with its equable climate, its superb situation, its rich hinterland, and its open, easy sea routes, seemed to answer every demand. When Constantine transferred his capital to the shores of the Golden Horn he chose a site which had all the economic advantages of a great trading city like Antioch, without any of the disadvantages accruing to its essentially Asiatic character. His new capital was so placed that it could make itself mistress of the East without losing contact with the West; it could stand aloof, yet at the same time maintain contact; it could open wide its gates to the East, and at the same time retain its European character. And if Constantinople was preferable to Antioch, it was still more preferable to the other cities. Alexandria thus lay isolated, on the fringe of the Empire; the site of Ephesus offered no outstanding geographical advantages; Nicomedia, which had been preferred by Diocletian, was nevertheless essentially provincial; Athens was too much a stronghold of old ideas. Nor was there any other city so admirably placed from the strategic point of view, as centre of a great Empire whose territory extended as far to the east as it did to the west, nor as admirably placed from the tactical point of view, with water on two sides of a great triangle, so that only a third of the city's periphery had to be defended against a threat of attack from the land. Indeed, the mightiness of the role that Constantinople played as bulwark of the West and apex of the East for so many centuries was in no small degree the result of its geographical situation.

The distribution of the other great cities of the Empire serves to bring out the essentially maritime basis of its structure to which reference has already been made. In the south there was Egypt, lost to the Moslems in the seventh century, though until then of very considerable importance. It had been the granary of Rome, and it remained a great commercial centre until the decline of the Empire after Justinian; the role that its principal city, Alexandria, was to play in the formation of Byzantine art was outstanding. In the north, almost equally far removed, were the colonies of the Chersonese on the north coasts of the Black Sea. They too were important commercially, though as a centre of a trade which was primarily in luxuries like furs their role was less vital. In the west, again, the greater part of Italy was of the first importance in early times; and even at a later date Sicily and Venice were never completely cut off. Of the role of Ravenna as a province of Byzantine art a great deal will have to be said, and in medieval times southern Italy was wellnigh equally important, though its character was more provincial. Finally the islands of the Aegean must be noted, for though much of their art was provincial in character, it was not always so, as the magnificent mosaics of the Nea Moni on Chios serve to prove.

It is impossible in a short survey to speak individually of every city, but a few additional outstanding names may be mentioned. Thus in early times the holy cities, Jerusalem and Bethlehem especially, were not only of religious significance, but were also important in the sphere of art, because endowed with magnificent churches by Constantine and his successors. Even more flourishing was northern Syria, and though it is today a desert as the result of desiccation, whole towns of magnificent stone-built architecture still survive there, to attest the former importance of the region, though they are today deserted and uninhabited. The cities of the Mesopotamian fringe, Edessa, Urfa, Nisibin, and others of lesser significance, were perhaps more important as frontier posts than as centres of art, but it may be that when the day comes to explore them they will prove to be of considerable interest; if not as rich and as important as Antioch, they probably imbibed something of the prosperity and culture of this great city, and flourished along with it until the Moslem conquests of the seventh and following centuries.

As already stated, the role of Asia Minor was twofold, and the coastal area must be clearly distinguished from the upland. It is the towns of the former that we know best, and to their number others were added as Byzantine civilization developed, notably Antalia, which was perhaps more important in mid-Byzantine times than the more famous Greek cities like Pergamon or Priene. But the towns of the upland, though now virtually deserted, once exercised a considerable influence on architectural and artistic developments; the famous Bin bir Kilisse, or Thousand and One Churches, may be noted among the many. There were perhaps not as many as a thousand churches there, but the ruins of a very large number survive, and they serve to attest the vital role that the whole of the region played in the story of architecture. Its part in the story of painting was no less considerable, and the painted caves of Latmos or the rock-cut churches of Cappadocia are not only extremely interesting in themselves, but are also important because of the influence that the monastic art of the poor communities of the region exercised on the development of painting in more prosperous areas all over Greece and the Balkans, and even, probably, in the capital itself. Nor can such towns as Nicaea and Nicomedia be passed without mention, for they were a good deal more important in later Byzantine times than they were in Roman days; it is only necessary to remember that the former was the centre in which the Nicene creed was composed. Of the towns of the Black Sea coast, Trebizond was certainly the most outstanding, first as the main station on the northern trade route to the East, and later as the capital of a small independent Empire which was to outlive Constantinople itself as an independent Christian power.

In Europe the most important city of pure Byzantine culture, both in early and in later times, was undoubtedly Salonica; it still remains one of the richest centres where Byzantine architecture and mosaics can be studied. Elsewhere in Greece the most active centres of

Principal sites of Byzantine
works of art

0   200   400 km

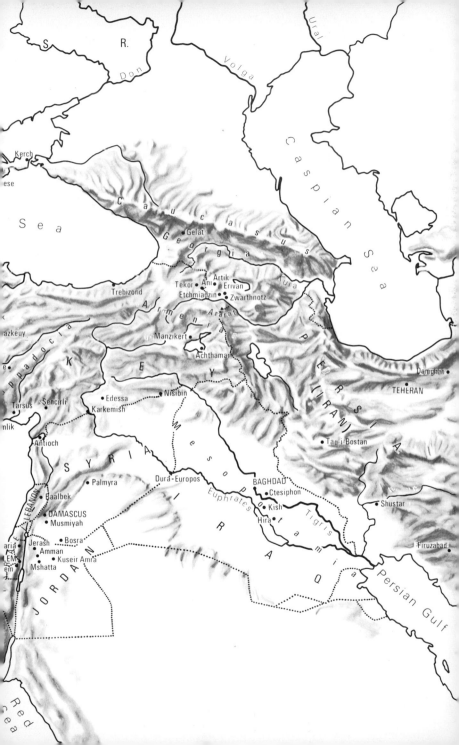

architectural development and of artistic production were probably the monasteries rather than the cities; Hosios Lukas, near Delphi, Megaspeleion in the Peloponnese, and, above all, the peninsula of Mount Athos were thus all outstanding, and Athos remains to this day the one surviving stronghold of Byzantine culture and Byzantine life, alike unaffected by Moslem domination and Western progress.

The area that now composes the Balkans comes on to the scene at a comparatively late date, but both in Bulgaria and in what is now Yugoslavia there are important remains, more especially in the way of architecture and painting. Mesembria, Tirnovo, Preslav, and Sofia in the former country may all be noted; all were considerable towns, and all were centres of art and culture, whether the country was at the time independent or whether it was under Byzantine rule. In Yugoslavia, on the other hand, it was primarily in the monasteries that the best work was done, and there are a considerable number of them that survive, dating from the thirteenth century onwards; they contain both churches and wall paintings of the very highest quality.

Finally a word must be said of Italy, for in early times Ravenna, and to some extent Rome, and in later times Sicily and Venice and its region were the centres of a more or less completely Byzantine culture and art. The early mosaics and paintings of Rome are thus probably as much Byzantine as were those produced in the East, and there is reason to believe that in Iconoclast times artists who fled from Constantinople because of the ban on figural art were given commissions to work there by some of the popes; many of the mosaics of the late eighth and ninth centuries which exist in Rome are thus markedly Byzantine in style, notably those in the chapel of St Zeno in Sta Prassede. Ravenna was virtually a Byzantine city, there were Byzantine mosaics in Milan, and numerous other towns were centres of more casual Byzantine influence, for example Monte Cassino in the south. The close relationship to Byzantine art of Benedictine painting, as practised for example at Sant'Angelo in Formis near Capua, must also be noted. Similar influences extended into northern Italy and France, but they have little significance from the geographical point of view.

A few additional factors of a geographical character which may also have exercised an influence on artistic developments of one sort or another may also be noted. In architecture, for instance, there were two main methods of construction, in brick and in stone. Stone was in general procurable in the highlands, but it was not by any means always of the same quality, and brick was quite often employed in preference to it, even in stone-producing areas, either because the stone was too poor to provide the finish required by the architects, or because the architect came from elsewhere and preferred to build in a material which he knew. It is thus the poorer buildings that are most affected by locality in this respect; only a rich patron could afford to bring his architect and his material from elsewhere. But even so, brick buildings in the uplands of Anatolia are few and far between, and in Syria and Armenia brick was never used at all. In Constantinople the case was somewhat different, for there brick and stone were very frequently used together, a number of courses of brick alternating with a number of courses of stone in the same wall. Basically the division there was primarily a chronological one, but it was not very rigid, and it is perhaps safer to say that stone was most favoured in early times and brick in later ones.

Another interesting factor is that of the influence exercised on sculpture by the character of the material available. Thus the soft limestone of the Nile valley which was habitually used by the Copts favoured, and perhaps even helped to bring into being, that rather florid, loose style which became characteristic of Coptic work, first in stone and later in ivory, while the brilliant, rather soapy marble of the quarries of the Proconnesos permitted a precise, clear treatment, and favoured those silhouette-like effects of deep shadow and brilliant light which were so strikingly developed by the sculptors employed by Justinian, not only at Constantinople, but also in all regions which were in contact with the capital. There is, however, reason to believe that the marble from the quarries of the Proconnesos was much exported, and in many cases it would seem that the carving was done on the spot, and capitals and closure slabs, the more usual forms of sculpture from the sixth century onwards, were probably carried long distances in a finished or partly finished state.

This influence of material, and hence of environment, is an important factor in the study of any particular art, though it is frequently neglected. It is most clearly to be seen in architecture or sculpture, where the material is a fundamental element: but a similar influence was doubtless brought to bear on other arts, even if it was exercised in a more esoteric manner. Thus the arid deserts of Arabia and the nature of the life that they necessitated probably exercised a considerable effect on the development of that type of art which is usually termed the Semitic, while the beauty of the surroundings and the ease of life of the eastern Mediterranean were similarly responsible for the art centred there which we term Hellenic. The former was a harsh, severe art, seeking for expression or inner meaning rather than for pleasing forms or delightful surfaces; the latter was an elegant, delicate, refined art, seeking an imaginary ideal rather than truthful realism. But these are problems of aesthetics which cannot be entered upon here; the reader may inquire into them for himself if he will. Let it be stressed, however, that an understanding of the build and form of a land, a knowledge of the routes of communication, and an idea of the character of the natural resources which any area has to offer are all of them factors which should be considered at the outset by every historian of art in the course of his examination of a particular area or a particular civilization.

3 The Origins of Byzantine Art

No civilization passes without leaving some heritage behind it; no civilization of any advanced degree is born without antecedents. To consider in turn each of the predecessors of Byzantine culture which did or could affect its development, and to give a general outline of the character of the contribution of each is the aim of this chapter. The reader will thus conceive some idea of the nature of the various sources which exercised an effect on Byzantine art, both in the earliest days, and also later, when the distinguishing characteristics of the Byzantine style had already been formulated. Yet, however important these elements culled from external sources may be – and of recent years the authorities have been very much concerned with stressing the role of one area at the cost of the others – it must always be borne in mind that the chief glory of creating a style or producing an object has always been the task of the particular culture to which it belongs. Thus a Byzantine ivory may be fundamentally Hellenistic or Roman or Eastern in character – it may exemplify the idealistic spirit of Greek art; it may follow the more matter-of-fact canons of the Roman style; it may be conceived in the expressive manner of the Semitic world, or show formal, non-figural ornament of a Persian or Islamic character – yet there is beyond such factors something about the ivory which makes it first and foremost Byzantine. It is the definition of the true nature of this quality that presents itself as one of the foremost problems that concern the art historian. But even when he is thoroughly familiar with every facet of the style with which he is concerned, his appreciation must remain incomplete and his understanding limited unless he also have some knowledge of what had gone before and of what was going on at the same time in adjacent and related areas.

The cultures that concern us in respect of the origins of Byzantine art fall into six principal groups, namely Greece and the Hellenistic

1 Agios Eleutherios (Little Metropolis), Athens. Detail of gable with built-in panels from elsewhere

world, Rome and Italy, Asia Minor, Syria and the Semitic East, western Persia (Iran) and lower Mesopotamia (Iraq), and finally north-eastern Persia, or what Strzygowski has termed Altai-Iran.[1]

1. Greece and the Hellenistic World

The story of the dissemination of Greek culture all over the Nearer East as a result of the conquests of Alexander falls outside the scope of this survey, though the effects must concern us, for the extent to which elements that were basically Greek were spread as far to the east as India at this time was very considerable, and these

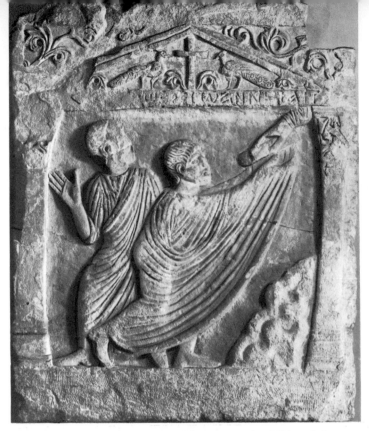

2 The Archaeological Museum, Istanbul. Tomb carving. Fifth or sixth century

elements at a later date found their way back to the Byzantine world
in an indirect manner by way of Persia and Syria. More important,
however, was the role played by the Greek cities of the Mediterranean coastlands, for they were a stronghold of Greek culture and
all of them were large and prosperous at the time of the foundation
of Byzantium. In these towns the pure Greek culture of the old
city-states had been maintained, and as Greece itself gradually
declined in power and influence, and assumed the role of a conserver
rather than a creator so far as art was concerned, so the great cities
of Asia Minor, Syria, and Egypt progressed, keeping up a live and
vital culture of their own. As time went on this culture tended to
become rather less purely Greek, for it was penetrated to a greater
or lesser degree by Oriental elements. But nevertheless the basis of
idealism that characterized Greek art was definitely maintained in

3 Archaeological Museum, Athens. Ivory carving. Mycenean. Confronted sphinxes. *c.* 1400 B.C.

all of them until, and in many places long after, the dawn of the Christian era.

It must of course be borne in mind that from around the end of the third century B.C. these cities had formed a part of the Roman Empire, and they had become to some degree affected by the intrusion of Roman elements in art and culture. Some writers would even insist that by the third century of the Christian era there was little in the make-up of their life that was not really more Roman than it was Greek,[2] with the possible exception of the Greek language, which was most generally spoken by their inhabitants. But such conclusions are extreme, and are not borne out by the evidence. It would rather seem that much that was basically Greek was preserved, and of the

4 Agios Eleutherios (Little Metropolis), Athens. Detail of built-in panels of diverse origin. Tenth to eleventh centuries

new ideas in art that were being invented throughout the first three centuries A.D., quite a number would seem to be essentially the products of the Greek rather than of the Roman genius. Thus the narrative or continuous method in the depiction of scenes in art was probably a Hellenistic rather than a Roman system; a great deal of the ornament most commonly employed in sculpture was in essence entirely Greek; the use of large circular domical buildings as martyria was very probably common in the Greek world before they were further developed in the Roman, and the idealistic style in the depiction of human forms was again essentially a part of the Greek rather than the Roman outlook. It is, no doubt, an exaggeration to describe Roman art as no more than Greek art in its imperial phase, but it is equally wrong to denigrate the power of the Greek spirit in the late Classical or early Christian age.

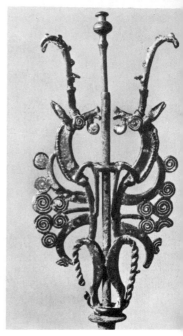

5 Archaeological Museum, Ankara. Stone relief. Hittite, from Kara Tepe. Confronted rams. 800 B.C.

6 Luristan (Persia). Bronze affronted rams and Tree of Life. Eighth to seventh century B.C.

2. *Rome and Italy*

Roman culture, like that of the Hellenistic cities, was based in the main on that of Greece, but by the beginning of the Christian era it had taken on a definitely individual form, owing to local influences. Yet, though Rome was the capital of the civilized world, she did not, during her prosperity, impose her art lock, stock, and barrel upon any but her more immediate dependencies. When Constantine transferred his capital to the shores of the Marmora in 330 he took with him all the panoply of an imperial court. Buildings were constructed in the Roman manner, to answer Roman demands; statues, which were purely Roman in appearance and Roman in spirit, were set up in public places; Roman law, the Latin language, and indeed every other aspect of Roman culture were imposed there. The city was the new Rome in all its superficial aspects. Two strong forces, however,

7 Baptistery of the Orthodox, Ravenna. Stucco reliefs. *c.* 450

opposed the complete assimilation of Roman culture by Byzantium, namely geography and race. Thus by the sixth century we find that the Greek tongue had replaced Latin in general usage, and before the ninth century the latter had been entirely forgotten. In art affairs were closely parallel, and purely Roman forms, such as the imperial portrait bust, or the conception of Christ as a youthful, beardless figure, were similarly abandoned. Thus, though Roman influence was considerable, it was by no means the only influence that went to the making of Byzantine art. Even if Strzygowski's theories as to the predominant importance of Oriental influence can be shown to be exaggerated, there is no reason why the contribution of Rome should be overstressed in opposition.

8 Agios Eleutherios (Little Metropolis), Athens. Eagle attacking hare. Relief on outer wall. Twelfth century

9 Sancta Sophia, Trebizond. Round marble plaque. Eagle attacking hare. Now at Salonica. Thirteenth century

10 Church, Achthamar (Armenia). Eagle attacking hare. Relief on the outer wall. 915–21

3. Asia Minor

It has already been noted that the coastal belt and the highlands of Asia Minor form two distinct regions, but in art it is necessary to go

11 Cifte Minara Medrese, Erzurum. Seljuk sculpture. Tree of Life and lions. 1253

even further and distinguish between the Hellenistic art of the coastal cities and the indigenous art of the uplands. The culture of the uplands was founded upon very long antecedents, established in the land, so far as one can tell, even before the days of the Hittites.[3] We know little of this early Anatolian art, and for our purposes here it will suffice to note that certain particular animal motifs, more especially the lion and the eagle, were popular in the uplands from early Hittite times onwards. In the Hellenistic period, indeed, their reproduction continued in a way which is hardly to be reconciled with Hellenistic culture alone.[4] We can trace these motifs and a particular style or manner in their depiction which was associated with them in Byzantine art, more especially in sculpture, both in Constantinople and in Greece, where contacts with Asia Minor were especially close. Exactly the same animal motifs and the same style of treatment reappear at a rather later date in the Seljuk art of Asia Minor. This sudden reappearance of the old motifs was by no means fortuitous;

it represents rather the revival of an age-old tradition in Asia Minor, and there can be little doubt but that this tradition also exercised an influence on Byzantine art in the intervening periods. But exactly how much this influence was exerted and how important was its role will only be disclosed when further first-hand researches have been conducted in Asia Minor. Only then will it be possible to establish what is the Anatolian element in art, and to show what exactly were the architectural systems that were developed on the uplands, as opposed to those of the coastal belt and elsewhere.

4. *Syria and the Semitic East*

The term Syrian is rather a confusing one for the student of Byzantine art, for it is used in a number of different ways by different writers. On the one hand, for example, it has been used to describe the culture of the great Hellenistic cities of northern Syria, more especially Antioch; on the other it has been employed to describe the rather more Orientalized products of the Caravan cities, the most important of which was probably Dura.[5] Or again, it has been used to describe a decided but a less definitely localized trend in art, where expressionism supplants the idealism of the Hellenistic world. An ivory in the British Museum will serve to illustrate this manner: the Adoration is depicted above and the Nativity below. In both scenes the figures are almost grotesque in their proportions; there is no elegance, no beauty; yet in spite of this, there is a certain force and vigour about the work, which tells the tale vividly, and attracts the attention of the beholder more forcibly than would many a more elegant and superficially attractive rendering of the scene. We are, in fact, in the presence of an art which aims at conveying an idea, rather than pleasing at first sight, and if necessary, as in modern art, extremes are resorted to in order to achieve this object. Certain features characterize the art, such as a preference for the frontal pose, a habit of enlarging the head out of all proportion to the body, the enlargement of figures of outstanding importance to a scale far greater than that of the other figures, and the deep undercutting of a bas-relief to produce a striking effect. The gradual intrusion of these elements into art of Hellenistic times took place simultaneously with the decline of Greek supremacy, and they became of outstanding importance in the first centuries of the Christian era, affecting the art of the Roman world wellnigh as considerably as that of the Hellenistic sphere and the eastern Mediterranean.

12 British Museum, London. Ivory panel. Adoration of the Magi and Nativity. Syrio-Palestinian. Sixth century

13 Louvre, Paris. Sculpture from Palmyra. Palmyrene Triad: Aglibol, Baal-
    schamin, Malakbel. First century A.D.

At the back of this trend were all the forces of the ancient Semitic
civilizations of the Middle East, for it was an art which ran in line
with the old religious doctrines of the region. The divine was thus
conceived as something awesome, esoteric, and of deep significance,
where gentle comprehensions of kindliness and charm were not
allowed to enter in. Art became in consequence expressive and forceful, and delight was cast to the winds; where fear ruled, intimacy was
impossible. But though the character of the art was distorted to some
extent by religious ideas, it is possible that the development of the
style was also affected by the material conditions of the age. It was
a period in which the desiccation which was finally to bring about
the depopulation of vast areas of Hither Asia had already set in, and,
as the country grew drier, life no doubt became more and more
difficult. In art these difficulties probably found expression in an
interest in realism rather than delicacy, and in an avoidance of anything that might savour of the superficial. Just as the severe conditions

14 Museum of the History of Art, Vienna. Marble relief. St Menas. Fifth
century

of industrialism on the one hand and of political instability on the
other have produced in the art of today a love of abstraction and an
avoidance of mere prettiness, so in the early Christian age did the
trouble of life bring about similar results.

Where exactly the first monuments of this expressive style were
produced it is as yet impossible to say; its development was probably
long drawn out. But we see it already dominant in the style known as

15 Benaki Museum, Athens. Ivory relief. Coptic. Sixth century

Parthian,[6] in the sculptures and tomb paintings of Palmyra, in much of the sculpture of Baalbek, and in the Jewish and early Christian wall paintings at Dura. At a later date the same manner was manifested in some at least of the mosaics and sculptures produced for Christian patrons at Antioch and elsewhere; it was responsible for the sudden change of style which affected ivory carving in Alexandria in the fifth century; it was perpetuated in the wall paintings of Cappadocia executed between the ninth and eleventh centuries, and it continued to show itself in the art of numerous regions almost until the Turkish conquest. This and the Hellenistic stem were, indeed, perhaps the two most important elements at the basis of the Byzantine style as a whole.[7]

While dealing with this trend, mention should be made of Egypt, for, though the Hellenistic style was retained at Alexandria until the sixth century to a degree of purity unknown elsewhere, there developed in the Nile basin at an early date a Christian art of a severer and more expressive type, akin to that of Syria. That art later came to be known as Coptic. Many of the elements that went to form Coptic art may be attributed to ancient Egypt; many were basically Hellenistic. But these two elements alone could never have produced the Coptic style had not the expressionist Syrian element also exercised its influence. The influence first penetrated by way of the Red Sea or the isthmus of Suez, along trade routes which had been in use for many thousands of years. It was an influence

16 Taq-i-Bostan (Persia). Stone relief. Detail of raiment of Persian king Chosroes II. Seventh century

17 Cathedral treasury, Sens. Byzantine damask reproducing motif of Sasanian winged lion. Eleventh century

conveyed from and by way of the arid deserts, and it avoided at first the great cities and the more clement shores of the Mediterranean. The degree to which it affected the hinterland of Egypt can, however, be appreciated if a piece of Coptic sculpture is compared with an Egyptian or a Greek statue.

5. *Iran and Iraq*

The lowland area of Mesopotamia, a flat plain where brick was the only available building material, may be considered together with western Persia, for both areas through a great part of their history had boasted a common culture and had been under the same rule. It is not so much their art in very ancient times that concerns us here, however, as the developments that took place in the area as a whole in the early Christian age, and so far as this region is concerned contemporary influence on the Byzantine world was more important than what was inherited from the past. Under the rule of the Sasanian emperors (222–650) a very distinctive and vigorous art was developed, founded in part on Greek elements introduced at the time of Alexander and subsequently, and in part on the earlier culture of Persia. Excavations at Kish and Hira in Iraq, at Damghan in Persia and elsewhere, have shown the marked individuality of this art and prove that Sasanian culture was very widely spread over the Nearer East. Further, the influence of Sasanian art elsewhere was considerable, for the Sasanian element was of great importance in Moslem art, and certain elements for which it was responsible came to the Byzantine world by way of Islam. We see the direct influence most to the fore in textiles, and it is indeed often impossible to determine whether some of the superb silks of the Middle Ages should be assigned to a Persian or to a Byzantine factory. Mid-Byzantine sculptures, objects in metal and ceramics also attest links with Persia which were first established in Sasanian times.[8]

6. *Altai-Iran*

The Sacian area to the north of Persia is in some ways easier to deal with than the Sasanian in the south, for Strzygowski associates with it a very distinct and definite type of art, and the importance of the region so far as we are concerned here must stand or fall with his theories. His main thesis may be briefly summarized. Among the nomads of Turkish race living in the Altai region, he thinks, there sprang into being a formalistic, non-representational art which was

18 Sancta Sophia, Istanbul. Capital and cornice. 532–7

characterized by low relief carving which covered every available space with floral or geometric forms, executed in a silhouette-like manner. Again, a special technique which he terms the slanting cut (*Kerbschnitt*) was invariably used. These features spread westwards at quite an early date in the form of what may be termed an art-complex. Three main routes were followed, a southern, which affected Syria and Egypt, a central, which touched Asia Minor and the Byzantine world, and a northern, which carried the art into the heart of Europe and ultimately to Scandinavia.

There can be no disputing the existence of this trend in art, wherever and however it may first have been conceived, but whether or not certain architectural elements, notably the use of dome over square plan, are also to be associated with the trend, as Strzygowski asserts, is a more doubtful question, and in the light of recent research it is likely that many of Strzygowski's conclusions with regard to architectural origins should be discarded. His ideas as to the dissemination of the non-representational style in early Christian times, on the other hand, are of considerable importance, and the value of his work in calling attention to the existence of the style, which was before his day more or less disregarded, cannot be exaggerated.

The nature of this art and of the ideas underlying it are both entirely opposed to those of Classical art, though as it travelled westwards elements of the non-representational style tended to become much confused with those proper to other styles. The non-representational style exercised an even more important role on developments in the Byzantine world, and the capitals of Justinian's Sancta Sophia show this clearly. But exactly how the elements which are to be seen in ornament of this nature reached the Byzantine world is a more complicated question, for they had become generally disseminated over the Nearer East long before the days of Justinian, and it may well be that the influence on Byzantium which is to be traced in such works came in a very indirect manner.

A further and rather distinct element in art which is again to be assigned fundamentally to central Asia may also be considered here, though it was not of the first importance in the formation of Byzantine art. It is that known as the 'animal style'. In the last few centuries of the pre-Christian era a particular art which Rostovtzeff was the first to catalogue under this heading was brought into wide popularity by the culture known as Scythian. It was a highly formalized art, and in this respect owed much to the non-representa-

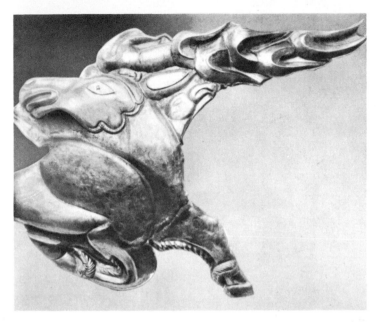

19 National Museum, Budapest. Gold stag from Zoldhalompuszta. Scythian. Fifth to fourth century B.C.

tional trend, but its motifs were founded on the living animal. The Far East has been suggested as its place of origin, as has the extreme north. Wherever it was first developed, however, it travelled westwards by way of the northern shores of the Black Sea and what is today southern Russia and Rumania, and some of the finest manifestations of the art have been unearthed in Hungary.[9] It also exercised an influence in Bulgaria, where the 'animal style' nomads were established for a time, and Filow has suggested that the great popularity of animals in ninth-century Bulgarian sculpture is due to a great extent to this ancestry. This may be so. But we find very similar animals in Byzantine sculptures in Greece, which are to be attributed to the influence of Sasanian art, and this seems a more likely immediate source, especially as there are marked Sasanian influences in Bulgaria, to be seen in the plans of palaces at Aboba Pliska and perhaps in the ninth-century rock reliefs at Madara.[10]

The suggestion that the 'animal style' was carried westwards primarily as a result of racial migration has also been questioned,

59

20 Agios Eleutherios (Little Metropolis), Athens. Relief on outer wall. Eleventh to twelfth century

and the researches of certain writers in Soviet Russia have aimed at proving that archaeological ethnography as we know it is a science which cannot be relied upon. These writers maintain that certain types of art arise inevitably at certain stages of cultural development, without any necessary connexion between the two.[11] The question of independent invention is a very vexed one, but there can be little doubt but that in many cases like results were produced by like effects quite independently. We have thus already suggested that non-representational art may have been developed in more than one place independently. But how far this explanation can be relied upon when some very definite motif such as the Scythian stag is concerned is a very different matter, and when we have to deal with the elements composing such developed arts as the Byzantine or the Sasanian, the importance of interconnexions and influences is not to be disputed.

21 Sant'Ambrogio, Milan. Stone carving. Detail of pulpit. Ninth century

Though primitive nomad tribes in different areas would naturally tend to represent the same animals provided they both knew them, or primitive settled tribes to conceive the same type of building provided the same materials were available, the probability of a more civilized community inventing exactly the same details in the portrayal of a stag seems much less probable.

To disentangle the eventual interplay of all these elements is far beyond the scope of this volume. The existence of practically every possible contributor to the Byzantine panorama has, however, been noted, so that the student of Byzantine art who knows little of the Nearer East may be in some degree prepared to understand manifestations which are not necessarily related to the Classical world. For at its best Byzantine art was the outcome of a fusion of elements from East and West alike. The two elements that concern us most are the Hellenic and the Syrian, the one responsible for delicacy and elegance, the other for strength and expression. But the realism of Roman portraiture, the formalistic, all-embracing ornament of the East, the fantastic animals of Sasanian or Hittite art, the rigidity of Anatolian sculpture; all are present also, especially in the minor arts, even if in painting it is to the Classical world on the one hand and to Syria on the other that the primary roles must be accorded. In fact, the very essence of Byzantine art is that of fusion, and it is absurd to seek to deny the multiplicity of influences in favour of one region or the other, as many recent writers, protagonists of Rome, of Alexandria, or of the East, have sought to do. Art, after all, is a reflection of thought, and for those who prefer to read rather than to look the different phases of doctrine illustrate the same point. Thus in the Iconoclastic age ideas were dominated by an essentially Eastern or Semitic belief, according to which the depiction of divine forms was regarded as evil; with the Macedonian revival there was a complete reversal of outlook, and thought turned once more to the anthropomorphic ideas of ancient Greece and Rome.

Yet in addition to all this there was one thing more that helped to make Byzantine art markedly distinctive, namely the Christian faith. Until the sixth century the religious basis was subservient to some extent to imperialism of a Roman type, but in the age of Justinian the triumph of religion was secured, and the energies of this emperor were concentrated on building and adorning numerous churches throughout the Empire, including one of the vastest and most glorious cathedrals of all time, while the Great Palace remained little more than a conglomeration of detached halls and small apartments. The everyday life of the population was alike affected by religious concerns, and a historian records that in the bazaar discourses upon

22 Byzantine coin, with likenesses of Constantine VII and Romanos I. Seventh
century

theological matters were indulged in by the tradesmen, who could
hardly even sell a loaf of bread without entering into a discussion on
the nature of the Trinity. By the following century this preoccupation
with religious matters had assumed even more dominant proportions,
for it was a religious dispute that racked the state for some two
hundred years, and not a political one. During the brilliant period
between the ninth and the thirteenth centuries all the best art was of
a religious character; so much so, indeed, that we know practically
no secular art of the time, and all the more important writings were

theological. The Palaeologue age, again, is remembered primarily because of its churches and monastic foundations and the religious paintings or mosaics that decorate them.

Christianity was thus not only one of the principal factors governing the development of Byzantine art; it was also one of the most important in its creation. It moulded and influenced that art as a sculptor moulds his clay; it set certain bounds upon the art which could never be transgressed; it dictated its form and limitations. Like the services and liturgies of the Church, art was little affected by external events, and like the liturgy it developed from within, shaped by the nature of the faith it served. It sought to express the infinity of the Christian God, not the finite perfection of Greek thought. But in doing this, set forms were followed, and as time went on a very complicated system of iconography was developed, which in its turn had an important influence on the subsequent character of art. The role of iconography, however, can hardly be discussed under the heading of 'origins'; it must be dealt with in connexion with the art in which it was primarily manifested, namely painting.

Basilica Euphrasiana, Parenzo (Poreč), Istria. Mosaic in lower part of apse. Head of the Virgin, from the Annunciation. 530–5

4 The Architectural Background

To unravel all the problems that beset the field of Byzantine architectural history, or to provide sufficient material to enable the student to date at a glance any building on stylistic grounds, is not the purpose of this chapter. Its aim is rather that of an appreciation, and an attempt will be made to point out the main features of the developed Byzantine style, to show how the buildings served as a background for the other arts, and to summarize the history of the various architectural elements which played a part in the development of the style. But owing to the new forms and the new types of building which came into vogue with the triumph of Christianity, and owing to the diversity of influences which were at play, the subject is extremely controversial, and the principal theories which have been put forward with regard to the origins of these forms must first be considered.

Any survey of Byzantine architecture must be devoted primarily to churches. Few secular buildings have survived, and from what we know of the finest of them, the Great Palace of the Emperors at Constantinople, it seems wellnigh certain that they presented no very important architectural features of their own. No palace in the Western sense was ever built; like the Turkish sultans, the Byzantine emperors preferred a series of detached pavilions to a single edifice, and these pavilions were either of simple plan, where no particular architectural problems arose, or were closely related to the churches, and so do not demand consideration apart. The walls of Constantinople again, though most spectacular, and in every way satisfactory from the structural point of view, present no truly architectural problems, and when once small-scale vaults and arches had been developed the same is true of the cisterns. They are today perhaps the most intriguing architectural remains in Constantinople, and fall into a special group which is outside the scope of this book; but the

65

23 Bin-bir-Derek, Istanbul. 'The Cistern of 1001 Pillars.' Sixth century

24 Cordova. The Great Mosque. 786–990

heritage they left is to be seen in the small dome chambers of many of the mosques of Constantinople.[1] Private houses and monasteries again cannot be dealt with here; practically no houses certainly of Byzantine date survive and the monasteries, though many of them, more especially those of Athos, are amazingly spectacular, are also mostly comparatively late, and show Western influence to a greater or lesser degree.

The whole area with which we have to deal can be roughly divided according to the material which was employed for building purposes, since a rather different class of edifice was developed as a result of the use of brick from that which dominated in the areas where stone was more readily available. In the central and lowland regions, Constantinople, Greece, the Balkans, south-west Russia, southern Mesopotamia, and Egypt, bricks were thus the usual material, though stones were sometimes used to reinforce them. In the uplands, Armenia, the Caucasus, Anatolia proper, Syria, Crete, and Cyprus, where good quarries were at hand, stone was universally used. In the later periods the use of the one material or the other produced a considerable effect on the decorative details of the edifice, even if the plans were the same. At an early date it seems that certain major features were equally affected by the material. Thus in Hellenistic Syria, where stone was universally employed, the hemispherical dome was the rule, while in Sasanian Persia, where large bricks were used, the domes were of an ovoid form. The Syrian domes were either of wood or were built with the aid of centring; the Persian, like the vaults, could be erected course by course without any additional support, the large flat bricks being tilted backwards, so that each successive layer rested on the one below.[2]

Apart from such considerations dependent on material, the most satisfactory classification of buildings of a religious type is on a basis of their plans, and in this respect four main groups may be distinguished. These are the basilica, the centralized building, the domed basilica, and the cruciform church. As time went on the basic plans peculiar to each type were most subtly combined and intermingled. Initially, however, each was distinct, and it will be best to begin by looking at them in turn in their simplest forms.

1. The Basilica

The basilica was in use in the Classical world long before Christian times, but whether it was first developed in the Hellenistic world or in Rome has given rise to some argument. It was, however, probably first in Rome that timber-roofed basilicas were first adopted to Christian usage, and the Christian ritual and the subsequent arrangement of the church interior owed quite a lot to the nature of the disposition of the basilical plan. For example, the inclusion of a throne at the end of the apse, for the use of the bishop, was a pagan feature, taken over along with the basilical plan; it was, in the original basilicas, the seat of the Judex. Such a disposition is still to be seen at Torcello, near Venice (rebuilt 1008) as well as in other churches of earlier date. In early times, again, the churches of basilical plan had apses at both ends, and though this disposition is not to be found in Byzantine architecture, it survived in the West, and became usual first in Carolingian architecture, and subsequently in the Romanesque architecture of southern Germany. In early times, again, the principal entrance was sometimes at the east instead of the west, but by the fourth or fifth century the western entrance had become usual. Rivoira maintains that the earliest instance of an eastern apse is that in the Basilica Ursiana at Ravenna (370–84), and in Constantine's day in any case western apses were still quite usual. Thus the Constantinian church at Baalbek has three apses facing

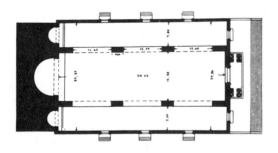

25 Baalbek. Plan of the Emperor Constantine's Basilica, after Creswell

west, and the same Emperor's Church of the Holy Sepulchre at Jerusalem had its main doors at the east.[3] The idea of directing the church towards the east was, indeed, probably an Oriental feature, and Strzygowski attributes it to Armenia, where he thinks it was usual in religious architecture owing to the fact that the Mazdaean cult had been universal since about 500 B.C. Persia itself is perhaps a more likely source. But the marked absence of any systematic orientation in the early churches of Rome, where Classical influence

26 Old St Peter's, Rome. Fresco in San Martino ai Monti

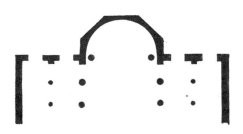

27 Ravenna. Plan of
Basilica Ursiana,
after Rivoira

69

was always uppermost, supports the theory that the idea of eastern orientation was of Eastern origin. But in the absence of early buildings on Armenian soil it seems unsafe to attribute too much to that country; it was probably the natural unification of new and old religious ideas that was taking place in Rome and all over the Hellenistic world that occasioned the adoption of such Eastern ideas by local architects, rather than the influence of actual plans or buildings from some outside region.[4]

Basilicas, with the characteristic three aisles divided by columns, were much in favour all over the Christian world during the first two or three centuries of official Christianity, for they were economical and simple to build, and at the same time held a large body of people. Marble columns could easily be looted from pagan buildings, while the construction of their wooden roofs presented no very complicated building problems. Such basilicas were indeed set up in large numbers, often on the sites of houses or Mithraic sanctuaries where Christians had previously gathered before the faith was officially accepted. There is a large series of them in Rome, and many are of great size and simple beauty. It was at Rome, more than anywhere, that this type of structure was developed, and it is there that the finest examples are to be seen today.

Similar longitudinal structures were, however, also erected at an early date in Syria, but there stone or vaulted roofs took the place of the timber ones of Rome, with consequent modifications on the nature of the structure. With a wooden roof, for example, the columns could be slender and the walls light; in order to support a masonry vault both had to be stout and strong. As a natural outcome the built pier was introduced to alternate with or take the place of the columns, as for instance in the fifth-century Church of St Demetrius at Salonica.

A further development, which was entirely due to Christian architects, was the arcade, which took the place of the Classical architrave, and resulted in the employment of a new kind of capital. The marble slab of the architrave could rest without difficulty on a small surface; the brick foundation of an arch required a more extensive form of support, and this was provided by the use of an impost or second and more extended capital above the first one. The impost was shaped like a truncated pyramid, upside-down, and its face was decorated only with low relief ornament, so as not to weaken it in the way that the carving weakened a Corinthian capital. By the fifth

28 Sta Sabina, Rome. Interior. 425

29 Basilica Euphrasiana, Parenzo (Poreč), Istria. Interior

71

30–1 San Vitale, Ravenna. Capitals. *c.* 530

or sixth century the impost block above the capital was in universal employment in buildings of every type; slightly later an impost capital was evolved, which combined the functions of the two in a single, wide-spreading capital, the ornament of which could not be undercut in the Classical manner, since all the upper surface was required to support the mass of brickwork above it. The demands set upon sculpture by architecture here coincided with the turn which

32 Archaeological Museum, Istanbul.
   Capital. Eleventh century

33 Archaeological Museum, Istanbul.
   Marble capital. Fifth century

34 St Demetrius, Salonica (in process of restoration). Fifth century

architectural ornament was taking independently in the course of the development of the new style which we know as Byzantine.

Certain variations in the plans of these basilicas were made in the early centuries. Thus the usual three aisles were sometimes increased to five; polygonal apses, as at Ravenna, sometimes replaced the original semicircular ones; apsidal terminations were added to the side aisles, as well as to the main one. But beyond such features, the plan was incapable of much development. It was inevitably somewhat pedestrian, and was not wholly suited to Byzantine liturgical demands or to Byzantine esoteric thought, and with the end of the fifth century the plan began to fall out of favour except in Rome. Of later basilicas elsewhere those at Mesembria in Bulgaria and at Kalabaka in northern Greece are the most important.

Before leaving this type of building, a primitive group, found only in northern Mesopotamia, must be briefly noted. The naves of the buildings of this group are disposed transversely, and as far as plan is concerned the group stands apart. But all of them have stone vaulted roofs, and as the stone vaulted roof replaced the timber one all over the upland of Anatolia, as opposed to the coastal belt, it is possible that the basilicas of that area, of conventional plan, owe something to those of the mountains of northern Mesopotamia, where the transverse nave is usual. In addition to the vaulted roofs, the churches of upland Asia Minor show certain other features which are not paralleled in the lowland area or in the Roman world, notably a preference for side doors instead of a western entrance, and the presence of two tower-like chambers at the western end, instead of the Classical atrium. It is probable that in this an old Hittite plan was followed. Indeed, what may be termed the Anatolian element in basilical construction was undoubtedly important, and it is high time that the monuments of Asia Minor were re-examined, special attention being paid to the contribution of the upland area. Millet has shown that the influence of this area was a vital one in Greece and the Balkans in full Byzantine times.[5] It was probably just as vital in the days of the formation of the Byzantine style.

35 Pantheon, Rome. Exterior. 120

2. The Centralized Building

The essential element in this group of buildings is the dome, but in early times two main groups may even so be distinguished: that where the building is of circular plan, and that where it is square. These may be considered in turn, though the second group is the more interesting and the more important.

Round buildings were in fairly common use as pagan mausoleums. Hitherto their origin has usually been attributed to Rome, and it

36 St George, Salonica. Exterior. Fourth century

37 Sta Costanza, Rome. Interior. 324–6

38 San Stefano Rotunda, Rome. *c.* 475

is true that the earliest dated examples are to be found there. But recent discoveries in the East, most notably at Pergamon and Constantinople, show that large circular buildings were known there at an early date also, so that the idea of posing a masonry dome over a drum may as easily be an invention of the Hellenistic as of the Roman mind.[6] The most important instance of the type, however, is undoubtedly the Pantheon at Rome, founded by Agrippa in 27 B.C., but reconstructed more or less in its present form by Hadrian between A.D. 120 and 124. The plans of these round buildings in East and West alike have a great deal in common, and wherever they originated, they must have been closely related. Subsequently they gave birth to a considerable number of later and smaller variants, the most important of which is probably the mausoleum in Diocletian's Palace at Spalato (Split) (early fourth century).

With the adoption of Christianity, buildings of circular plan were

39 Mausoleum of Diocletian, Spalato (Split). Early fourth century

soon exploited in the service of the new faith, and a number of
variations on the theme, some of them quite elaborate, were produced between the fourth and sixth centuries.[7] The first in date was
Sta Costanza at Rome (324–6), where the dome is supported on an

40 Jerusalem. Ground-plan and section of the
Church of the Resurrection, after Creswell

41 St John Lateran, Rome. Baptistery. Fourth to fifth century

inner rotunda of columns, surrounded by a circular aisle, the vaulted roof of which serves to buttress the inner rotunda most effectively. Next is Constantine's Church of the Resurrection at Jerusalem (327–35), where an inner circle on columns was surrounded by an octagon. In the next stage of development an inner octagon is enclosed within an outer one, as in the Dome of the Rock at Jerusalem (691–2). The final elaboration was achieved apparently simultaneously in Italy and in Byzantium at the time of Justinian in the churches of San Vitale at Ravenna (526–47) and SS. Sergius and Bacchus at Constantinople (526–37). In the latter there is an octagon to uphold the dome, which is in turn enclosed in a square. Both of these buildings are of great beauty and show a new appreciation of architectural ornament in their decoration.

42 San Vitale, Ravenna. Aerial photograph. *c.* 530

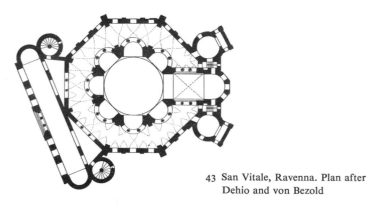

43 San Vitale, Ravenna. Plan after
Dehio and von Bezold

44 San Vitale, Ravenna. View towards the apse. *c.* 530

46 San Vitale, Ravenna. Capital. *c.* 530

San Vitale, Ravenna. View from the ambulatory. *c.* 530

47 Church of SS. Sergius and Bacchus, Istanbul. 526–37

Allied to this group are certain other buildings where the dome stands on four piers, with an apse-like construction on each of the four sides. On the basis of the church at Zwarthnotz (641) in Armenia, which is of this type, Strzygowski originally held that this was an Armenian form, but excavations by Crowfoot have shown that the cathedral at Bosra in Syria (512–13) was of the same type,[8] and it would seem probable that the idea was a Syrian one, and that it spread to Armenia from there. Indeed, the role of Syria was very important so far as the evolution of centralized buildings was concerned, and it must be borne in mind that the Dome of the Rock, the culmination of the evolution in point of size and grandeur, though erected by a Moslem patron, was set up at an age when Islamic art as such had not yet been formulated, in a country which

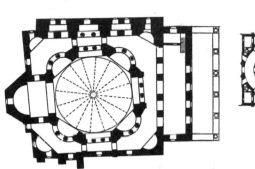

48 Church of SS. Sergius and Bacchus, Istanbul, after Dehio and von Bezold

49 San Lorenzo, Milan. Plan after Dehio and von Bezold

until a few years before had been an important part of the Byzantine Empire. There were also important developments in Italy, as for example in the Church of San Lorenzo at Milan (fourth century), where a central square is composed of large piers, with an exedra-like projection at each of its four sides.

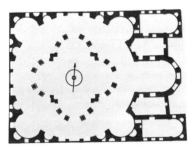

50 Bosra Cathedral, Syria. Plan after Creswell

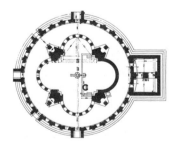

51 St Gregory, Zwarthnotz, Armenia. Plan after Strzygowski

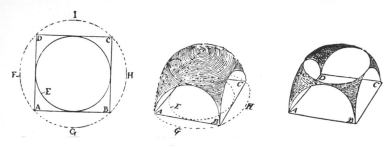

52 The Pendentive. After T. E. Jackson

But however elaborate these constructions, they were still limited with regard to the ground-plan, and it was only when some means of placing the circular base of a dome upon a square or rectangular ground-plan had been devised that really extensive developments were possible. Architects seem to have been preoccupied with solving this problem all over the Nearer East in the first centuries of Christendom, and it is with regard to the area in which the problem was first overcome that some of the bitterest controversies of all archaeology or art history have raged since the early years of this century. Thus certain authorities, most notably Rivoira in the last generation and Swift in this, would assign the honour to Italy; others, most notably Creswell, favour the Hellenistic world, and Syria in particular; others, with Strzygowski as their prophet, favour the East, especially Persia and Armenia. The problems are extremely complicated, and the evidence is still far from complete, but it would seem that the answer depends to a great extent on the means of transition from the square plan of the base to the circle of the dome, for two quite distinct methods were used, the one usually called the pendentive and the other the squinch. The former consists of a triangular-shaped section of a dome which fills up the corner of the square and so transforms it into a circle; the latter is a small arch spanning the corner of the square, and so converting it into an octagon, on to which the circular base of the dome could be conveniently fitted.

Everything goes to suggest that the squinch was an Eastern invention, for the earliest surviving example is in the Sasanian palace of Firuzabad in Persia, which is almost certainly to be dated to the

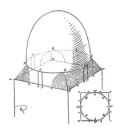

53 Sancta Sophia, Istanbul. Diagram
    of pendentive's dome

54 Palace of Firuzabad, Persia.
   Diagram of a dome on squinches

third century, and the system was considerably developed by the
Sasanian builders. According to Strzygowski, it was first evolved
thanks to the inspiration of wooden prototypes, wooden dome-like
roofs being formed by corbelling, that is to say, by placing beams
across the corners of a square, and then over the corners of the
octagon so formed, until something approaching a circle was arrived
at. Wooden domes of this type, he thinks, were used in the Altai
region, and from there the idea spread to Persia, to be elaborated in
brick and stone. For Strzygowski, Armenia played an important part
in the development of this idea, but the buildings that survive there
are all of fairly late date and, though interesting, are not to be
regarded as of fundamental importance.

The pendentive, on the other hand, was not known in Persia, and
though it occurs in Armenia, it would not seem to be indigenous
there. Nor is Rivoira's case for Rome very convincing, for Creswell
has shown that the earliest example he cites, the Domus Augustana
(A.D. 85), was roofed with a domical vault and not with a true

55 Palace of Firuzabad, Persia. Section after Flandin et Coste

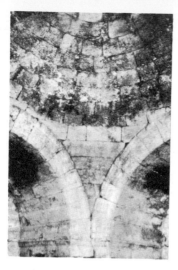

56 The Mausoleum of Qusayr
an-Nuwayis, Amman.
Pendentive. Second century

57 Molfetta, Apulia. Squinch in the
dome. Ninth century

pendentive. The case for Syria, on the other hand, is far better substantiated, for examples survive at Amman, Jerash, and Samaria from the second or early third century, and it is probable that the idea was carried from there to Byzantium, to Italy, and to Armenia.[9] Recently, however, Egypt has been brought into the discussion, for examples there, though on a small scale, are probably as early as the Syrian ones.[10] But the two areas were in close contact, and both are equally associated with the Hellenistic rather than with the Roman or the Eastern spheres.

Though the pendentive was the more efficient solution architecturally speaking, and found greater favour with the Byzantine architects, the squinch continued to be used both in Italy and the Byzantine world, and the Baptistery of Soter at Naples (465–81) or the great church of the monastery of Hosios Lukas, near Delphi (1000–25), may be cited as examples. It was the pendentive, however, that was used in the main by Justinian's architects, notably in the greatest triumph of Byzantine architecture, Sancta Sophia at Constantinople.

When once the possibility of placing the dome over the square base had been realized, a wide series of elaborations of building plans opened up before the architect's eyes. Thus the square could be extended in one or more of four directions, and a plan could be envisaged which was of greater interest and significance than a mere rectangle. In fact, a cruciform building, with the crossing topped by a dome, had a particular appeal to the more mystical aspect of Christian teaching, for it combined the emblem of the faith with something that symbolized heaven above, and from Justinian's time onwards the nature of the building itself and the ideas of the faith to which it was consecrated developed alongside one another. But from the architectural point of view the subsequent story of Byzantine building is really that of variations on the theme of dome over square.

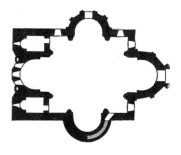

58 Artik Cathedral, Armenia

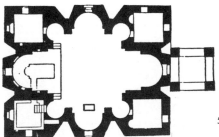

59 St Hripsimeh, Etchmiadzin, Armenia

The possible variations on this theme are admirably illustrated by a series of fifth- and sixth-century churches in Armenia, most of which were originally published by Strzygowski. Thus the simplest variant, the apse-buttressed square, appears at Mastara (c. 641) and Artik (seventh century). In the Church of St Hripsimeh at Etchmiadzin (618) angle chambers appear as well as the apse buttresses. But these Armenian examples though they illustrate admirably the

60 The Praetorium, Musmiyah (Syria). *c.* 400

61 Basilica of Maxentius, Rome. Reconstruction by G. Gateschi and
A. Trabacchi. *c.* 300

62 Mausoleum of Galla Placidia, Ravenna. Interior. *c.* 440

various stages of evolution, are all late in date, and there are earlier, if less clearly developed, instances in Syria. The Praetorium at Musmiyah (A.D. 160; altered *c.* 400) is thus a cruciform building, with vaults to roof the arms of the cross, and the Mausoleum of Galla Placidia at Ravenna (*c.* 440) follows the same plan at a later date; it is roofed with a domical vault.

Perhaps the most important elaboration of the dome resulted from its combination with the basilical plan, and the earliest examples of this idea seem to be associated with Asia Minor, for there are churches of the type at Bin bir Kilisse, Sivri Hissar and Meriamlik; all would seem to belong to the fifth century.[11] It was also in Asia Minor that vaults were extensively used for churches of basilical

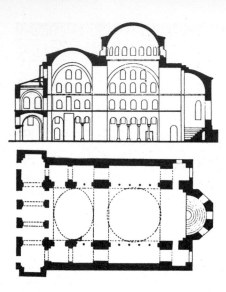

63 Church of St Irene,
Istanbul. Section and
plan after Salzenberg

plan, and the transition from this to dome, or, more often, a combination of the two, was natural. But it must not be forgotten that longitudinal chambers of large scale which were roofed with vaults were known in the great baths and palaces of Rome in imperial times, and these must also have played an important part in the development of early Christian architecture.

Wherever the idea originated, however, it was in Constantinople that the first really important domed basilicas were set up; the Church of St Irene was the earliest of them (532). Its plan is fairly simple, for it shows what is virtually a basilica at ground-level, though the central aisle is unusually wide. Above, however, instead of the usual timber roof or barrel vault there are two domes end to end, each set on pendentives above great transverse arches.

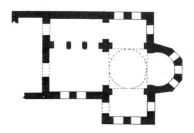

64 Sivri Hissar, near Smyrna.
Plan after Ramsay

92

65 Church of St Irene, Istanbul. Interior. 532

Justinian's Cathedral of Sancta Sophia (532–7) represents a further and more experimental development of this idea. Below, the basilical plan is still preserved, though the central aisle is even wider than in St Irene; above there is a single vast dome at the centre; length is given by the addition of large semi-domes at east and west, which serve simultaneously to roof the space below and to buttress the great central dome itself. Discussion has once more raged as to how this idea of buttressing the main dome with semi-domes was first conceived. Strzygowski regards the semi-domes as elaborations of the niche buttresses which were usual in Armenia; the protagonists of Hellenistic origins regard them as developments of the niches

93

66 Sancta Sophia, Istanbul. Section after A. M. Schneider

which appear in the walls of the great circular martyria or in many of the stone buildings of Syria; Diehl and others think that they were arrived at by bisecting, as it were, a domed building of centralized plan like SS. Sergius and Bacchus, and enlarging it upwards and lengthways by pushing out the ends, filling the intermediary area with columns, and imposing a new and larger dome above the bisected ends. Millet, taking a less complicated and more common-sense view, believes that Sancta Sophia represents the result of a synthesis of the various ideas known at the time. His is the most plausible explanation of the evolution of the plan, for the elements belonging to the square building topped by a dome, the columned longitudinal basilica, and the free-cross type are all combined together, and all of them are seen at once in the interior of Sancta Sophia. Such a synthesis would naturally arise in the mind of an architect of intelligence who was familiar with buildings of the various types; indeed excavations recently undertaken on the site of the Church of St Polyeuktos in Constantinople, built soon after A.D. 500, suggest that the fusion of ideas was first arrived at there. But only a genius could have produced from such diverse elements a building which was in itself so definite a unity as Sancta Sophia, and which was not only to mark a stage in the history of architecture, but was also to survive for some fourteen hundred years as the most glorious representative of its class. Nothing exactly similar, as large, or as fine as Sancta Sophia was ever built again in the Byzantine world,

94

67 Sancta Sophia, Istanbul. View from the south-west. 53

68 Sancta Sophia, Istanbul. Interior from a lithograph by Gaspard Fossati

69 Sancta Sophia, Istanbul. View towards the east. 53

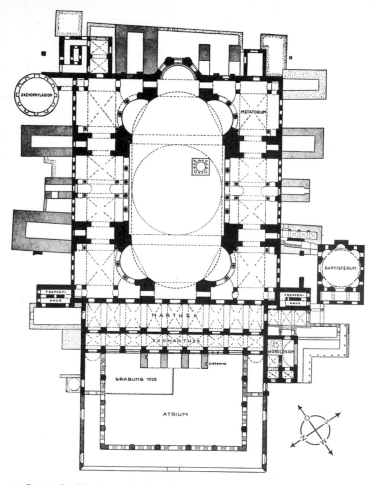

70 Sancta Sophia, Istanbul. Plan after A. M. Schneider

but we can trace the influence of the great cathedral in numerous churches, like Sancta Sophia at Salonica (sixth century) or the Church of the Assumption at Nicaea, now destroyed. In the sixteenth and seventeenth centuries again the magnificent series of mosques built by the Turks in Constantinople and the neighbourhood also owed much to the Byzantine model.

A number of other plans were also developed by Justinian's architects, the most important of which was probably that known as the five-domed plan. The buildings of this group are cruciform, with one dome at the crossing, and one on each of the four arms of the cross. The most important building of the type was Justinian's Church of the Holy Apostles at Constantinople (536–46); it was copied in numerous other places, but the most important surviving example is St Mark's at Venice (1063–95). The Church of the Holy Apostles

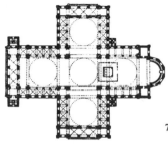

71 Holy Apostles, Istanbul. Plan after Dehio and von Bezold

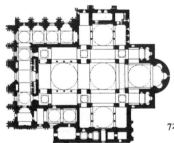

72 St Mark's, Venice. Plan after Dehio and von Bezold

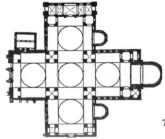

73 St Front, Périgueux. Plan after Dehio and von Bezold

was destroyed by the Turks to make room for the Mosque of Fatih. The plan also penetrated to the West, for it was followed in the twelfth-century Church of St Front at Périgueux.[12] The five-domed type of church is the most important of the multiple-domed types; it must be distinguished from a later variety, especially common on Mount Athos, where one dome tops the crossing and others the side chapels, but not the actual arms of the cross. A good example of this group of rather later date is to be seen in the Church of the Holy Apostles at Salonica.

Even if Sancta Sophia at Salonica and a few other buildings are close to Sancta Sophia at Constantinople in that they are buildings whose interiors represent a great spatial unity, this conception passed

74 St Mark's, Venice. View towards the altar. 1063–95

75 St Front, Périgueux. Twelfth century

76 St Mark's, Venice. Aerial photograph, showing the five domes. 1063–95

out of fashion soon after the days of Justinian, and later Byzantine churches were universally of far more modest proportions. In addition their plans tended to become more and more complicated as time went on. But the idea of a three-aisled, longitudinal building was never lost sight of, and a cruciform upper structure was in some

77 Holy Apostles, Salonica. Exterior. 1312

78 La Cattolica, Stilo (Calabria). Eleventh century

way or another invariably imposed upon it. The general tendency of later structures was to add numerous small chapels and subsidiary structures to this basic essential. These additions follow no very set plan; but the main structure almost always follows one of two formulas, the free-standing or the obscured cross plan. In the former the transepts project and the cross is at once visible; the Church of the Kapnikaria at Athens serves as a good example, though chapels have been built into the spaces between the arms of the cross. In the latter the chapels between the arms form an essential part of the structure, so that below the building appears to be rectangular. But above the arms of the cross are carried up rather higher, so that the cruciform plan is visible at roof-level, though not on the ground. The tenth-century Church of the Myrelaion at Constantinople may be cited as an example.

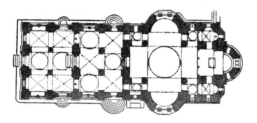

79 Monastery of Chilandari, Mount Athos.
Plan after G. Millet

A number of variations in the manner of construction in churches of both groups appear to be associated with locality rather than with the different groups. Thus in Constantinople and the places most nearly dependent, Salonica and Mount Athos especially, the dome was usually supported on four columns, whereas in Greece, Anatolia, and Armenia there were two columns to the west, while at the east the two walls of the apse were carried forward to take the place of the other pair of columns. It was probably as a result of this that the horseshoe apse was arrived at, for it was automatically produced when the extremities of the walls had to be narrowed to do duty as columns to uphold the dome above. This is not the only feature in

80 Church of the Pantanassa, Mistra (Peloponnese). Fourteenth century

which the churches of Greece show Eastern affinities, and Millet, in his detailed analysis of the Greek schools, has proved that they are generally more closely akin to those of Anatolia than to those of Constantinople.

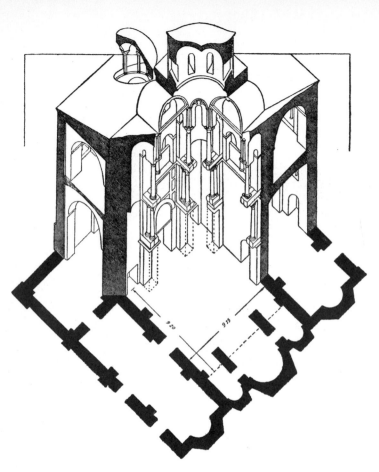

81 Panaghia Parigoritissa, Arta (Epirus). Christ as Pantocrator. 1295

From the tenth century onwards no completely new plans were evolved, but churches underwent considerable developments in structural detail, and more especially with regard to decorative treatment. There was a general tendency towards an increase in height and a reduction in the scale of the ground-plan in proportion. The windows were elongated, till they became long niches in the walls. Carved stone closure slabs were often fitted into the lower extremities. The domes were set upon taller and taller drums as time proceeded,[13] and the exteriors were richly decorated with ornamental

82 St Gregory of Tigrane Honentz, Ani (eastern Turkey). *c.* 1215

brickwork or stonework, to give a mosaic-like effect, and blank arcading was extensively employed; glazed vessels were in later days sometimes built into the walls to add colour to the masonry; in Bulgaria it appears that special 'plates' were made for the purpose, which retained the form of plates, though their bases were never finished off, so that they could never have been used on a table. They offer an interesting instance of conservatism in art, an old form being retained for a new use, to which it was really not very well adapted.

83 Hosios Lukas (near Delphi). Older church, right, and second church, left. Tenth century

84 Church of St Theodore (Kilisse Camii), Istar
West front. Tenth to eleventh century

85 Holy Apostles, Salonica. Decorative brickwork on the apse. 1312

Churches in which one or more of these later developments are to be seen exist all over the Byzantine world. Blank arcading was thus extensively developed in Bulgaria, as for example at Tirnovo and Mesembria, as well as in Constantinople; the Church of St Mary Pammakaristos in the latter city affords an excellent example (1315). Decorative brickwork was much used in Greece; there are lovely examples at Mistra, but the Church of the Holy Apostles at Salonica affords an especially attractive example (1312). But nowhere, perhaps, are there finer late Byzantine churches than on Mount Athos, where a distinctive plan, with long double nave and large outer transverse narthex, was developed to suit the demands of the monastic communities. Here again the exteriors were usually quite elaborately decorated, and, like the rest of later Byzantine architecture, a marked contrast is to be seen with earlier work, where the outsides were almost always extremely plain. This love of external decoration seems to have developed as time went on, and in the fifteenth century the exteriors were quite often adorned with paintings. It is possible that this idea was of Eastern origin, for the

86 Church of St Mary Pammakaristos (Fetiye Camii), Istanbul. South side. *c.* 1315

interesting Armenian church on the island of Achthamar on Lake Van (915–21) was sculptured all over outside, and churches in the region of Trebizond were in part sculptured and in part painted. From there the idea perhaps travelled to central Russia on the one

87 The monastery church, Voronet (Rumania). Wall painting. Our Lady in Paradise. 1547

88 The church, Achthamar (Armenia). 915–

hand and to Rumania on the other, where the painted exteriors were especially popular. There the churches were built of brick, and the exteriors were plastered and then painted with biblical scenes, just like the interiors. The idea was never adopted in Constantinople. In Russia the most important churches with external decoration are those of Yuriev-Polskij (1230–4) and Vladimir (1190), both stone-built churches with carved decoration.

A few other features of general interest may be noted. Thus open porticoes were a late feature, which was probably adopted from the West. Bell towers are a late feature, for in the Orthodox East the service was announced by a rhythmical beating on a wooden bar, the symantron.[14] The idea must again have been introduced from the West. But essentially Byzantine is the love of dim but very elaborately

89 The church, Achthamar (Armenia). Reliefs on the outer wall. 915–21

90 St George's Church, Yuriev-Polskij. Reliefs on the outer wall. 1230–4

91 Byzantine Museum, Athens. Iconostasis. Eighteenth century

decorated interiors. Columns of the finest marble, piers, and walls covered below with polished marble slabs and above with mosaics or wall paintings, capitals delicately sculptured, a profusion of church furniture, and an elaborate iconostasis separating the eastern sanctuary from the body of the church are all features which were developed in the Byzantine world. Indeed, it is hardly possible to think of a Byzantine interior without wall paintings and iconostasis, for the painted picture was a very essential feature in the liturgy, and the iconostasis was in fact a sort of frame on to which additional pictures could be attached. In early times it was of stone, and was comparatively modest in size, but by the twelfth century wood had generally replaced stone, and the iconostasis had been increased considerably in height, and to it was affixed tier above tier of painted panels, or icons, showing Christ and the Virgin and the more important saints below, and certain essential scenes of the New Testament story above, with at the summit the Crucifixion.[15] In the area immediately to the west of the iconostasis was placed an ambon or pulpit of carved wood, with carved reading-desks on either side; to the east was the altar, covered by a ciborium or canopy on four columns. In appropriate shrines reliquaries, set in gorgeous frames of jewelled metal work or enamel, were preserved; and the general note was one of richness and luxury. The rich vestments of the clergy completed the scene. Massive doors of wrought bronze or carved wood secured the entrance.

The larger Orthodox churches of today in Greece or the Balkans retain something of this magnificence, but in general ornateness has often taken the place of a more profound grandeur, and in general it must be left to the imagination to re-create an impression of the original glory. The architectural structure, however, really constituted the basis of all this. It served not so much to house the pictures and the treasures, as to envelop them like a superb garment. The glory of the one enhanced the glory of the other; separate, their perfection was apparent; combined it was wellnigh overwhelming.

5 Byzantine Mosaics

In this chapter we will be mainly concerned with wall mosaics showing figural subjects of Christian character. Though figures often
formed part of the decoration of floor mosaics in Roman and
Hellenistic times, these were of pagan character, and the story of
such mosaics belongs to a different chapter in the history of art.
Attention must, however, be drawn to a number of pavements laid
between about 300 and 600, notably those at Antioch and in the
Great Palace at Constantinople, for, even if their subject-matter
belongs to a pagan repertory, the style is already to some extent
Byzantine, and it is possible that the animals and hunting scenes
depicted on many of them may even have had an esoteric Christian
significance, in that they were designed to depict the Christian
paradise.[1] But even if this was the case, such pavements appear to
have been more generally associated with houses and palaces than
with churches, and in the latter pavements were usually in another
technique, where small shaped pieces of marble fit one with the other
to compose a pattern which is in the main geometric, even if small
animals and birds are sometimes included. Work of this type is
designated by the name 'opus Alexandrinum' or 'opus sectile'; the
latter is a more delicate, the former a bolder form.

The earliest use of mosaics in a vertical position for wall decoration was probably at Pompeii, but any that have been found there or
in similar sites are on a small scale, appearing in niches only, and it
was really only after the adoption of Christianity as the official faith
that the possibility of mosaic as a covering for walls or vaults came
to be fully exploited. At first the conch of the apse was the place
most usually adorned, and in many of the later basilicas of Rome or
Ravenna it was still only in the apse that the mosaics were placed.
But the earliest mosaics in a Christian building that survive, those in
Sta Costanza at Rome, cover the vaults, and by the fifth century

whole wall faces were also being adorned. A large series of scenes could be set up on the flat wall surfaces, and as time went on these scenes tended to become a more and more important part of the church decoration. It was there that the Bible story was unfolded for the faithful to follow, while the more sacred figures of the Christian story were placed above, on the vaults or, later, in the domes. It became the custom to adorn all the richer churches in this way; in the poorer ones paintings took the place of mosaics. Mosaics remained popular until the Empire became so impoverished that patrons were no longer able to sustain the immense expense of furnishing a mosaic decoration for a whole building. Throughout the long period from the fourth to the fourteenth century, mosaics were

92 Great Palace, Istanbul. Mosaic floor. Detail of the border. Sixth century

93 Great Palace, Istanbul. Detail from the mosaic floor. Eagle attacking snake. Sixth century

things of primary importance, and it is to them that the highest place must be assigned in a study of Byzantine art, just as it is to sculpture in ancient Greece and to panel painting in Renaissance Italy that the student turns when in search of the characteristic and most accomplished art.

The fundamentally religious character of Byzantine art as a whole has already been stressed, and it has been suggested that the greatest achievement in architecture for which the Byzantines were responsible was the development of a plan suited above any other to the demands of the Orthodox faith. The decoration of the buildings was concentrated inside, in opposition to the practice of the Classical world, where the most important decoration was without. In concentrating the decoration inside the building in this way the idea at the back of the artist's and of the patron's mind seems to have been twofold. First, they sought to glorify God by beautifying his house and by dedicating to him the most sumptuous offering in their power. Secondly, they sought to instruct those who were illiterate or who were not sufficiently well equipped to understand the purpose of the

94 Sta Costanza, Rome. Detail of the vault mosaic. 324–6

95 Sant'Apollinare Nuovo, Ravenna. Mosaic. The Raising of Lazarus. *c.* 520

ritual, by placing before them a series of pictures which would make clear to them the story of the Bible without the necessity of reading, and which would enable them to follow the ritual of the actual service with their eyes as well as with their ears. The first full series of such doctrinal mosaics was probably that set up in the Church of the Holy Apostles, built by Justinian at Constantinople between 536 and 546. These mosaics have perished, but panels showing scenes from the Bible of a similar narrative character and which must have been very closely akin in appearance survive on the walls of Sant' Apollinare Nuovo at Ravenna (520–6); they illustrate practically the whole of our Lord's life, scene by scene.

In addition to the dedicatory and doctrinal intentions, it is also possible to discern a certain desire to overawe the spectator by means of an inconceivable splendour which would, when combined with the impression produced by the chanting, the vestments, and the wealth of relics, leave him spellbound and astounded. Indeed, the records tell us that this impression was a normal one, and it is probable that it was to some extent thanks to the impression produced by the interior of Sancta Sophia on the Russians sent by Vladimir to report on the nature of the Orthodox faith that he chose that faith, rather than Catholicism, Judaism, or Islam, for the new state he was founding in Russia.

The interiors of the later churches were entirely covered with mosaics or paintings portraying Christ, the Virgin, or the saints, or illustrating particular scenes of the Bible; where the space was too small for figures or scenes, lovely decorative patterns were set up. Every advantage was taken of the architectural frame offered by the building, for the numerous semi-domes, niches, and curves of Byzantine architecture afforded admirable opportunity for the scintillating lights and colours of the material to play a full part; for, though admirable enough on a flat wall, as we see at Ravenna, mosaics have an additional beauty when set on a curved surface. In such a position the cubes take up and reflect the light with an effect that is ever changing and which in itself alone is of the rarest beauty.

When once Byzantine art had been developed, certain scenes and certain figures tended to become identified with particular parts of the wall surface almost as much because of the way that they could be adapted to fit each given area as because of liturgical claims. Often indeed the two seemed to synchronize the one with the other in an almost mysterious way. Thus, following the dictates of liturgy, the more sacred figures were placed in the upper parts of the building. But no more appropriate place for Christ could be devised than the dome, nor for the Virgin than the conch of the apse. The great bust of the Pantocrator at Daphni or the lovely tall figure of the Virgin in the apse at Nicaea or Torcello are among the greatest glories of all art, not only because of their quality, but also because of the subtle way in which these figures are fitted to the areas they adorn. Similarly the portraits of the four Evangelists were often set in the four pendentives of the dome; not only were they ideally suited to the shape of the triangular pendentive, but also they corresponded admirably with the demands of the liturgy, for it was in every way

96 Church of the Assumption, Nicaea (destroyed 1919). Mosaic in the pendentive of the dome. St Mark. *c.* 1065

appropriate that they should be placed in close association with the figure of Christ, whose life they had recorded, and whose most intimate companions they had been. Lower down, upon the actual walls, the scenes of our Lord's life were portrayed, where they could be easily seen by the congregation, and where flat spaces were available for their showing. At the lowest level of all more mundane figures, the Fathers of the Church, the general hierarchy of saints, and so on, occupied the wall space nearest to the ground, and

97 Church of the Assumption, Nicaea. Apse mosaic. Madonna and Child. *c.* 850

consequently in closest association with everyday life. Yet once again the tall figures formed an admirable part of a subtle artistic composition, for they served to uphold the more varied and elaborate scenes above and to give proportion and balance to the whole interior. Their importance purely from the point of view of composition is attested by the fact that throughout the Renaissance similar standing figures were often employed at the bottom of a picture of such a scene as the Resurrection or the Assumption to enhance its beauty and mystery, and at the same time to give balance to the picture and to give weight to the deep significance of the scene portrayed.

All these developments, of course, came slowly, and the story of the evolution of Christian mosaics is just as complicated as that of Christian architecture. A number of distinct and to some extent conflicting influences were thus at play. Of these the Hellenic and the Semitic were probably the most important. The one favoured a refined, balanced, premeditated, and idealistic type of art; it knew the rudiments of true perspective, and was attached to 'antique' models. The art of the other sought to express a significant idea rather than to please; it was forceful and assertive, expressive in conception, and favoured vivid, impressive colouring; figures were represented frontally, there was no attempt at illusion or true perspective; harsh realism took the place of idealism. The one art looked upon Christ as a charming, youthful figure – almost as the Apollo of Greek mythology. The other represented him as an awesome, bearded personage, possessed of all the mysterious majesty of one of the old Semitic gods of Assyria. Linked with this tradition we find the use of vertical perspective, where scenes in the background are placed above those in the foreground, without any reduction in size, or of a hierarchical arrangement, where certain figures are enlarged because of their greater importance. The two trends, the Hellenic and the Semitic, were continually at variance, yet at the same time they continually mingled one with the other, and the presence of both can be traced until the very end of Byzantine art. But in the greatest masterpieces something of the best was culled from each, and the two diverse elements were blended, thanks to Byzantine genius, to form a subtle yet forceful whole, which could never have been achieved had only one of the influences been at work.

These are the main trends: Hellenic grace, Semitic significance; and the two were blended and attuned to the service of Christianity

98 Mausoleum of Galla Placidia, Ravenna. Mosaic. Christ as the Good Shepherd. *c.* 440

99 SS. Cosmas and Damian, Rome. Apse mosaic. Christ in Majesty. 526–30

100 San Vitale, Ravenna. Apse mosaic. Christ enthroned. First quarter sixth century

thanks to Byzantine taste. But the role of one further element from the art of the past must also be noted, namely that of the non-representational art of the East. The importance of art of a more abstract character, where human or, indeed, living figures were only employed as parts of a decorative pattern, was very considerable in the East, notably in Persia and Mesopotamia, and it had even affected the Roman world, along with a good many other elements from the eastern area which need not be discussed here. Strzygowski even goes so far as to explain the non-representational character of the mosaics on the vaults of Sta Costanza at Rome as the result of Eastern influence, but if this was indeed so the influence must have penetrated a long time before the period at which the mosaics were set up (326–37), for as they stand they are essentially Roman in style.

Eastern trends, however, are exemplified for Strzygowski not only in purely non-representational and decorative compositions like those of the Sta Costanza mosaics, but also in others where the landscape background has a symbolic significance and takes on a role as important as that of the figures; such elements as clouds, water, or the earth, and such figures as the phoenix or sheep in a flowered background, are, for him, part of an elaborate Eastern symbolism, taken over by the Romans, and later by Christianity, from the old religious beliefs of Mesopotamia. A good example is offered by the apse of SS. Cosmas and Damian in Rome, where clouds and water form the background, and where sheep appear in a row below. It is hardly justifiable to go as far as Strzygowski and assert that all the early mosaics of Rome were of this character, but it is fair to say that Mazdaean symbolism was certainly one of the elements from which the repertory of early Christian art was enriched. A love of symbolism was kept alive in the Byzantine mind by contacts with the East, and it is worthy of note that when a dynasty of Eastern origin came to the throne in the Iconoclast period figural art was precluded, and symbolism of a non-representational type held sway for a century or more.

In studying the mosaics of the Byzantine world two periods of primary importance have hitherto been distinguished, the first from the fourth to the seventh centuries, the second from the ninth to the twelfth; the two are separated by the Iconoclast age. Recent research, however, suggests that anyhow in secular work the Iconoclast age was perhaps not so barren from the artistic point of view as was at one time believed, and the mosaics of the Great Mosque of

101 San Giovanni Evangelista, Rome. Ceiling mosaic in side chapel of Baptistery. 641

102 Sta Costanza, Rome. Vault mosaic. 324–6

103 Kuseir Amra (Jordan). Ceiling painting in the bath building. 724–43

104 Sta Costanza, Rome. Vault mosaic. 324–6

Damascus (c. 715), set up for a Moslem patron, the Caliph al Walid, show to what a high degree of beauty a composition could attain in which no figures at all are present. Again, some of the most beautiful of all the mosaics that survive, those in Kariye Camii at Constantinople, are to be assigned to the fourteenth century, as are other works in Constantinople, of which only fragments survive. The fourteenth century, in fact, seems to have been one of the most glorious ages of mosaic production, and it should not be dismissed in the summary terms that have been applied to it by certain writers of the last generation, notably Peirce and Tyler, in their *Byzantine Art*.

In the first age, Rome, Ravenna, and Salonica were the most important centres – or rather, it is in those cities that the most important mosaics of the early centuries survive today. The mosaics may be divided into two main groups, the one where Classical feeling was uppermost, the other where the Byzantine style had already developed and become predominant. Between the extremes of these groups there are naturally a number of intermediary examples, and the dividing-line is at times wellnigh imperceptible. Often the change towards the Byzantine spirit had gone a long way in a part of the work, while in another part it had hardly begun. This is clearly to be seen, for example, in San Vitale at Ravenna, where the Christ in the apse is the youthful beardless figure of Classical art, whereas the portrait groups of Justinian and Theodora are completely Byzantinized, and owe a greater debt to the Eastern than to the Roman heritage. In general, however, the old Classical elements were perhaps more to the fore in Rome than elsewhere.

In Rome there are four churches which contain decorations of major importance. Of these Sta Costanza (324–6), a rotunda surrounded by a ring, was probably originally the most elaborate. The mosaics which adorned the dome no longer survive, but we know something of them from drawings and descriptions. They showed scenes from the Bible, principally from the Old Testament, which were bounded by a river at the outside. In this Strzygowski saw Mazdaean influence; Eastern traits were no doubt present, though the composition and iconography as a whole owed a good deal more to Roman art. The mosaics that survive on the vaults of the surrounding ring are more definitely Roman. The vault is divided into eight compartments, the eastern one now being bare, and the western occupied by a simple geometric composition; the compartments opposite one another at the sides have identical designs, increasing

105 Sta Costanza, Rome. Apse mosaic. Fifth century

in elaboration and quality from west to east, so that the sacred
character of the edifice is stressed by the disposition of the decoration.
The work is all of the highest quality, and the colouring harmonious
and subtle though pale. Characteristic of the early date is the white
background; later we see blue, and later still gold invariably
employed. This white background, and the Roman character of the
designs, tends to intensify the Classical appearance of these mosaics.
Mosaics in the conches of niches in the outer wall are more Byzantine,
for they not only show Christian scenes, but the figures are tall and
elongated in the characteristic Byzantine manner. Further, gold
tesserae are here used with great effect to bring out the highlights.
These mosaics were set rather later than those of the vault, for they
belong to the fifth century, at which date the building became a
baptistery. They have subsequently been much restored.

135

106 Sta Pudenziana, Rome. Apse mosaic. 384–9

The apse mosaic of Sta Pudenziana (384–9) shows our Lord enthroned between SS. Peter and Paul, who each head a group of five Apostles. There are also two female figures, one on either side, who represent the Ecclesia ex Circumcisione (crowning Peter) and the Ecclesia ex Gentibus (crowning Paul). Behind the figures is an elaborate architectural composition, which appears to copy a manuscript model, though the ultimate source of such backgrounds is to be found in the architecture-scapes of Pompeiian and Alexandrine wall painting. A similar model must have served for the rather later mosaics of St George at Salonica. Both are of outstanding beauty. The composition of those in Sta Pudenziana is one of the finest that survive in Rome; the technical quality and colouring of those in St George at Salonica are unsurpassed. They are particularly important for, though battered, they have not suffered from inept

Text on scroll:
DOMINVS ECCLESIAE
CONSER PVDENTI
VATOR ANAE

107 Sta Pudenziana, Rome. Christ, from the apse mosaic. 384–9

restorations, as have nearly all the mosaics of Rome and Ravenna. They perhaps date from as early as the reign of Theodosios I (379–95).

In Sta Maria Maggiore there are mosaics in the apse, on the triumphal arch in front of the apse, and on a number of isolated panels now set at a high level along the nave walls. The technique is impressionist, the backgrounds are of the light colour characteristic of early work as a whole, and the mosaics are close to the antique in style; there must have been a definite attempt to preserve the picturesque manner of Pompeiian art in a new medium. There were forty-two plaques; twenty-seven remain. All illustrated scenes from the Old Testament in a most vivid and expressive manner; it is a pity that they are placed so high that their beauty cannot be appreciated. They have been assigned to various dates; one between 432 and 440 is most probable.[2] The mosaics of the triumphal arch are more monumental. They are devoted to the glorification of the Virgin, as patroness of the church to which they belong, and were set up by Pope Sixtus III (432–40) perhaps to commemorate the decisions of the Council of Ephesus, where the doctrine of Nestorius, who regarded the Virgin merely as the mother of Christ and not also as the mother of God, was refuted. In these mosaics the Classical element has to a great extent been superseded, and the inner conception of the subject shows the birth of a new and essentially Christian style, heralding the greater glories to come. The apse mosaic, of the fourth or fifth century, was very severely remodelled in 1295 by Jacopo Torriti; the original appears to have been of a non-representational character, with great scrolls like those at the sides, which are all that survive of the original work. Strzygowski again sees Mazdaean symbolism here, but there is nothing in the mosaic which could not have been directly inspired by Roman art. A similar symbolical and non-representational scene is preserved in the apse of San Clemente; it is dated to 1299, but follows a fifth-century original very closely.

With the apse mosaics of SS. Cosmas and Damian (526–30), where Christ is shown in the centre before a background of flame-coloured clouds, with figures on either side, we find the Byzantine style fully developed. The Christ is bearded, the costumes are treated in the Byzantine manner, and the heads and faces show that elongation which was later to become characteristic, first of Byzantine art, and then of the paintings of El Greco. Below the main composition

108 Sta Maria Maggiore, Rome. Detail of the mosaics on the triumphal arch.
432–40

109 Sta Maria Maggiore, Rome. Above, mosaics of the triumphal arch,
432–40; below, the apse, restored in 1295 by Jacopo Torriti

110 San Clemente, Rome. Apse mosaic. *c.* 1200

111 The Lateran, Rome. SS. Rufinus and Secundus. Apse mosaic. Fourth
century

112 Palazzo Mattei, Rome. Stucco relief. Second century A.D.

113 Mausoleum of Galla Placidia, Ravenna. Mosaic. Detail of north lunette.
c. 440

114 National Museum, Rome. Fragment of the Ara Pacis of Augustus. First
century A.D.

115 Dome of the Rock, Jerusalem. Mosaic in the octagon. 691-2

twelve sheep, symbolizing the Apostles, appear in procession. The sheep of this mosaic served as models for a number of later compositions both in mosaic and in wall painting; most important are the mosaics of Sta Maria in Trastevere, in Rome.

A number of other mosaic compositions of the early period survive in Rome, though they are less outstanding in importance than the four just mentioned. Of these the Byzantine style is to the fore in those of St Lawrence-without-the-Walls (578–80), but the artist was not a great master, for the effect is rather wooden. The apse of the small chapel of SS. Rufinus and Secundus in the Lateran, executed in the fourth century, bears a formalistic acanthus composition, comparable to that which originally filled the apse of Sta Maria Maggiore. Sta Sabina was originally also elaborately decorated, but an inscription of the fifth century on the west wall is all that now

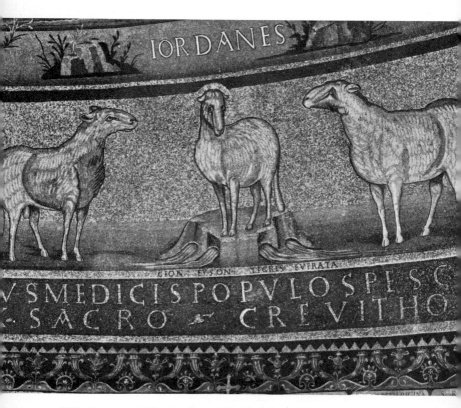

116 SS. Cosmas and Damian, Rome. Detail of the apse mosaic. 526–30

SANC THEODORVS

117 SS. Cosmas and Damian, Rome. Detail of the apse mosaic. 526–30

118 SS. Cosmas and Damian, Rome. Detail of the apse mosaic. 526–30

remains. The fine fifth-century decoration of St Paul's-without-the-Walls has again perished; it was destroyed by the great fire of 1823, though the mosaics were restored, like the building, to follow the original scheme as closely as possible. Except for a few small fragments in the Lateran Baptistery, most of the other mosaics in Rome are of later date. The decoration of the Lateran Baptistery itself is thus in the main to be attributed to 641, while mosaics in the apse of St Agnes-without-the-Walls date from between 625 and 638; here the patron saint of the church takes the place of precedence in the

119 St Lawrence-without-the-Walls, Rome. Mosaic on the triumphal arch. 578–80

120 St Agnes-without-the-Walls, Rome. Apse mosaic. 625–38

centre of the apse. They are delicate as regards technique, and essentially Byzantine in style. Two saints and a cross in the apse of San Stefano Rotondo were set up by Pope Theodore (642–9); the cross probably represents that which stood on Mount Golgotha, and the mosaics were intended to commemorate the destruction of the actual cross by the invading Moslems. Rather earlier, dating from *c.* 550, are some not very important mosaics in the Church of St Theodore.

Though this list includes but a modicum of what once existed, the series of early mosaics in Rome is none the less impressive, and

147

121 Mausoleum of Galla Placidia, Ravenna. Exterior. *c.* 440

nothing so well distributed in respect of dating or so varied as regards style is to be seen elsewhere. The next most important centre, Ravenna, however, boasts certain monuments which are more elaborate and more ambitious than any at Rome. Mosaics there were executed at three distinct periods, that of Galla Placidia (388–440), that of Theodoric (493–526), and that of Justinian (527–65). The most striking monument of the first age is the Mausoleum of Galla Placidia (*c.* 440), a small cruciform building containing a rich decoration with a deep blue ground which gives a wonderful atmosphere to the building. Indeed, small though it is, the decoration is one of the most complete and most thoroughly successful that survives from early times. Figures and ornamental compositions alternate one with the other, and both are equally effective. Strzygowski sees in the decorative work the influence of the Mazdaean landscape; Van Marle states categorically that there is no Eastern influence. The work thus offers a clear instance of how disputed are the questions of origin. But Van Marle is probably right as far as more immediate influences are concerned, for there is nothing that could not have come from Rome. But how much of

122 Mausoleum of Galla Placidia, Ravenna. Mosaics of the vault. c. 440

123 Mausoleum of Galla Placidia, Ravenna. Pendentive mosaic. The Eagle of
John. *c.* 440

124 Mausoleum of Galla Placidia, Ravenna. Mosaics over entrance and crossing. *c.* 440

125 Baptistery of the Orthodox, Ravenna. Interior. 440–50

the ornament that appears here, as well as in many other examples of Roman and Hellenistic art, actually emanated from the East at a much earlier date is another matter, which art historians are still debating and which it is impossible to attempt to answer here.

To much the same period belong the dome mosaics of the Baptistery of the Orthodox, San Giovanni in Fonte (440–50). There are elaborate architectural compositions below, with the Apostles above

126 Baptistery of the Orthodox, Ravenna. Mosaics of the lower arcade. 440–50

127 Baptistery of the Orthodox, Ravenna. Mosaic in the dome. 440–50

128 Arian Baptistery (Sta Maria in Cosmedin), Ravenna. The dome. *c.* 520

129 Sant'Apollinare Nuovo, Ravenna. Mosaic. Christ at the Well. *c.* 520

them, and, at the centre of the dome, the Baptism. The architectural compositions are important, for they show the influence of the architecture-scapes of Hellenistic or Pompeiian art, but the candelabra motifs probably owe their origin to the inspiration of Sasanian models, though the influence no doubt came by way of Syria, where such motifs were extensively used; we see them, for instance, in the mosaics of the Church of the Nativity at Bethlehem, and rather later in those of the Dome of the Rock at Jerusalem (691–2).

Of the second period at Ravenna are the dome mosaics of the Arian Baptistery, also known as Sta Maria in Cosmedin (*c.* 520), and

130 Sant'Apollinare Nuovo, Ravenna. Mosaic. The Betrayal. *c.* 520

the scriptural scenes along the nave walls of Sant'Apollinare Nuovo
(520–30). The latter constitute one of the earliest and most complete
series of New Testament scenes that survive, and tell the story of
Christ's life and passion with great vividness and expression. Classical and Eastern ideas are here once more blended. The bearded
Christ, of Eastern origin, thus appears in the Passion scenes, and he
is larger than the other figures in accordance with the Eastern idea
of indicating his importance. The women at the well, on the other
hand, are completely antique in style, and in such scenes as depict
Christ's early life he is shown beardless. The lovely processions of

131 Sant'Apollinare Nuovo, Ravenna. Mosaic. Saint on north wall. *c.* 561

saints at a lower level are to be assigned to the third period, that of Justinian. They were set up soon after 561 when the church was rededicated as an Orthodox instead of an Arian sanctuary.

In the third period an art which is more truly Byzantine had emerged, and San Vitale is an essentially Byzantine church with an

132 Sant'Apollinare Nuovo, Ravenna. Mosaic. South wall. Christ blessing.
    c. 561

essentially Byzantine mosaic decoration inside it, even if certain
Eastern and certain Classical elements can be isolated by means of
a careful stylistic analysis. The main apse of San Vitale (526–47) is
occupied by a very beautiful composition, showing Christ enthroned
upon the orb of heaven. The treatment is basically idealistic and

133 San Vitale, Ravenna. Detail of arcade arch in presbytery. First quarter
sixth century

naturalistic, and the colouring is particularly fresh and lovely. The
panels at the sides of the presbytery, which include portraits of
Justinian and Theodora and their courts, on the other hand, are
much more Eastern in conception. The treatment is realistic rather
than idealistic, the colours are heavy and impressive, the figures stand
in frontal attitudes, and many details of the costumes, such as
Theodora's crown and the stuffs from which the clothes of the
courtiers were made, are quite Persian.

134 San Vitale, Ravenna. View of the presbytery. First quarter sixth cent

135 San Vitale, Ravenna. South wall of the presbytery. First quarter sixth
century

136 San Vitale, Ravenna. North wall of the presbytery. First quarter sixth
century

The apse mosaic of Sant'Apollinare in Classe (535–49) shows an allegorical representation of the Transfiguration, the large cross which occupies the central position symbolizing the transfigured

137 San Vitale, Ravenna. Mosaic. Detail of Justinian panel. Maximian. First quarter sixth century

138 San Vitale, Ravenna. Mosaic. Head of the Emperor Justin First quarter sixth century

139 San Vitale, Ravenna. Mosaics of the presbytery vault. First quarter sixth century

140 Sant'Apollinare in Classe, Ravenna. Apse mosaic. 535-49

Christ, and the sheep close beside it the three Apostles who witnessed the scene. This type of symbolism belongs to the Semitic world, and it probably came to Italy from Syria along with the Christian faith. But though the symbolism is Eastern, the treatment is at the same time almost idealistic, and the lovely flowers of the background and the glorious colouring lift this mosaic out of the Eastern category. It is, indeed, one of the most successful pieces of decoration that have come down to us.

Other mosaics at Ravenna are less important, and may be dismissed very briefly. They comprise work in the Archbishop's palace (494-520) which is good, though much restored, some fragments in

141 Basilica Euphrasiana, Parenzo (Poreč), Istria. Mosaic. Detail. 530–5

the chapel of the Tutti Santi, and an apse mosaic from San Michele in Frigiselo (545), which was removed to the Kaiser Friedrich Museum at Berlin in the last century. The Christ here is beardless, but the style is otherwise in the main Oriental. It has, however, been very much restored, and some of the figures are recent additions.

Elsewhere in Italy a few other mosaics of the early period also survive. In the Baptistery of Soter at Naples there are portions of elaborate decorative compositions in the antique tradition; the work dates from between 470 and 490. It is more clumsy than contemporary work farther to the north, and was probably done by local artists. Though not actually in Italy, Parenzo must also be mentioned here, for the apse mosaics there are of very high quality indeed. Christ appears as a beardless figure, but there are Oriental elements. Most interesting, however, is the great importance accorded to the Virgin, who here for the first time fills the principal position in the centre of the apse. The mosaics date from between 530 and 535. Fragmentary mosaics in the chapel of Sant'Aquilino in the Church of San Lorenzo at Milan are to be dated between 355 and 397 and are among the earliest in Italy; they are still very antique in character.

Throughout this sketch of the mosaics of the early period attention

142 Basilica Euphrasiana, Parenzo (Poreč), Istria. Apse mosaic. 530–5

143 San Lorenzo, Milan. Apse mosaic in the chapel of Sant'Aquilino. *c.* 500

has been drawn to the gradual intrusion of Eastern elements, more especially those of an iconographical character like the bearded Christ. But in addition to these more or less concrete changes, evolution of a more subtle character was also taking place with regard to style. And if Syria was in the main responsible for the Eastern features in ornament or iconography, it was the new capital of the Byzantine world, Constantinople, that was primarily responsible for new ideas in style. Unfortunately, however, we can only follow these developments at the capital in works on a minor scale, for no monuments of major size in mosaic or painting survive there. At Salonica, on the other hand, there is rather more to be seen, and it is probable that mosaics there give a rather clearer idea of what was being done in Constantinople than do those in Italy. The technique in any case is extremely fine, and shows that the very best craftsmen were employed. The tesserae were more carefully graded and more cunningly set than was usual in Italy, the colours were more subtly blended, and more attention was paid to shading.

The earliest mosaics at Salonica are probably the architectural compositions in the drum of the dome of the Church of St George. They perhaps date from as early as the end of the fourth century and reproduce once more the architecture-scapes of Pompeiian art that we have seen at Ravenna and elsewhere, and which reappear with such striking effect at a later date at Damascus. The colouring is of outstanding mastery, and the mosaics in this building are some of the finest that survive. Of Classical inspiration again, though quite different, are the extremely lovely floral scrolls, with animals and birds in their branches, decorating the surfaces below the arcades in the basilica of the Acheiropoietos, formerly known as Eski-Djouma.

144 San Vittore in Ciel d'Oro, Milan. Mosaics on north wall. SS. Ambrose and Gervase. *c.* 470

145 St George, Salonica. Mosaics in Dome. Fourth century

This work is again of high quality. To the fifth century are to be
assigned mosaics discovered in 1921 in the small Church of Hosios
David, where the Vision of Ezekiel is shown. It is in the antique style
with a beardless Christ; the work is not unlike that in the niches of
Sta Costanza at Rome.

Of figural work the most important is that in the basilica of
St Demetrius. The best known shows the figure of the saint himself,
standing between the donors of the church. It is on the south pier of
the apse and, with most of the other mosaics in the church, dates

from the seventh century. Similar compositions balance it on the other faces of the pier, as well as on the corresponding pier on the opposite side of the apse. These mosaics are among the most accomplished that have come down to us from the earlier age; they show

146 Hosios David, Salonica. Apse mosaic. The Vision of Ezekiel. Detail. Fifth century

a complete fusion of Hellenic and Oriental elements, and in their severe but delicate line and rather abstract comprehension are already completely Byzantine. Compositions which adorned the walls of the central aisle and also the side aisles, though rather less

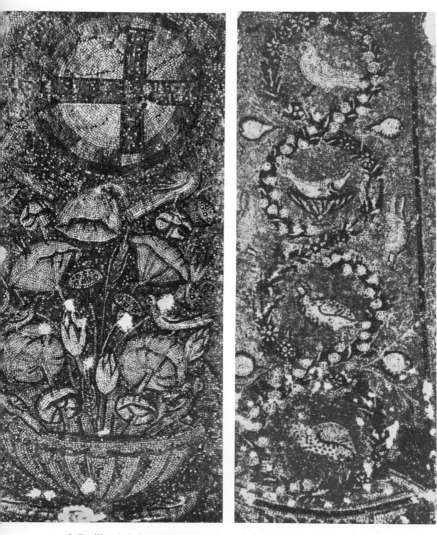

147–8 Basilica Acheiropoietos (Eski-Djouma), Salonica. Details of the mosaics of the arcade arches. Fifth century

149 Basilica Acheiropoietos (Eski-Djouma), Salonica. Detail of plate 148.
Fifth century

accomplished, were of considerable historical interest. They were destroyed in the fire of 1917, which laid low the main portion of the church. The building has been reconstructed, but records of most of these mosaics survive only in sketches and photographs.

A few other mosaics of this age are preserved in more distant places; most important are those in the apse of the church of the monastery of St Catherine on Mount Sinai, where the Transfiguration is shown. This little-known monument is of high quality and considerable interest from the iconographical point of view, but until recently only very poor photographs have been available. It is

150 St Demetrius, Salonica. Mosaic. West wall. St Demetrius and suppliant. Sixth century

151 St Demetrius, Salonica. Mosaic on pier to south of the apse. St Demetrius and donors. *c.* 635

152 St Demetrius, Salonica. Mosaic on west wall. St Demetrius and angel.
Fifth century

probably to be dated to 565.[3] Mosaics in the apse of the church at
Chiti near Larnaca in Cyprus show the Virgin and Child between
Archangels. Both here and in another mosaic in Cyprus, in the
Church of the Panaghia Kanakaria at Lythrangomi, the technique

178

153 St Demetrius, Salonica. Mosaic north of the apse. Seventh or eighth
century

154 St Catherine's monastery, Mount Sinai. Apse mosaic. The Transfiguration.
Sixth century

is careful and the composition balanced; it is astonishing to find
work of such high quality in such out-of-the-way regions.

The date of these mosaics was disputed; they have, however, been
recently cleaned, and there can now be little doubt but that those at
Chiti are to be assigned to the seventh century and those in the
Panaghia Kanakaria to the sixth.[4]

Though the Iconoclast period lasted for more than a century
(726–843), it is surprising how hard it is to distinguish works which
were produced immediately after it from those produced just before;
the severe ban which was exercised on representational art during

155 Panaghia Angeloktistos Church, Chiti (Cyprus). The Archang
Gabriel, from the apse mosaic. Seventh century

156 Metropolitan Museum, New York. Fresco from Boscoreale. First
century B.C.

the period probably accounts for this difficulty, for, except in out-of-the-way monasteries, where art was essentially primitive, development and change must have been impossible, and in monumental work things began at the end of the period where they had left off at its commencement. But the age itself was not completely barren, and it is probable that quite a lot of work which was still naturalistic, though figures were excluded, was done, as well as that which was purely decorative or symbolic in character. Indeed, the very lovely mosaics of the Dome of the Rock at Jerusalem (691–2) and the Great Mosque of Damascus, set up by the Caliph al Walid in 715, may be

157 Damascus. Mosaic in court of the Great Mosque. 715

regarded as Iconoclast monuments to all intents and purposes. At
the Dome of the Rock the mosaics are formal and decorative, with
Hellenistic and Persian influences curiously combined. At Damascus,
in addition to work akin to that at Jerusalem, there are a number of
huge compositions made up of trees and architectural elements.
Colonnades, basilicas, towers, balconies, and niches rise up, one
poised above the other as if in some hill town of Italy. Vine plants
twist round the columns; roofs which appear almost Chinese top
Classical rotundas; trees spring from the banks of a wide river; at
the summit of all stands a great temple. Elaborate shading in darker

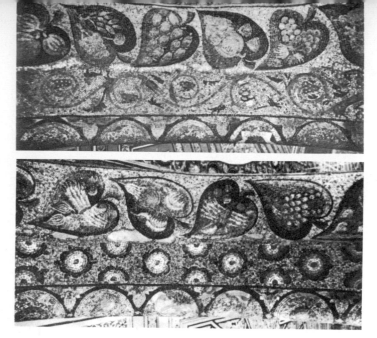

158–9 Dome of the Rock, Jerusalem. Mosaics on the arches of the arcade.
691–2

tones serves to accentuate at the same time the naturalism and the
fantasy of these lovely compositions. Huge trees looming up from
behind the buildings suggest infinite possibilities of exploration and
call up delightful visions of mossy terraces, springs and fountains.[5]

In the churches of the Byzantine world nothing so elaborate
survives, the religious art of the age being extremely severe and
restrained. But there are one or two mosaics of the period, the most
important of which are those in the apse of St Irene, in Constantinople, where a plain but finely proportioned cross stands out with
considerable effect against a gold background. A similar cross,
which was later replaced by a figure of the Virgin, occupied the
apse of Sancta Sophia at Salonica. It was set up by the Emperor
Constantine VI (780–97), the Empress Irene, and Bishop Theophilus,
who was at Nicaea in 787, and the monograms of these persons were
left when the cross was replaced by the figure of the Virgin shortly
after the lifting of the Iconoclast ban. There was a similar cross in the

160 Sta Maria in Domnica, Rome. Apse mosaic. 917–24

apse of the Church of the Assumption at Nicaea, which was also subsequently replaced by a full-length figure of the Virgin.

Though the Iconoclast ban was sternly enforced at Constantinople and in the more important centres, it was disregarded in more distant places, and when we come to deal with wall paintings, quite a lot will have to be said of figural work which was executed at this time

185

161 Sta Prassede, Rome. Mosaic in the chapel of San Zeno. 817–24

in out-of-the-way regions. As regards mosaics, however, the more out-of-the-way places were too poor to sponsor work in the more expensive technique. But in Rome, where the popes did not admit Byzantine control, the situation was very different; their patronage was lavish, craftsmen from the Greek world who favoured the figural style sought refuge there, and figural mosaics were set up not only to beautify the churches, but also, probably, to stress the disapproval of what was considered the heretical attitude of the Byzantine rulers. Much of this Italian work is not of very high quality, but all of it is

162 Sta Prassede, Rome. Lunette over the entrance
the chapel of San Zeno. 817–24

interesting iconographically and technically, and much of it can be fairly exactly dated. Thus the apse mosaics of Sta Maria in Cosmedin belong to between 705 and 707; those in Sta Maria in Domnica, Sta Prassede and Sta Cecilia to between 817 and 824, and those in St Mark's to between 827 and 844. Those in the apse of Sta Maria in Trastevere are post-Iconoclast, and date from between 1139 and 1153. Other mosaics of minor importance exist in San Pietro in Vincoli and in the oratory of John VII and in the Triclinium at the Lateran. Those in the apse of the Lateran basilica itself are thirteenth-century and are signed by Jacopo Torriti. Many of these mosaics show signs of considerable restoration at subsequent dates. The subject of the Sta Maria in Domnica mosaics is the glorification of the Virgin, a theme which was probably chosen to emphasize the importance of the cult of the Virgin in face of Iconoclasm. That of those in the apses of Sta Prassede and Sta Cecilia was the glorification of the saints to whom the churches were dedicated, and whose relics were brought to the churches at the time; the choice of subject again represents the iconodule policy of the popes in opposition to that of the Eastern Church. But there are many Byzantine elements in these mosaics, iconographic, to be seen in the Eastern form of blessing, colouristic, to be seen in the rich and brilliant harmonies, and stylistic, to be seen in the stylized forms and transcendental comprehension. Most truly Byzantine of all is the decoration of the little chapel of St Zeno in Sta Prassede, where the mosaics are not only very beautiful in colouring, but also have a very profound appeal. They are set very roughly, in order to catch and reflect the light to the best possible advantage in the dark little chapel. They deserve, as indeed does much of this Roman work, much closer attention than has usually been accorded to it either by the visitor to Rome or by the Byzantine specialist.

Yet it was the post-Iconoclast age that was in many ways the most important for the production of mosaic decorations on a full scale. A very wide field must now be embraced, for Venice and Sicily were, during part of the period, within the Byzantine sphere; work was done by Byzantine as well as by native craftsmen in Russia, and western Asia Minor, Greece, and the Balkans were wellnigh as important as Constantinople itself. Work of the age was invariably characterized by a new, very sublime, grandeur, and by an essentially transcendental approach. There was an ethereal elongation of the proportions of the human figure and the fullest advantage was taken of the nature of the building to produce a moving, at times almost an awesome, effect. A new preoccupation with liturgical affairs characterized a good deal of the work, unfamiliar as well as the more usual New Testament scenes appearing around the walls of the churches. Their titles accompanied the scenes, their names the figures, in Greek characters, and the lettering was usually designed to constitute an integral part of the composition. The backgrounds were uniformly of gold, and the colours were rich and varied.

It would seem that as soon as the Iconoclast ban was lifted, mosaics and paintings containing figures were at once set up. The most interesting series, although it is in a very fragmentary state, is in an upper chamber over the south porch in Sancta Sophia at Constantinople, where there are mosaics which comprised a Deesis and the portraits of a number of Apostles, Saints, and Patriarchs. The latter included Methodius, who presided at the Council which sanctioned the restoration of images, and three other Patriarchs who had always defended their cult: there is reason to believe that these mosaics were set up almost immediately after the lifting of the ban, that is, about 843.[6]

More spectacular, though not so firmly dated on external evidence, were some of the mosaics that survived until 1919 in the Church of the Assumption at Nicaea. Good photographs are fortunately available, and a recent study of them has made possible a dating which seems reliable. The four archangels on the vault in front of the apse and the full-length figure of the Virgin in the apse are thus to be assigned to about 850, while the decorative work on the bema roof and the four evangelists in the pendentives are to be dated to about 1065. Work of both periods is of very high quality, the archangels being extremely impressive, while the evangelists are particularly delicate and spiritual in conception.[7]

The standing Virgin may be contrasted with the seated one in the apse of Sancta Sophia at Constantinople, a recent examination of which proves that it must date from 867; it was set at the same time as the two archangels on the vault in front of the apse.[8] The figure of the Virgin in the apse of Sancta Sophia at Salonica was also set up to replace a cross very soon after the end of Iconoclasm. The more impressive mosaics in the dome of the same church, which show the prophets around the drum, are probably slightly later; though their date has been disputed, there is weighty evidence in favour of the year 886.[9]

163 Church of the Assumption, Nicaea (destroyed 1919). Mosaic. Head of an archangel. *c.* 850

From the end of the ninth century onwards mosaic decorations on a large scale were numerous, and enough examples survive to give an idea of the style at most of the various periods; from soon after Iconoclasm, however, the setting of the cubes in curves rather than straight lines has become virtually universal. In Sancta Sophia at Constantinople, for example, cleaning activities undertaken by the Byzantine Institute of America have disclosed eight separate series of different dates.[10] The earliest is probably the great lunette over the

164 Sancta Sophia, Istanbul. Mosaic in apse. Head of Archangel Gabriel. *c.* 861

165 Sancta Sophia, Istanbul. Mosaic in the south gallery. The Deesis. Probably twelfth century

main door from the narthex, showing the seated Christ with an emperor at his feet, whom Whittemore identifies as Leo VI (886–912).[11] Next in date is the lunette over the door of the southern porch, which shows the Virgin between Justinian and Constantine; Whittemore assigns it to the time of Basil II (986–94) but Morey thinks that the reign of Basil I (867–86) is more likely.[12] The work is rather arid, and on purely stylistic grounds the later date is the more probable. Two panels in the southern gallery, called by Whittemore the Zoe and the John panels, date from between 1042 and 1057 and c. 1120 respectively. The work is decorative, but not of very high artistic quality. Finest of all as regards quality is a panel bearing the

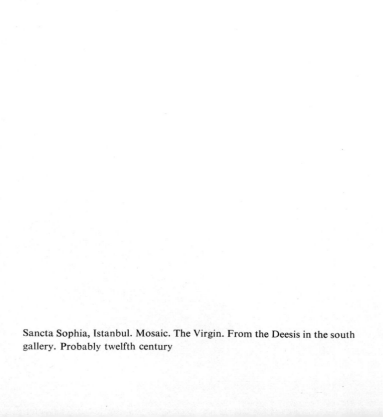

Sancta Sophia, Istanbul. Mosaic. The Virgin. From the Deesis in the south gallery. Probably twelfth century

166 Sancta Sophia, Istanbul. Mosaic in the lunette over the main portal in the narthex. 886–912

Deesis on the middle wall of the south gallery. It is not dated by an inscription or by any external evidence, as were the Zoe and the John panels, but it is in a very humanist style, and on the grounds of its similarity to work in Kariye Camii (1310–20) it has been suggested that it is to be assigned to the fourteenth century. But as research into the story of later Byzantine painting progresses, the more clear does it become that there was a definite Renaissance in the twelfth century, and that there was continuous development of a new manner anyhow from about 1130 (see pp. 266–74). In view of this, there are grounds for believing that the Sancta Sophia Deesis should be assigned to the middle of the twelfth century, and that it represents one of the earlier experiments in the new manner. In any case, it is a work of very rare beauty; to the writer it appears as perhaps the most lovely Byzantine mosaic that has come down to us. In addition, the Fathers of the Church occupy the spaces between the windows of the great lunettes to north and south, and more recently a portrait of Emperor Alexander (912–13) has been uncovered in the north gallery.

Outside Constantinople and Rome the next important mosaics in point of date are those of the monastery of Hosios Lukas, not far from Delphi, in Greece. They date from the early eleventh century. The finest work is on the vaults of the church; scenes from the Passion cycle in the narthex are rather cruder. Those that remain

167 Sancta Sophia, Salonica. Apse mosaic. The Virgin and Child. Ninth century

168 Sancta Sophia, Istanbul. Mosaic in apse. The Virgin and Child. c. 8

show brilliant and very lovely colouring, and they are of great interest iconographically. But though the work is very accomplished from the technical point of view, it is in the hieratic, primitive style associated with the monasteries rather than the capital, and may be contrasted with the more delicate work at Daphni near Athens, where the Constantinopolitan style, with its elegance and greater subtlety, is to the fore. The figures and scenes here are distinguished by an almost Classical beauty, and even though much has perished

169 Sancta Sophia, Istanbul. Mosaic in the lunette over the south portal. The Virgin between Justinian and Constantine. Probably 986–94

170 Hosios Lukas (near Delphi). Mosaic on roof of presbytery. The Virgin and
Pentecost. *c.* 1000

and much of that which remains has been over-restored, the impression is still overpowering. In fact, the Daphni mosaics constitute what is perhaps the most perfect monument of the age. The Crucifixion is typical, but even more impressive is the Christ the Almighty which dominates the church from the centre of the dome. Here Classicism is less to the fore, and Oriental realism plays a part. It is one of the most mysterious and at the same time one of the most impressive portrayals of Christ that Christian art has produced. The work at Daphni is all to be assigned to about 1100.

171 San Vitale, Ravenna. Mosaic on north wall of presbytery. Israelites awaiting Moses. First quarter sixth century

172 Hosios Lukas (near Delphi). Mosaic in exo-narthex. Group of apostles. *c.* 1000

173 Sancta Sophia, Salonica. Detail of dome mosaic. The Ascension. Ninth
century

174 Hosios Lukas (near Delphi). Mosaic in south transept. Virgin and Child.
c. 1000

175 Daphni (near Athens). Dome mosaic. Christ Pantocrator. *c.* 1100

Another important though fragmentary decoration survives in the
Church of the Nea Moni on the island of Chios. The work is of very
high quality and the style nearer to the expressionism of Hosios
Lukas than the Classicism of Daphni. The mosaics have recently
been disencumbered of a great deal of dirt which had collected on
them throughout the centuries. They are to be dated between 1042
and 1056. Of the same period are the mosaics in the Church of
Sancta Sophia at Kiev, in Russia, dating from between 1037 and
1061. Though provincial, they are still probably to be attributed to
Greek rather than to Russian craftsmen. On the other hand, Russian
craftsmen, who were perhaps taught by the Greeks who worked in

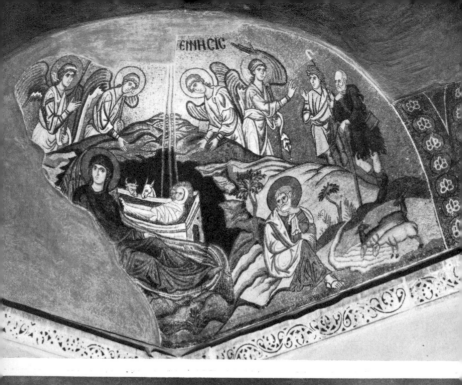

178 Daphni (near Athens). Mosaic on the north wall. The Crucifixion. *c.* 1100

7 Daphni (near Athens). Mosaics in pendentives.
Nativity and Transfiguration. *c.* 1100

179 Daphni (near Athens). Mosaics in the narthex. Christ. *c.* 1100

180 Daphni (near Athens). Mosaics in the narthex. Head of an angel. *c.* 1100

181 Nea Moni monastery, Chios. The Virgin. 1042–56

182 St Michael, Kiev. Mosaic. Head of an angel. 1108

Sancta Sophia, were responsible for other mosaics in the same town, notably some rather more intimate ones in the Church of St Michael, which date from 1108.

Of work outside actual Byzantine territory, however, by far the most important is that in Sicily, for the quality is far higher than that at Kiev, and the extent of wall space covered is very much greater.

183 Sancta Sophia, Kiev. Detail of mosaic on pier. 1043-6

184 Sancta Sophia, Kiev. Mosaic. Detail of the Communion of the Apostles.
1043–6

There are decorations there on a major scale in four separate buildings. Probably the finest from the artistic point of view is the work at
Cefalù. As the church is of Western character, with no dome, the
figure of Christ the Almighty has been transferred from its usual
position in the dome to the conch of the apse, while the Virgin,
whose normal place is in the conch of the apse, has been moved

185 Cefalù. Apse mosaic in cathedral. 1148

186 Sta Maria dell'Amiraglio (Martorana). Mosaic: the dome. *c.* 1151

down on to the eastern wall. Below and on the side walls of the apse are decorative compositions, saints and apostles. The mosaics are not all of the same date. Those on the curved walls of the apse are part of the orginal scheme and date from around 1148; those on the walls of the presbytery probably date from around 1175, and those on the presbytery vault from between 1150 and 1160; the later mosaics are to be attributed to Sicilian craftsmen, while the earlier ones were probably done by Greeks who were brought to Sicily from Byzantium at the request of the Norman rulers. Dêmus, in his penetrating study of the mosaics of Sicily, has shown that the dates at which mosaics were set up can to some extent be correlated with the periods at which the Sicilian and the Byzantine emperors were on good terms.[13]

The decoration of the Martorana, or Sta Maria dell'Amiraglio at Palermo, on the other hand, is uniform in style and date; the work was done around 1151, and it is likely that the Greek craftsmen from Cefalù passed on to the Martorana when their work in the apse at the former place was done. Here the arrangement is more truly Byzantine, for the church is an Eastern rather than a Western building. The Pantocrator thus occupied his usual position in the dome, and the vaults and upper portions of the walls were covered with New Testament scenes, mostly from the life of the Virgin. The majority of the scenes around the crossing still survive, and there are two panels in the narthex which are especially interesting, for one shows Christ crowning the Emperor Roger and the other shows the donor, Admiral George of Antioch, at the feet of the Virgin. These mosaics are all of very fine quality, brilliant in colour and delicate in technique; had the choir not been redecorated in the rococo style,

187–8 Sta Maria dell'Amiraglio (Martorana). Mosaics of the narthex. c. 1151

189 Sta Maria dell'Amiraglio (Martorana). Mosaic. Dormition of the Virgin.
c. 1151

190 Palatine Chapel, Royal Palace, Palermo. Mosaics of the nave. *c.* 1160

this would have been the most lovely interior in Sicily and one of the finest of Byzantine art.

The Palatine Chapel in the Royal Palace of Palermo consists of a basilica-like nave, with a cruciform eastern end with dome at the crossing. All the wall space is entirely covered with mosaics, comprising very full cycles of Old and New Testament scenes. The work was done by a large number of hands and at different times; it has subsequently suffered very severely from deceptive restorations. The best work is that at the east end, which is to be assigned to Greek workmen; it was done about 1143; that in the nave is to be assigned

191 Monreale. Mosaics in apse

to the fifties and sixties of the twelfth century. Here local craftsmen, who had been taught by the Greeks, were employed; their work is accomplished, but is sometimes rather lacking in delicacy and feeling.

At Monreale, a few miles from Palermo, the whole church, which is of very considerable size, is again decorated, but if it is more impressive than the Palatine Chapel on account of the immensity of the scheme, the work is in no way comparable in quality, even if full allowance be made for the effect of the numerous later restorations. The building was erected between 1174 and 1182, and, immediately on its completion, work on the mosaics began; it was finished, Demus concludes, within about ten years; and, in the light of the evidence he puts forward, an old theory that some of it was actually done in the thirteenth century can be discarded. Indeed, the Monreale mosaics have nothing in common, so far as style or colouring are concerned, with fourteenth-century work in Constantinople; they are more wooden, and lack the superlative excellence which distinguishes the mosaics of Kariye Camii there or those of the Holy Apostles at Salonica (1312).

Some mosaics which survive in a small chamber of the palace at Palermo, and on a less extensive scale in a villa in the town known as La Ziza, are interesting, for they constitute the only important secular work that has come down to us. The former scheme is strikingly Persian in appearance, archers, birds, and fantastic animals being depicted either confronted or addorsed, with formal trees in between, much as on textiles. Persian influence was probably to the fore in a good deal of secular decoration in the Byzantine world as a whole, and the Palermo mosaics are not necessarily to be attributed to the very marked Islamic character of Sicilian culture at the time. The motifs of the mosaics are, in any case, close to those which we see on Byzantine textiles, and both attest the importance of Persian influence. The two decorations at Palermo are both to be assigned to about 1170.

Another area outside the actual limits of the Byzantine Empire where important mosaic work was done was Venice. In spite of the fact that glass tesserae were made there as early as the ninth century, none of the mosaics in St Mark's are probably earlier than the twelfth century, with the possible exception of the Ascension in the central dome and some scenes illustrating the life of the Virgin in the north aisle, which may belong to the late eleventh. They cannot

192 Camera di Ruggero, Royal Palace, Palermo. Mosaic over the entrance. *c.* 1170

193 La Ziza, Palermo. Detail of mosaic. *c.* 1170

be earlier than 1063, for the structure was begun only in that year. These mosaics are in a rather archaic style, and the artistic quality of the work is not outstanding. From the twelfth century onwards additions were made to the decoration of the church at every period and in every style until the fifteenth century, and the later contributions serve to prove how ill adapted the mosaic medium was to

Renaissance art. Some of the twelfth- and thirteenth-century work, which is Romanesque in style, is, however, quite effective, though never does it compare with the best of the Byzantine.[14]

Mosaics of rather higher quality survive at two places close to Venice; most important is Torcello, where there are mosaics of three periods. The Apostles in the apse belong to the beginning of the twelfth century; the Virgin in the conch of the apse and the Last Judgement at the west end belong to the latter part of the twelfth; and mosaics in the apse of the southern aisle may perhaps be rather earlier, though they were certainly restored in the thirteenth century. The church itself was rebuilt in 1008, so they can hardly be earlier than the eleventh century. Of all of them, the twelfth-century work in the apse is the best, and the tall figure of the Virgin there, isolated against a background of dull gold, is a thing of very great effect and very rare beauty. A similar Virgin occupies the apse of the church at Murano near by. It is probably to be assigned to the thirteenth

194 St Mark's, Venice. Mosaic. The Archangels Michael and Gabriel holding a medallion of Christ. Thirteenth century

195 Cappella del Sacramento, the Cathedral, Trieste. Apse mosaic. Twelfth
   century

century. It lacks the compelling beauty of the Torcello composition,
but is none the less very graceful and elegant. The work at Torcello
must have been done by Greek workmen. Some mosaics in the
Cathedral of San Giusto at Trieste belong to the Venetian school,
and show quite good work of the late twelfth century.

In Greece itself the most important twelfth-century work, exclud-
ing Daphni, is a Communion of the Apostles formerly at Serres in
Macedonia. Diez and Demus regard it as typical of the Byzantine
Renaissance,[15] and Serres seems to occupy in the story of mosaics
something of the same position as is to be assigned in painting to

ΜΡ ΘΥ

196 SS. Maria e Donato, Murano. Apse mosaic. The Virgin. Fourteenth
century

197 Torcello. Apse mosaic. The Virgin and Child. Twelfth cen

198 St Theodore, Serres (Macedonia). Mosaic. Communion of the Apostles (destroyed 1913). Fourteenth century

Nerez. But not all the monuments of the age show the same feeling for vitality and humanism as is to be seen at Serres and Nerez, and the Pantocrator in the dome in the Church of the Panaghia Parigoritissa at Arta in Epirus is in a more monumental manner, even though the mosaics belong to the thirteenth rather than the twelfth century. Nor is there much of the spirit of the Renaissance in two panels showing St George and St Demetrius in the monastery of Xenophontos on Mount Athos, and panels with the Annunciation and the Deesis in the monastery of Vatopedi are again in the monumental style. They are to be dated to the twelfth, perhaps even to the

199 St Theodore, Serres (Macedonia). Mosaic. Communion of the Apostles. Fourteenth century

eleventh century, and are earlier than the church in which they now stand.[16] A mosaic at Gelat in Georgia, to be dated to the second quarter of the twelfth century, shows a local interpretation of the Constantinopolitan manner of the period.[17]

The last age of Byzantine mosaic production, the fourteenth century, was at one time represented by two monuments only, a composition showing the Pantocrator, surrounded by Prophets, in the dome of the Church of St Mary Pammakaristos (Fetiye Camii) at Constantinople, and a more extensive decoration in the better-known Church of the Chora, or Kariye Camii, in the same town. Recently, however, a number of additional monuments have come to light, notably more scenes in St Mary Pammakaristos, and some panels with figures in the Church of St Theodore Tiro (Kilisse Camii) at Constantinople, and a number of scenes in the Church of the Holy Apostles at Salonica. The latter were probably set up very soon after the completion of the church, that is to say about 1312. All these mosaics are interesting, but those of Kariye Camii are quite

200 Monastery of Vatopedi, Mount Athos. Mosaic. The Deesis in the narthex. Twelfth century

Church of the Chora (Kariye Camii), Istanbul. Mosaic. The Assumption.
c. 1315

201 Panaghia Parigoritissa, Arta (Epirus). Christ as Pantocrator. 1295

203 Holy Apostles, Salonica. Mosaic. The Transfiguration. *c.* 1315

St Theodore, Serres (Macedonia). Mosaic. St Andrew
Fourteenth century

204 Church of St Mary Pammakaristos (Fetiye Camii), Istanbul. Mosaic:
dome of the southern side chapel. Christ Pantocrator. *c.* 1315

outstanding, not only because of the comparative completeness and
fullness of the cycle of scenes, but also because of the artistic quality
of the work. The little church is in fact a gem of the finest degree,
comparable as regards quality to Giotto's Arena Chapel at Padua.

A great change has come over Byzantine art as we see it in these
mosaics. There is a new lightness, a new delicacy, the approach is
more human, and though none of the old ethereal quality of the art
has been lost, it has at the same time gained a new intimacy. The
revival that we see here is more fully exemplified in wall paintings,
and a full discussion of it is reserved for the next chapter; here it is
necessary only to stress the importance of this renaissance in general
and of Kariye Camii in particular in the story of Byzantine art.

The majority of the scenes that have survived are on the vaults of the outer and the vaults and walls of the inner narthex. They comprise full cycles of the lives of Christ and the Virgin. The Nativity is typical of the attention to detail of this new art, while the childhood of the Virgin shows its humanism. There is an important panel which shows the donor presenting a model of the church to Christ, which serves to date the mosaics to between 1310 and 1320. A composition showing the death of the Virgin inside the body of the church, over the western door, which was discovered in 1920, belongs to the same series. A large panel, in the inner narthex, showing our Lord and the Virgin, is clearly by a different hand from the other mosaics. It was at one time regarded as of earlier date, but recent investigations have revealed two figures of donors below the main figures and also an inscription which establishes a date soon after 1307. In any case, its quality is quite outstanding, even among the superb mosaics of Kariye Camii. These mosaics have recently

205 Church of the Chora (Kariye Camii), Istanbul. Mosaic in the inner narthex. The Deesis. *c.* 1315

been completely cleaned and fixed by the Byzantine Institute of America.[18]

Before leaving the subject of mosaics, a word must be said of miniature mosaics, which constitute one of the most delicate and most successful of Byzantine minor arts. But so minute are the tesserae, and so fragile is the wax ground-work in which they are set, that very few examples have survived to the present day. True portable mosaics of this type were probably first made in the tenth

206 Church of the Chora (Kariye Camii), Istanbul. Mosaic in the inner narthex. The founder presents a model of the church to Christ. *c.* 1315

207–8 Church of the Chora (Kariye Camii), Istanbul. Mos in the outer narthex. Nativity and Census. *c.* 1315

209–10 Monastery of Xenophontos, Mount Athos. Mosaics. SS. Demetrius and George. Twelfth century

or eleventh century; by the twelfth they were already very popular, but even then they were considered as rare and precious. A few examples are probably to be assigned to this date, notably a fine panel bearing the figure of Christ in the National Museum at Florence, which shows certain affinities with the mural mosaics of

211 Museo Nazionale del Bargello, Florence. Miniature mosaic. Christ. Twelfth century

Sicily, and one with the Virgin and Child at Chilandari on Mount Athos.[19] A small panel, bearing the Virgin and Child, in the Church of Sta Maria della Salute at Venice, on which there is an inscription with the date 1115, is probably actually not quite so early, for the style, more especially the method of treating the highlights as a single

212 Monastery of Chilandari, Mount Athos. Miniature mosaic. The Virgin and Child. Twelfth century

band of light colour, is hardly what one would expect to find before the end of the thirteenth century. Other examples that are known would seem to belong either to the later thirteenth or to the four-

213 Museo Civico, Sassoferrato. Miniature mosaic. St George. Fourteenth century

teenth centuries. There are quite a number of them in different places. The most important comprise a superb Crucifixion, now in the State Museum at Berlin, a Transfiguration in the Louvre, and two panels in the Opera del Duomo at Florence, each bearing six of the Twelve Feasts of the Church. A very delicate little panel bearing the Annunciation in the Victoria and Albert Museum is probably of the fourteenth century; it is of outstanding quality. A number of miniature mosaics preserved in various of the monasteries of Mount

214 State Museums, Berlin. Miniature mosaic. Crucifixion, with The Virgin and St John. Thirteenth century

215 Opera del Duomo, Florence. Mosaic diptych. The Twelve Feasts of the Church. Left wing. Fourteenth century

Athos should also be noted; they comprise a Crucifixion, a panel with St Anne and the Virgin, given by the Tsarina Anastasia, wife of Ivan the Terrible, and a panel with St John Chrysostom, all at

216 Victoria and Albert Museum, London. Miniature mosaic. The Annunciation. Fourteenth century

Vatopedi; a standing figure of Christ at Esphigmenou, a Virgin and
Child at Chilandari, and a bust of St Nicholas at Stavronikita. A
St John the Baptist in St Mark's at Venice may also be noted, as

217 Monastery of Esphigmenou, Mount Athos. Miniature mosaic with embossed frame. Christ and the Twelve Apostles. Fourteenth century

may a St Nicholas at Patmos, and one bearing Christ as the Man of Sorrows from Evrytania, both of which were made known for the first time at the Byzantine Exhibition at Athens in 1964. All these

218 Monastery of Stavronikita, Mount Athos. Miniature mosaic. St Nicholas.
Fourteenth century

are to be dated to the thirteenth or early fourteenth centuries. The
workmanship in all of them is invariably delicate, there is developed
modelling in the features, and subtle and very lovely colouring; the
general effect is close to that of Sienese painting.

6 Wall Paintings

In many ways it is hard to dissociate wall paintings from mosaics. The designs for the mosaics were in most cases painted in colour upon the walls in a more or less finished state before the tesserae were laid; the masters who set out the designs were no doubt in many cases the same people who executed paintings proper; both arts made use of the same system of iconography and the same models, either sketches or manuscript illustrations. Yet the techniques of the finished work differentiate the arts in style as well as in material, and there is a further difference in that until fairly late times the majority of the paintings that have survived come from poorer or smaller churches or more distant sites, and hence do not represent the finest court art, whereas the mosaics mostly belong to the greater churches, and were in many cases executed under direct imperial patronage. It is primarily for this reason that it is most satisfactory to treat the two arts apart.

Broadly speaking, the same periods or ages may be distinguished in the story of painting as in that of mosaics. Except in the first of them, from which a good deal of work survives in catacombs and early churches in Rome, the paintings were seldom in true fresco, a very specialized technique, where the paint is laid on damp plaster, so that it penetrates and becomes one with it. We have to do instead with paintings in a glue or tempera medium, laid upon hard plaster, in much the same way as they might be laid upon the gesso ground of a panel. The plaster, however, was usually good, and often has set in the course of centuries to a rocklike hardness. The actual nature of the plaster varied of course from region to region, but it is on stylistic rather than technical evidence that the work of the various areas is to be distinguished.

Throughout the period from the third to the ninth century three main regions concern us, namely Italy, Syria, and Egypt. Today, as a result of the work of N. and M. Thierry and Jerphanion in Cappadocia, one must also consider Anatolia. At the outset, however, Egypt and Italy seem to have been closely allied, for there appears to have flourished both in Alexandria and in Rome and the Roman cities a naturalistic, landscape style – or rather one should say architecture-scape style, for buildings, colonnades, and perspectives were perhaps more important than the actual landscapes in which they stood. It has been suggested that paintings of this type were derived from the scenes made for the Hellenistic theatre, and Alexandria has been proposed as the original home of the style. But Pompeii, with its numerous surviving monuments, furnishes a more satisfactory centre in which to study the development of the art, and the case for Rome as the original centre of the style has also been convincingly argued. Wherever it originated, it was in the Roman world that the style was most developed in the first centuries of the Christian era, and with the adoption of Christianity as the official faith it served to inspire a good deal of work in churches and sacred buildings. Attention has already been called to the influence of the Pompeiian architecture-scapes on mosaics like those of Sta Pudenziana at Rome, or the Baptistery of the Orthodox at Ravenna; they were extensively used in manuscript illumination, and they inspired the backgrounds made up of buildings which, as Christian iconography developed, came to be universally adopted as an essential part of the Old and New Testament illustration.

But this picturesque style was not the only one that was available to the Christian artists. Alongside it there flourished a realist manner, where figures were shown frontally and where the whole attention was concentrated on the essential personages and very little care was paid to the backgrounds. Again, a system where greater attention was paid to esoteric symbolism than to actual representation must also be noted. According to this system birds, fish, or animals which at first glance would seem purely decorative were depicted because they conveyed some profound idea to the initiated; the peacock was popular, for example, because its flesh was believed to be incorruptible, and it therefore served as symbol of the Resurrection. The dove was revered as symbol of the peace of Christ, and the fish was sacred because the word for fish in Greek, ἰχθὺς, stood for the phrase, Ἰησοῦς Χριστὸς Θεοῦ υἱὸς Σωτήρ, 'Jesus Christ, son of God, Saviour'.

The earliest examples of purely Christian paintings that survive

are preserved in the catacombs of Rome. Most of them are on a comparatively small scale, and they were executed by little-known artists who had had but scanty training. But sincerity made up for lack of elegance, and many of them were extremely expressive and at times even very beautiful. The individual figures were mostly drawn from Classical models; Christ followed the prototype of the youthful Apollo; Eirene, personification of the peace of the Church, had the appearance of a Roman tutelary goddess; the Apostles looked like Classical philosophers. The scenes, however, showed greater originality, and even before the acceptance of Christianity as the state religion, the depiction of the various scenes of the Bible

221 San Ermete, Rome. Wall painting in the catacomb chapel. The Virgin.
Eighth century

o San Clemente, Rome. Wall painting. The Virgin. 869

222 Sta Maria Antiqua, Rome. Wall painting. St Andrew. Seventh or eighth century

story had begun to assume the set forms which were rapidly to be developed into a strictly controlled system of Christian iconography. Sometimes the Christian subjects were modelled on some Classical scene; sometimes they were completely new, showing great freshness and originality of mind, even if the actual figures were often clumsy and inelegant or were taken from elsewhere.

On a rather more grandiose scale than the catacomb paintings were those which were done for the decoration of some of the early churches in Rome, though there is little that survives which is earlier than the eighth cnetury. The most important of the paintings are to be found in San Clemente and in Sta Maria Antiqua in the Forum. Those in the latter church are of varying dates and in different styles. Thus the well-known Crucifixion (705–8) follows a Syrian iconographical model, for Christ wears a long robe in place of the Classical loin-cloth, and its whole style is Eastern. St Andrew, on

223 Sta Maria Antiqua, Rome. Wall painting. The Crucifixion. 705–8

247

224 Sant'Angelo in Formis, Capua. Wall painting in the apse. Archangel
Michael. Eleventh century

the other hand, is in a style which heralds the fully developed
Byzantine, with white highlights and emaciated face. Others, like the
Angel in the Annunciation scene, are wholly Hellenistic, while
others, like the Virgin and Christ, done under the patronage of
Pope Leo V (847–55), are more Latin, and herald the paintings
executed in Italy during the Dark Ages, which culminated in the
Romanesque.[1]

During the Iconoclast age the development of this Latin style in
Italy was affected to some extent, as were the mosaics, by the arrival

225 Sant'Angelo in Formis, Capua. Head of an angel. Twelfth century

of exiles from Constantinople, who fled to Italy on account of their belief in representational art. They appear to have established a colony in Rome, and to have executed quite a number of works, so that throughout the eighth century the Byzantine and the Latin trends were both practised at Rome. The native strain was for a time supported by anti-Byzantine social feeling, but by the ninth century it had lost practically all the vigour that had been inherited from the Classical world, and from then onwards art was almost of a peasant type. At the same time the Byzantine trend, divorced from its true roots, also tended to decadence, though it was sustained to some extent by the Benedictine school of Monte Cassino right down to the twelfth century. The most important examples of the Byzantinizing Benedictine school are the paintings of Sant'Angelo in Formis, near Capua (1056–86), where Orthodox influence is clearly to the fore. This is the case with the paintings in the church; renderings of the Virgin and the Archangel Michael in the porch are truly Byzantine works; an icon of much the same date, now in Russia, and known as the 'Golden-haired Virgin', may be compared.[2]

Even if the story of painting in Italy was one of gentle decadence, it was nevertheless also one of continuous production. In the eastern part of the Byzantine world, on the other hand, though none the less interesting in early times, it was rudely interrupted by the Moslem advances in the seventh century. The area to the east of the Mediterranean, owing to its ready connexion with the Red Sea and the Persian Gulf, seems to have drawn many of the elements of its culture from Hither Asia as well as from the Classical world, so that Syria was actually a great cultural entrepôt between East and West. This blending of elements was already in progress in pagan times, as for instance in the sculptured tombs of Palmyra, and it was carried forward in the early centuries of the Christian age. Nowhere are the results more apparent than in monuments discovered in the excavations conducted at Dura on the middle Euphrates in the years between the two world wars. Most striking, perhaps, are the paintings of the Temple of the Palmyrene Gods, dating from the year A.D. 85, where there appeared a number of figures standing with their faces directly turned towards the observer, and engaged in a ritual scene in the temple, which was probably connected with the Mazdaean faith. Beside them stood other figures, the most important of which were those of the Palmyrene Gods themselves; they seem beyond doubt to be prototypes of the warrior-saints of later times. But the importance of these paintings in the story of Christian art goes deeper than this, for in colour, style, and arrangement it is clearly apparent that the 'hieratic' art of the developed Byzantine phase owed a very great deal to such monuments as these. With the overthrow of Zenobia in 272 Christians in Syria were allowed a very free hand, and it is probable that their churches from this time onward were frequently decorated with paintings not unlike those in the Temple of the Palmyrene Gods.[3] But the only paintings from Christian buildings of early times that have so far been discovered

226 Temple of the Palmyrene gods, Dura (Syria). Wall painting. Ritual scene.
A.D. 85

are in a rather less accomplished manner. They come from a church
at Dura dating from shortly before A.D. 250 and show such scenes
as the Good Shépherd bringing the lost sheep to the flock, the three
Marys bringing myrrh to the tomb of our Lord, Christ walking on
the water, and other miracles. This is the earliest figure of Christ that

251

227 The Church, Dura (Syria). Wall painting. Christ healing the Paralytic.
c. 250

is known in Christian art, and it is of a far more Oriental type than
the early renderings in the catacombs. The frontal pose is universal;
the colours are bright and striking, and the general effect is forceful
and impressive. Most important of all, however, is the stage to which
the iconography of the Bible scenes had already progressed at this
early date in Syria. The development seems to have been well in
advance of Rome.[4]

Perhaps of even greater importance than the paintings of the
church at Dura are those in a synagogue at the same place, dated to
about 245. Its walls were covered with scenes from the Old Testament, which could have served equally well for the decoration of a
Christian building. It is interesting to find them in a synagogue, for
even at this date there was a definite dislike of depicting the human

228 The Synagogue, Dura (Syria). Wall painting. Moses before the Burning
Bush. *c.* 245

form in Jewish art, and if the paintings of the Temple of the
Palmyrene Gods indicate the influence of an Eastern style, those of
the synagogue show how deeply Hellenistic ideas had penetrated.
Even apart from the effect it exercised on Semitic thought, Hellenistic
influence is to be seen here in other ways also, notably the animated
scenes and the elaborate architectural backgrounds. The figures, too,
are mostly of a Hellenistic type, though the style is in some ways

Persian at the same time. Eastern elements are exemplified in the frontal pose of the figures, which is usual, though not universal, in the system of vertical projection, where the figures in the background are placed vertically above those in the foreground; again the enlarged size of the principal personages is very characteristic of this style. Moses, for instance, is almost twice the size of his companions. In the centre of the main wall of the synagogue was a niche with a single panel above it. On either side were three rows of paintings, separated one from the other by ornamental bands. Above was the cycle of Moses, in the middle that of the Ark of the Covenant, and below, to the right the life of Elijah and to the left that of Ezekiel. In fact, the Synagogue vies with the Church in affording the first instance of Bible illustration on a large scale. On Syrian soil, and in a Jewish synagogue, we see the first beginnings of the elaborate pictorial art which was to become of such supreme importance in the Byzantine world, and it is probable that such prototypes as these played a more important role in the formation of Christian art than did the catacomb paintings of Rome or Alexandria, confined as they were in the main to an antique mannerism or to an obscure symbolism.

What form Christian painting took in regions farther to the east is still somewhat uncertain, though a few fragments bearing figures as well as purely non-representational motifs like crosses are known from Hira, Samarra, and elsewhere in the eighth and ninth centuries. But the importance laid upon paintings in Manichaean texts suggests that the art was widely practised in Mesopotamia and Persia from the sixth century onwards, and it must be remembered that Christianity was the most important religion in the area for quite a time before the rise of Islam, and that it also remained important for several centuries after.[5] There was doubtless a developed church architecture, and the churches were probably decorated with paintings. Secular work in the desert palace of Kuseir Amra, dating from between 724 and 743, serves to give some idea of what character these paintings had assumed by the eighth century. Hellenistic elements are still very much to the fore, in spite of the Persian style of some of the work.[6]

Another important area throughout the early centuries was Egypt. The earliest work, in any case at Alexandria, was in the picturesque style of architecture-scape which we have already discussed in connexion with Pompeii. By the fifth century, however, a new style

229 Kuseir Amra (Syria).
Wall painting.
A female figure. 724–43

255

had evolved, if not in Alexandria, which was always a very conservative centre, at least in the Christian monasteries of the Nile valley. This new style was deeply influenced by the Orient, and was characterized by the same love of frontality and vertical perspective, the same harsh realism, the same dumpy figures, and the same stress upon inner significance rather than outward elegance that characterized much of the Syrian work. The most important examples of this style of painting that survive are at Baouit, at al Baggarat, and in the Church of St Jeremiah at Saqqara. All are interesting and of considerable importance in the history of Christian Iconography, but none is of any very great artistic quality. Some paintings dating from between the eighth and the eleventh centuries recently discovered by a Polish expedition at Faras in Nubia should also be noted; they are of finer quality than anything known in Egypt. As the Church of Egypt broke away from Orthodoxy at quite an early date, the iconography also developed along particular lines, and certain scenes or interpretations of the biblical texts that appear in Egypt were peculiar to that country alone.

Outside Italy, Syria, and Egypt there is very little work indeed that can be attributed to a pre-ninth-century date. At Perustica in Bulgaria there are a few fragments which, in Grabar's opinion, serve to indicate the character of Constantinopolitan wall painting in the ninth century.[7] But in the capital itself nothing survives, nor has anything been found in any of the other great cities which remained important after the fall of Alexandria and Antioch to the Moslems in the seventh century. Most of what there once was must have been destroyed at the order of the Iconoclast rulers between 726 and 843. Only in the monastic sanctuaries of Cappadocia and Latmos, in Asia Minor, are any extensive remains to be found, and though these are of great interest and sometimes of real quality, they do not represent the accomplished work of specialists employed under imperial patronage, but rather that of uneducated hermits, who were in general more interested in dogma than in art.

The monastic paintings of Cappadocia are practically all to be dated to between the ninth and eleventh centuries, and a considerable number of them survive there in rock-cut chapels and sometimes also in larger built churches. The region seems to have been little affected by the Iconoclast ban. Monastic circles were always in opposition to the idea, and in Cappadocia they were far enough away from the great cities to ignore the decree with impunity. In

St Panteleimon, Nerez (Macedonia). Wall painting. Detail from the
Lamentation for Christ. 1164

230 The New Church, Tokale Kilisse, Cappadocia. Wall paintings. Two super-imposed strata of different periods. Upper layer, figural work of the tenth century. Lower layer, decorative work of the Iconoclast period. 730–843

fact, the monks and hermits of the region seem to have continued to decorate their churches without interruption. The inaccessibility of the region has again helped to preserve the work, and most of the paintings are in comparatively good condition. Happily they have been very fully published, so that their study is possible without arduous journeys to see the originals.[8]

The earliest of these paintings belong to the eighth century; they are purely decorative and were no doubt done in Iconoclast times. Others are admirable examples of a crude but vigorous monastic art in which we see perpetuated the features that were characteristic of the art of Syria some five or six centuries earlier. But the iconography, as might be expected, had developed very considerably since

231 Göreme, Cappadocia. Wall painting. Probably of the Iconoclast period. 730–843

232 Elmale Kilisse, Cappadocia. Ceiling painting. Angel. Eleventh century

the days when the Dura church and synagogue were decorated, and
the tastes of the hermits of Cappadocia are clearly reflected in the
attention that was given to unfamiliar apocryphal scenes or to long
and complicated biblical cycles, where the scenes follow one another
as in a frieze. The monks have, in fact, neither tried to make the
Bible story clear for the benefit of laymen, as was usually the main
intention in congregational churches, nor have they been concerned
with making beautiful pictures out of the more important scenes, as
was the object of the artists who decorated the great churches built
under the patronage of emperors or nobles. Their object was rather
to mirror the themes of their religious reflections in the paintings that
surrounded them.

Some of the earliest of these are to be found in the Peristrema
valley. More accomplished are those at Kiliclar or Tokale Kilisse
of the mid tenth century, where some of the finest work of the region
is to be seen. A very full cycle survives here, and the work is in a very
good state of preservation. It is, however, still in the narrative style,

and the art is completely unsophisticated, even if at times it is vivid and expressive. The Adoration of the Magi at Tokale may serve as an example. There are other paintings in the region to be dated to the ninth and tenth centuries, but the larger numbers belong to the eleventh and twelfth; among these may be mentioned another chapel at Karalek, and the churches of Elmale, Göreme, and Çaregli. One of the latest in date was the chapel of St Eustathius, which was decorated in the twelfth century; after this time no further work was done in Cappadocia, primarily as a result of the overrunning of most of Asia Minor by the Moslems.

The paintings of the Latmos caves, not far from Miletus, are similar in style and character to those of Cappadocia, though the standard of work is perhaps not so high. They have been dated by Wulff to the seventh or eighth century, and though so early a date is not precluded, since the Iconoclastic ban would hardly have been observed in these out-of-the-way sanctuaries, a tenth- or eleventh-century date seems more likely, owing to the close resemblances to work of that period in Cappadocia. The battle of Manzikert in 1071 seems a likely terminus, for not long after it the region became Turkish.[9]

The influence exercised by this monastic art of Asia Minor on subsequent developments all over the Byzantine world was considerable. The art penetrated to southern Italy, and the decoration of a large series of rather similar rock-cut chapels there is in much the same style.[10] The same realist manner is apparent in paintings and even in mosaics in Greece – some of the mosaics of Hosios Lukas, for example, show the influence of the crude but vigorous monastic art – and the style also penetrated to the Balkans, more especially to Bulgaria. In the opposite direction the influence was naturally even more vital. The illustration of a number of Syriac manuscripts of the thirteenth century is thus clearly related to Cappadocian work, and the few wall paintings that are known in Armenia are basically in the same style, though a strongly marked local style was developed there in the twelfth or thirteenth century; the distinction was made more obvious by the use of Armenian instead of Greek script for the names and titles of the figures and scenes. Of the Armenian paintings the most important are those at Thalish, Tekor, Ani, and Achthamar, where a full New Testament cycle is preserved. It is to be assigned to the tenth century; paintings in the church of Tigrane Honentz at Ani are dated to 1215.[11] It is recorded that Armenian painters

233 Sakli Kilisse, Göreme, Cappadocia. Wall painting. Angel. Twelfth century

worked at Sohag in Egypt, but, apart from this, the role played by Armenia in the history of Byzantine painting was of very little importance.

As has already been noted, the monastic style had some influence in Greece, and there are a few paintings in various places, like some of the eleventh century in the crypt of Hosios Lukas, which should be included in this group. But far more important are those in a more accomplished style, which reflect to a greater or lesser degree what was being done at Constantinople in the great Second Golden Age. Most important of these are paintings in the Church of Sancta Sophia at Ochrida, which can be dated to shortly before 1056. They comprise various Old and New Testament scenes, but the finest is undoubtedly the great composition showing the Dormition or Assumption of the Virgin on the western wall of the church. The colours are rather sombre, but the figure drawing is excellent, and the composition is balanced, dignified, and accomplished, and the quality of the work as a whole is quite outstanding. There is something much more than monastic vigour and sincerity here; in addition, real artistic genius is to the fore. This great composition is a truly admirable example of the grandest style of mid-Byzantine

234 Sancta Sophia, Ochrida (Serbia). Wall painting. The Assumption. *c.* 1050

235 St Gregory of Tigrane Honentz, Ani (eastern Turkey). Wall painting. The
Assumption. *c.* 1215

237 Sancta Sophia, Ochrida (Serbia). Wall painting. Two Apostles from the Assumption of the Virgin. *c.* 1050

monumental painting, and it must have been executed by a master who was in close touch with the capital. It is interesting to compare the work with some very fine, though more fragmentary, paintings at Castelseprio in Italy, which have been variously dated between the seventh and the tenth centuries, and which also attest the influence of Constantinople.[12] Both Ochrida and Castelseprio, whatever its date, can be drawn on in order to complete a picture of what was

6 Castelseprio (Lombardy). Wall painting, Sta Maria foris Portas. St Joseph.
Detail from the Journey into Bethlehem. Eighth to tenth century

265

238 St Panteleimon, Nerez (Macedonia). Wall painting. The Lamentation for Christ. 1164

being done in the capital on a monumental scale just before and just after the Iconoclast ban. Otherwise our ideas of the style which is now usually termed that of the first Byzantine Renaissance must depend almost entirely on the evidence afforded by the manuscripts. But even so there is enough to show that partly as a result of the return to figural art, and partly as a result of the Classical tastes of the Emperor Constantine Porphyrogenitus (913–59), there was not only a great revival at the capital, but also a definite turning to Hellenistic models for inspiration.

From the tenth century onwards the story of Byzantine painting is not one of gradual decadence, as writers were prone to assume till only three decades ago, but rather one of continual progress, and if

239 The Arena Chapel, Padua. Wall painting. The Lamentation by Giotto.
c. 1303

the tenth century saw a first Renaissance which was responsible for
the birth of mid-Byzantine monumental art, the twelfth century saw
a second, which produced a new interest in humanism and personality
in art in the Byzantine world at least a century and a half before a
similar change took place in Italy under the influence of Cimabue
and Giotto. And if Sancta Sophia at Ochrida may serve us as a type
monument in large-scale painting for the first Renaissance, another
church in Macedonia, Nerez, serves as the type monument of the
second Renaissance in the twelfth century.

The paintings of the little church at Nerez date from 1164; they
were executed under the patronage of a member of the Comnene
family, by an artist who must have been in the closest contact with

Constantinople, if indeed he did not come from there. The work is of the very finest and the conception gentle and tender; it is marked by an essentially humanist comprehension, which lays a new stress on personal emotion and feeling, unknown to the sublime, essentially unworldly art of the middle period. This is to be seen especially clearly in the Deposition, where the tender compassion and deep emotion of the Virgin and attendant figures strikes a note of profound feeling which, it was at one time held, only appeared with Giotto.[13] The paintings at Nerez also served as models for some much cruder ones in Macedonia, notably those at Kurbinovo (1191) and some at Kastoria.

240 St Panteleimon, Nerez (Macedonia). Wall painting. Detail from the birth of the Virgin. 1164

241 St Panteleimon, Nerez (Macedonia). Wall painting. Detail from the life of
    the Virgin. 1164

242 St Demetrius, Vladimir, Russia. Wall painting. Head of Apostle. Detail of Plate 243. *c.* 1195

This new approach was not universal, for paintings which showed little hint of it continued to be produced right down to the fifteenth century. They were often excellent, grand, and magnificent. But in general the monumental art gradually tended to become academic, and more and more paintings seem to have been executed in the new style, which we have termed that of the second Byzantine Renaissance. Various theories have been put forward by different authorities

243 St Demetrius, Vladimir, Russia. Wall painting. The Last Judgement,
   Apostles. *c.* 1195

to account for this Renaissance. Many of these may now be discarded, for the assumption that the Renaissance only began with the fourteenth century has been proved incorrect, and it is therefore impossible that it can have been due to Italian influence. The writings of Kondakov have thus assumed what is primarily an academic interest.[14] Again, those authorities who explain the revival as due primarily to a particularly proficient copying of Hellenistic models do not properly explain its character, for the mere copying of other works, however good, could never produce such spirited results.[15] Not only was the work of the revival essentially alive and vital, but it was also obviously due to the hands of artists who were creators and innovators, even if they did at the same time benefit

244 St Panteleimon, Nerez (Macedonia). Wall painting. The Deposition. 1164

245 St Demetrius, Vladimir, Russia. Wall painting. Head of an archangel.
c. 1195

from what was to be learnt from the past. And in addition to changes in style, the repertory of scenes and the number of figures in each scene was also considerably developed, in a way which can only be accounted for as the result of a great burst of creative energy. In fact, the revival can only be explained as due to a great upwelling of the human creative spirit, parallel with, but in no way dependent on, that which took place in Italy in the fourteenth century.

Though it was doubtless in Constantinople that the new art flourished most gloriously, no monuments from the twelfth or thirteenth century have survived there. Happily, however, a more or less continuous series of paintings which show the development of the new style is to be found in other parts of the Byzantine world, notably the Balkans and Russia in the earlier years and Greece in the later. It will perhaps be most satisfactory to mention the more important of these in chronological order. Thus the very fine paintings of the Church of St Demetrius at Vladimir in Russia belong to 1193; they show the same interest in personality and the same touch of humanism as the paintings of Nerez, and their master, who was a Greek, must have learnt in the same school, for he has many of the same stylistic mannerisms, notably in the way in which he makes use of light coloured highlights. This use of highlights to effect modelling was greatly developed at this time and is to be seen in many of the wall decorations of the later twelfth and earlier thirteenth centuries, even though the approach is more monumental and less intimate than it was at Nerez and Vladimir. Sometimes, indeed, the highlights are accentuated till they constitute what is almost a geometric art; this was the case in the Church of St George at Staraya Ladoga in Russia, where the paintings date from around 1180. How widespread was the style is shown if paintings of 1193 at Agios Neophytos in Cyprus are compared.

A particularly rich series of paintings in the new manner is preserved in the churches of what is today Yugoslavia. Some of these were the works of Greek masters, who must have been in close touch with the capital, but others were done by men of the locality, and there is reason to believe that the new style found a readier acceptance in Serbia than it did in Greece itself. At first, however, it is not easy to distinguish anything intrinsically Slavonic about the paintings, but as the thirteenth century progressed a new delicacy of form on the one hand and a new realism, savouring sometimes almost of caricature, on the other, came to distinguish Serbian work, while a

246 Agios Neophytos (Cyprus). Wall painting. Archangel Michael. 1193

more developed feeling for plasticity and a closer adherence to Classical models characterized the work of the Greek masters. Earliest of the Yugoslav decorations is that of Mileševa, which dates from around 1235; the work is perhaps closer to the monumental style than was that of Nerez, but many of the figures have an almost

247 The monastery church, Mileševa (Serbia). Wall painting. The Lamentation. *c.* 1235

248 The monastery church, Mileševa (Serbia). Wall painting. Angel at the
Sepulchre. *c.* 1235

249 The monastery church, Mileševa (Serbia). Wall painting. Portrait of the
Emperor Constantine

250 The monastery church, Mileševa (Serbia). Wall painting. Portrait of
St Cosmas. *c.* 1235

Classical beauty about them, as, for example, the Angel at the sepulchre; it is interesting to compare it with some of the work in Sta Maria Antiqua at Rome, which is in the Hellenistic style. Several masters, however, seem to have worked at Mileševa who had not all been taught in the same school. Thus other work there is more conservative, and seems to have been inspired by one of the great mosaic decorations of the middle period; the artist has even gone to the length of painting the backgrounds yellow, in imitation of the gold of mosaics. Other work again is later in date, belonging to the sixteenth century.[16]

More experimental than the work at Mileševa is the earliest among that at Sopoćani, which belongs to the same date as the church, that is around 1260. There is a new profusion of detail here, numerous subsidiary figures are included, and the backgrounds are elaborate and full; a portion of the scene of Christ's Descent into Hell may serve as an example. At times perhaps the profusion of detail makes for confusion, and one regrets the absence of the simplicity of the earlier work like that at Nerez. Yet the detail is very beautiful, the colouring is particularly subtle, and the bright, sweeping highlights are used with very great effect. The colouring here helps to distinguish the hands of the various masters who worked at the first decoration. Thus the main Bible scenes, where pinks, greys, and delicate half-tones predominate, would seem to be by one man, while the individual figures of saints, which are rather stronger in tone, would seem to be by another. By a different hand again are the portraits associated with the tomb of Anne, Mother of Uroš, done perhaps as early as 1256, which are rather sombre in tone and rather clumsier in handling. Other work in the church is later, notably that of two side chapels at the west end, which was done at the end of the thirteenth century, and that of the exo-narthex, which belongs to the fourteenth; that of the eastern side chapels is later still. All the work, however, is good, and all of it is to be attributed to local artists rather than to Greek masters.[17] Paintings which have recently been uncovered in the Church of Sancta Sophia at Trebizond are not dissimilar from those at Sopoćani, and show the humanism of the Revival style to a marked degree. They are probably to be dated to *c.* 1260.

Of the other wall paintings in Yugoslavia, those at Moraca (*c.* 1240), Staro Nagoričino (1317), Gračanica (*c.* 1320), and Dečani (*c.* 1330) are in a more dramatic style; those of a small church at

251 The monastery church, Sopoćani (Serbia). Wall painting. Detail from the Descent of Christ into Hell. *c.* 1265

252 The monastery church, Sopoćani (Serbia). Wall painting. Doubting
Thomas. *c.* 1265

253 The monastery church, Sopoćani (Serbia). Wall painting. John the Baptist.
   c. 1265

Vodoca in Macedonia should also be noted, for the scene of the
Forty Martyrs there is very expressive; the crowd is a living mass,
and the agony of feeling is clearly shown in the expression and

254 Church of St George, Staro Nagoričino (Serbia). Wall painting. The mocking of Christ. 1317–18

attitude of each figure; so often this scene was treated as a piece of mere symbolism. Many of the painters of these decorations were no doubt Slavs, like those men who worked at Mileševa. But some were Greeks, as was perhaps the man who worked at Nagoričino, who signs himself with the Greek name of Eutychios. But it must be remembered that Greek names were also employed by the Slavs, and Greek inscriptions continued to be used till quite a late date, since Greek was an ecclesiastical language, much as was Latin in the

255 The monastery church, Gračanica (Serbia). Wall painting. The Raisin Lazarus. c. 1320

ЛАZAPOBOBЬCKPЬШЄNIЄ

Western world in the Middle Ages, so that neither script nor name are absolutely positive indications. But stylistic considerations help, so far as the paintings are concerned, and Okunev distinguishes a separate group of paintings which he terms the Graeco-Slav, where local characteristics are as marked as, if not more marked than, the Greek. Especially characteristic is the absence of highlights, the modelling of the faces being achieved instead by opposition of light and shade. The principal monuments of this school are the Church of Milutin at Studenica (1314), the Church of St Nicholas at

256 The monastery church, Dečani (Serbia). The Prophet Isaiah. c. 1340

286

257 Church of King Milutin, the monastery of Studenica (Serbia). Wall painting. The Madonna and Child. 1314

Ljuboten (1337), the Church of St Nicetas at Cučer (early fourteenth century, restored 1483–4), the church at Peć (*c.* 1310), and the church at Berende in Bulgaria (fourteenth century).

Developing alongside these schools was a third group, the monastic, which owed less to the spirit of the Renaissance, and more to the old art of Cappadocia and the East. Its masters were less accomplished, its approach less refined; the colours were dark and

258 Lesnovo (Serbia). Wall painting. Illustration of Psalm. 1349

sombre, the drawing often rather graceless. The aim was didactic, and a preference was shown for scenes of an obscure, apocryphal character. But some of the figures were extremely expressive, none the less, though expression was achieved by the accentuation of particular features rather than by balance and delicacy. At times the art was almost one of caricature. The most important monuments of the group are at Lesnovo (1349), Markov Monastir (late fourteenth century), and Matejič (late fourteenth century).

288

Church of the Chora (Kariye Camii), Istanbul. Painting in the Pareccleseion. *c.* 1320

259 Markov Monastir (Serbia). Wall painting. Rachel weeping for her children. Fourteenth century

The true character of the second Byzantine Renaissance was rather less to the fore in Bulgaria than in Yugoslavia, but one monument of the first importance must be noted, namely Boiana, near Sofia, where there are paintings of very high quality dating from 1259. Much of the work shows the same understanding of personality, the same interest in expression, as at Nerez and Vladimir. The child Christ, from the scene of his discussion with the doctors in the Temple, may be noted. It is a figure of great beauty, as well as of great depth of understanding. At a later date the spirit of the Renaissance is also to be seen in some lovely fourteenth-century paintings in the Church of St George at Sofia, showing the Pantocrator and the Twenty-two Prophets; it is highly successful, both as a rhythmical composition, and because of the vitality of the individual figures. Other work in Bulgaria is less advanced, but several schools can be distinguished. Some twelfth-century paintings at Bačkovo are thus in a purely Byzantine style of monumental character, and at Tirnovo and elsewhere there is a good deal of work which must have been done either by Greeks or by locals who had learnt in Greek schools. But alongside this there grew up a more local style, as for example in the Church of the Forty Martyrs at Tirnovo (late fourteenth century), while in the mountainous districts work of a more primitive or monastic type was usual. By the end of the fifteenth century Western

260 Sancta Sophia, Trebizond. Wall painting in narthex. Christ among the Doctors. *c.* 1260

261 Church of Boiana (near Sophia, Bulgaria). Wall painting. Christ among the Doctors. 1259

influence had also penetrated, and paintings at Poganovo (1500) are in a new semi-Westernized manner. They are of little merit.

In Greece itself very much less work of thirteenth- and fourteenth-century date is now preserved than must at one time have existed, and it is really only at Mistra in the Peloponnese and at Kastoria and

262 The monastery, Bačkovo (Bulgaria). Wall painting in the burial chapel.
1083

Salonica in the north that anything of consequence is known.
Vestiges of paintings, all dating from the first quarter of the fourteenth century, survive in nearly all the churches in Salonica; the
best and most perfect are in Agios Nikolaos, a tiny building at the
eastern end of the town, containing a lovely decoration done
around 1320. In several churches at Mistra there are the vestiges of
large-scale decorations of the very first quality, and this little ruined

263 Church of Boiana (near Sophia, Bulgaria). Wall painting. Christ; detail
from the Transfiguration. 1259

264 The church of the Pantanassa, Mistra (Peloponnese). Wall painting. *c.* 1428

town is in its own way as important in the story of fourteenth-century painting as is the monastery church at Assisi in the West. The earliest paintings at Mistra are in the Church of St Demetrius, sometimes called the Metropolis; they date from around 1320. Some of the work is of a monumental character, close in style to mosaics; but the rest is more intimate and more delicate, combining feeling with a brilliant sense of decoration. The colours are bright and contrasting, and light shades are used on dark in wide splashes, to

265 The monastery of the Pantanassa, Mistra (Peloponnese). Wall painting.
The Madonna and Child. *c.* 1428

give life and relief. No attempt is made to reproduce the shades of
nature – an ox in the scene of the Nativity in the Brontocheion, for
example, is coloured bright green – yet the result is supremely
effective. The paintings of this church, though very fragmentary, are
extremely fine; they date from the second half of the fourteenth
century, and represent the continuation of the school which was
responsible for the decoration of the Metropolis earlier in the
century. The culmination of the style is to be found in the Church

266 Agios Nikolaos Kasnitsis, Kastoria (northern Greece). Wall painting.
St Nicholas. Twelfth century

of the Pantanassa, done around 1428. Here again there is little
attempt at pure naturalism, but the paintings are profoundly human.
We can see the artist's vivid joy in his work and his power to evoke
not only religious emotion, but also the concrete beauty of the
world. The Raising of Lazarus is perhaps the finest composition in
the church; it is also one of the finest of Byzantine paintings,
comparable in merit, as well as in composition and style, to much of
the best Quattrocento work in Italy.

267 The monastery of the Pantanassa, Mistra (Peloponnese). Wall painting.
The Raising of Lazarus. *c.* 1428

The school that was responsible for this work at Mistra was
termed by Millet the Macedonian,[18] and this connotation has
survived, though the term has perhaps rather too much of a geographical significance. A second school grew out of it, which he termed
the Cretan, though its first appearance seems also to have taken
place at Mistra, in the decoration of the Church of the Peribleptos
(1340–60). The work here is characterized by figures which are rather
more elongated than those of the Pantanassa; the highlights are
rather more severely stressed and the style is generally more minute,
in a manner more appropriate to panel than to wall painting. There
is a great profusion of detail, and the scenes, as well as the figures,

297

are probably at their best when full consideration is given to detail as well as to the general effect. Two painters worked in the Peribleptos, and the more accomplished of them, distinguished by his mastery of detail, was of the very first class. His rendering of Christ, from the scene of the Transfiguration, shows this clearly.

There are probably in the south of Greece numerous other monuments which will serve to supplement our knowledge of the painting of this school, but few of them have as yet been fully investigated. Some fourteenth-century churches at Geraki in the Peloponnese may be noted. There are also wall paintings in Crete itself, though the island was especially important as a centre of icon painting. The

268 Peribleptos Church, Mistra (Peloponnese). Wall painting. The Nativity. *c.* 1350

269 Peribleptos Church, Mistra (Peloponnese). Wall painting. The Transfiguration. *c.* 1350

manner penetrated to other portions of the Balkan area also, notably to Serbia. Quite a number of decorations there are in the Cretan rather than the pure Renaissance style; such are those of Kalenić (1405–10), Ljubostinja (1405), Ravanica (1381), Manasija (1407), and Rudenica (1410). The decorations of churches at Kalotino (late fifteenth century), Dragalevci (1476), and Arbanassi (1681) in Bulgaria may also be noted. A particular feature of many of them is the inclusion of founder portraits, and the minute manner of the Cretan style was particularly suited to these. The likenesses would appear to be striking; the costumes are brilliant and delightfully decorative, and the whole effect is most pleasing, even if the art is

270 The monastery church, Kalenić (Serbia). Wall painting. The Marriage in Cana. 1405–10

271 The abbey church, Manasija (Serbia). Wall painting. The Archangel
Michael. 1407–18

not one of the first importance. A stage of development somewhat
similar to that reached by the minor portraitists of Elizabethan times
in England had, in fact, been reached here, and these portraits are
worthy of some consideration in themselves, apart from the fact that
they afford the most valuable evidence for dating purposes, both

direct, in connexion with the churches to which they belong, and indirect, by way of the nature of the costumes that the people wear.

The inspiration of all this later work stemmed from Constantinople, and, thanks to the work of cleaning recently undertaken in a side chapel of Kariye Camii by the Byzantine Institute of America, it is now possible to study one really supreme monument virtually in its entirety. The paintings date from the second decade of the fourteenth century, that is to say, the same date as the mosaics in the

272 Church of the Chora (Kariye Camii), Istanbul. Wall painting in the apse of the Parecclesion. The Anastasis. *c.* 1320

273 Church of the Chora (Kariye Camii), Istanbul. Wall painting in the
Parecclesion. The Ascension. *c.* 1320

narthices of the church itself, so that both are closely contemporary
with Giotto's famous Arena Chapel at Padua. As regards quality the
Kariye paintings are no less outstanding, and the lovely drawing, the
delicate, subtle colouring, and the profoundly spiritual content com-
pensate completely for the absence of the interest in three-dimen-
sional form which is to be found in Giotto's work. It was at one time
suggested that these paintings represented an early work of the
famous painter Theophanes, the Greek, who was later responsible
for several great decorations in Russia, notably that of the Cathedral

303

of the Transfiguration at Novgorod, done in 1378.[19] This was probably not the case, but two facts nevertheless stand out, first that Theophanes the Greek must have learnt in Constantinople, and secondly that the painted aisle of Kariye Camii is one of the world's major monuments of painting.

Later manifestations of the second Renaissance are to be seen in the decorations of some of the monasteries of Mount Athos, which, with their large areas of wall space and their comparatively rich patronage, were in a position to foster the art of wall painting in the fifteenth century to a degree hardly possible elsewhere after the ravages of the Turkish conquest, for the monks there were left unmolested, and the monasteries were still in a position to own extensive properties. Vestiges of paintings, indeed, survive in practically all the monasteries, though some have suffered very severely at the hands of later restorers. They show the fullest development of the two schools originally distinguished by Millet at Mistra, namely the Macedonian and the Cretan. The most important paintings of the former are in the Protaton at Karyes (fourteenth century, restored and added to c. 1540), the Catholicon (monastery church) at Chilandari (c. 1302, severely restored in 1804), and in the Catholicon at Vatopedi (1312, restored 1819). Among the fine paintings of the Protaton a fragmentary head of the Virgin and a fine portrait of the child Christ may be noted. The name of a particular master, Manuel Panselinos, was associated with the Macedonian school on Athos as well as with work in the region of Salonica. Though he can hardly have been responsible for all the paintings which have been attributed to him by popular tradition, the suggestion put forward by certain authorities that he was a fictitious personage seems entirely groundless. Indeed, his style seems to have been fairly personal if paintings in the Protaton at Karyes which have recently been attributed to him are to be regarded as typical.[20] The effect is somewhat sombre, but there is a dignity and grandeur about his figures which recalls the beginnings of the Renaissance at Nerez nearly four hundred years earlier.

Of the Cretan paintings on Athos the most famous are in the refectory of the Lavra (c. 1530), the Catholicon of the Lavra (1535), the old Catholicon of Xenophontos (1544 and 1563), the Catholicon and refectory of Dionysiou (1547), the chapel of St George in the monastery of St Paul (1555), the chapel of St Nicholas at the Lavra (1560), the Catholicon at Docheriou (1568), and the refectory of the same

274–5 The Protaton, Karyes, Mount Athos. Wall paintings. The two Saints
Theodore and the Child Christ. *c.* 1300

monastery (late sixteenth century). Other paintings of the Cretan school are to be found all over the Greek mainland; the paintings in the Meteora monasteries are probably the best of them. Those in the principal monastery of the group were done in 1552. Of all these, the work at Xenophontos is perhaps the most effective. The artist who worked there was named Anthony, and his style was very personal; he made a very extensive use of white highlights slashed on with very great effect. The paintings in the apse there may serve as an example; though the work is less beautiful than that in the Peribleptos at Mistra, the painter had more feeling for his material, for what he produced was a wall painting in every sense of the term, and not just a panel transferred to the wall. But the personality and humanism of the Mistra work has given place to a more mystic outlook, the frontal pose has come in once more rather than the three-quarter or side-face attitude, and in many other ways in addition there has been something of a reversion to the old iconography and style of the monastic art of Cappadocia. This is no doubt to be explained by the demands of patronage, for Athos was a monastic community, and the tastes of the monks lay in the direction of doctrine and dogma rather than beauty and elegance, much as had those of the earlier monks of Cappadocia.

276-7 The Protaton, Karyes, Mount Athos. Wall painting. The Dormition of the Virgin. *c.* 1300

278 The Catholicon, monastery of Xenophontos, Mount Athos. Wall painting.
The Dormition. 1544

279 The monastery of the Lavra, Mount Athos. Wall painting in the refectory.
St Dorotheos and St John. 1512

280 Monastery of the Transfiguration, Meteora (Thessaly). Wall painting.
St Theodore. Sixteenth century

The last phase of the story of Byzantine painting was enacted in
Rumania, and the most important paintings there are to be found
in a church built under royal patronage at Curtea de Arges. The
work is by several different hands, but all of it dates from the

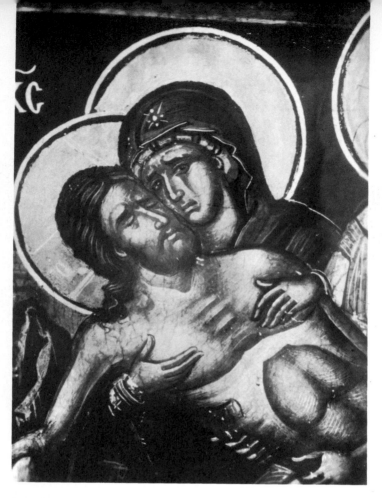

281 The monastery of the Lavra, Mount Athos. Wall painting in the Catholicon. The Lamentation for Christ. 1535

fourteenth century. The paintings of a second fine church there were
mostly destroyed at the time of a restoration in the nineteenth
century, but some fragments were preserved and are now in the
Bucharest Museum. There were several Greek artists in the country
at the time, though native schools were soon formed, and after about
1400 Serbians took the place of the Greeks among the strangers. Of
the buildings that survive, however, the majority should be attributed

282 St George's chapel, monastery of St Paul, Mount Athos. Wall painting. Madonna and Child. 1555

283 The monastery of Dionysiou. Wall painting. Detail from the Apocalypse.
1547

284 The monastery church, Humor (Rumania). Wall painting. The Visitation.
1535

to local craftsmen; good examples survive at Snagov, Hurezi, and
Humor. Those of Moldavia are particularly rich, and are often
painted outside as well as in; the most important are those at
Dolhesti-Mari (1480), Voronet, Arborei, Popauti (end of the

285 The abbey church, Arborei (Rumania). Wall painting. Saint on horseback.
1541

fifteenth century) and Roman (1550). Stefanescu distinguishes two
main influences at the base of these, which first came into Wallachia
in the middle of the fourteenth century; they are those of Byzantine
art from the south and of the peasant art proper to the locality. In
the fifteenth century there was also a certain amount of influence
from Mount Athos, and a further intrusive style was imposed from
the West. But in the opposite direction an influence was exercised by
Byzantine art on Poland, quite apart from the somewhat similar one
on that region from Russia.

The story of painting in Russia is extremely important, but it
constitutes to a great extent a chapter of its own, for from the four-

286 The monastery church, Voronet (Rumania). Wall painting. Our Lady in Paradise. 1547

teenth century a distinctive Russian manner had been developed, and the country was never actually a part of the Byzantine Empire, as were at one time or another the various lands of the Balkans. Moreover, the most important developments there were in the sphere

315

287 Sancta Sophia, Trebizond. Wall painting in Bema. Detail of the Tiberias
scene. *c.* 1260

of panel painting rather than in that of wall decoration. Where
Russian monuments entered into the general story of Byzantine wall
painting, however, they have been mentioned above, and something
more will be said about them in a later chapter, devoted to Byzantium
and the Slavonic world.

Of a similar distinctive character, again, was the painting of the
thirteenth and following centuries in the city and region of Trebizond.
This area was ruled by members of the Comnene dynasty as an independent state from the time of the Latin conquest of Constantinople
(1204) until the area was finally overcome by the Turks in 1461, and
though contacts with Constantinople were maintained throughout,
the art of the region developed to some extent along its own lines,
the influence of the old Cappadocian or Anatolian schools being
usually well to the fore. What little remains of early work, notably
in the Church of Sancta Sophia just outside the town, suggests that
there was a flourishing local school in the thirteenth century; it was

288 Sancta Sophia, Trebizond. Wall painting on apse vault. Christ in Majesty. *c.* 1260

perhaps set on foot by artists from Constantinople, for the style of the capital was more to the fore at this date than it was later. Of the fifteenth-century paintings the most important are those that decorate the three cave chapels dedicated to St Savas, one of them dated 1411, those in the bell tower of Sancta Sophia, dated 1443, and those in a little church at Kurt Boghan, some thirty miles from the city of Trebizond, which must belong to the sixteenth century. There is little of the spirit of the Renaissance in any of these. Portions of a more extensive decoration that survived in the Theoskepastos monastery in the city have been much restored, but the work was

289 Church of the monastery, Sumela (near Trebizond). Wall painting.
Perhaps twelfth century

closer to the Renaissance style as developed on Mount Athos. At the
Armenian monastery of Kaimakli, not far from the city, there are
two separate series of Armenian paintings, of very individualistic
style; one is dated 1622, but looks two centuries earlier; the other is
of the late eighteenth century. The work is apparently close in style
to that which survives in Armenia proper; relationships with
Cappadocia are marked, as they are also in what survives of the
decoration on the roof of the great cave church of the monastery
of Sumela, some thirty miles inland of Trebizond.[21]

Other interesting local schools also existed in other places, most notably Cyprus. Some of the work there, though by no means as fine as the best in Yugoslavia, at Mistra, or in Constantinople, is of very great importance because it can be accurately dated. In this respect the paintings at Asinou may be noted.[22] A somewhat similar local school existed on Rhodes, and in both places curious blendings of Eastern and Western ideas took place as a result of the presence

290 Church of the monastery, Sumela (near Trebizond). Paintings on the outer wall. Seventeenth century

291 Panaghia Phorbiotissa, Asinou (Cyprus). Wall painting. St Andrew. Detail from the Dormition of the Virgin. 1105–6

of large Western colonies in these islands. This blend heralds the penetration of Western ideas into the Byzantine world as a whole which began to take place in the sixteenth century, and was manifested both in style and in iconography, to a great extent as a result of the penetration of prints and woodcuts, which were extensively copied.[23] And with the seventeenth century work over the whole Orthodox world had usually become set in a wooden, semi-Westernized manner. But even at a later date good work was at times still produced, thanks to a great extent to the soundness of rules handed down originally by tradition and subsequently in the form of a written work called *The Painter's Guide*. This was compiled by a monk named Dionysios of Fourna, who appears to have lived at the end of the fourteenth century, though it is quite probable that it was founded on an earlier original. Similar guides, the *podlinniki*, were common in Russia from the sixteenth century onwards.[24]

Manuscripts have probably received more detailed attention from scholars than has any other branch of Byzantine art, and on account of this, as well as because quite a number of them are dated, the attribution of particular styles to definite periods is, with a few notable exceptions, more certain than in other branches of art. Hence, apart from their own intrinsic interest, the manuscripts are of special importance, in that they help in the dating of other works. Again, more manuscript illustrations are preserved from early times than wall paintings or panels, so that they help us to reconstruct a picture of the art as a whole; without them it would be extremely incomplete. The importance of manuscripts in any study of Byzantine art is thus outstanding.

At the outset a distinction must be made between the two principal types of book that were known to the Byzantines, the roll or rotulus, and the bound book or codex. The former, originating in Egypt and passing from there to the Classical world, was common only in early times, and in the Byzantine world was more popular for secular than for religious usage. But a few rolls bearing part of the Bible text have survived, and it seems likely that they were occasionally used right down to the tenth century. So far as biblical or ecclesiastical texts were concerned, bound books were far more common, and as often as not the more important ones were elaborately illustrated. Naturally, it is their illuminations that must be our chief concern here, but it may be noted that the actual script is often in itself very beautiful, and the decorative headings to chapters or paragraphs are also often of very great merit. All of these, text, headings, and illustrations, were probably usually the works of different individuals, though distinctions were probably rather less rigorous in the Byzantine world than they were in the later Middle Ages in the monasteries of the West. These books were usually on parchment, but paper was

292 Bibliothèque Nationale, Paris. The Sinope Fragment. Suppl. Gr. 1286.
Salome receives the head of John the Baptist. Fifth to sixth century

introduced from China early in the eighth century, and after the
tenth century it was used quite often.[1]

As in the wall paintings and the other arts, two distinct manners
are to be observed in manuscript illustrations, the Hellenistic and
the Eastern. The most important manuscript of early date that is

293 Laurentian Library, Florence. The Rabula Gospels. Crucifixion and
Resurrection. 586

entirely Eastern is a fragmentary one in the Bibliothèque Nationale
at Paris, known as the Sinope fragment. It is to be dated to the fifth
century, and was probably executed in Syria, as was another, though
less important fragmentary manuscript now in the British Museum,
known as the Cotton Genesis. The pages of the Sinope fragment, like
those of all the more important manuscripts, are coloured purple;
the text is in large gold letters, and the illustrations are at the bottom

294 Laurentian Library, Florence. The Rabula Gospels. The Ascension. 586

of the pages, occupying about a quarter of the page at most, but stretching right across from side to side. The colours are brilliant and effective, the figures small and dumpy with staring eyes, inelegant but very forceful; they are not unlike those of the wall paintings of about A.D. 245 in the synagogue at Dura, and represent the continuance of the Syrian style some two centuries later. The same style is to be seen again after the lapse of a further century or more in an important manuscript in the Laurentian Library at Florence, known as the Rabula Gospels, for it was illustrated by a monk of that name at a place called Zagba in Mesopotamia. It is exactly dated to the year 586. But though it was produced in the most easterly portion of the Byzantine Empire and though its text is in Syriac and not in Greek, the style is perhaps rather less Oriental than might be supposed, and in some of the scenes, notably the Ascension, the pictures have a distinct elegance about them. The iconography, however, is definitely Eastern, as for instance in the Crucifixion scene, where our Lord is shown in a long robe, and not in the simple loin-cloth which was usual in the Classical world and in the Byzantine sphere properly speaking. A further example of the Eastern style appears in the illustrations of an Armenian manuscript, the Etchmiadzin Gospels; they are much coarser and more primitive than the illustrations of the Rabula manuscript, but this is probably to be accounted for by the fact that the work is considerably later and represents what was in the East a decadent phase of art. The text of

295 Austrian National Library, Vienna. The Vienna Genesis. Cod. theol. Gr. 1.
Jacob's Prophecy and Departure. Sixth century

the book is actually dated to 989, and though the illustrations were at one time believed to be earlier, recent research suggests that there is little evidence to support this theory.[2]

More magnificent than any of these, and related more closely to the Sinope fragment than any of the others, is a copy of the Book of Genesis at Vienna. It has been assigned to the fourth, fifth, and sixth centuries by different authorities, and to practically every region in the Christian world except Greece. Some of the illustrations verge almost on the grotesque, but several hands must have worked on them, and others are of very high quality indeed. The style is in the main close to the antique, though Oriental influences are present, as for example in the stylized trees, which follow a manner that was probably derived from Parthian art.[3] They look rather like mushrooms. The scene where Laban and his sons seek Jacob and parley with him is vivid and full of spirit (Genesis xxxi. 23ff.). In contrast to the stylized trees, the expressive figures and the profound feeling for naturalism to be seen in the depiction of the flocks and camels

296 Austrian National Library, Vienna. The Vienna Genesis. Cod. theol. Gr. 31. The servant of Abraham makes a present to Rebecca. Sixth century

297 Archiepiscopal Library, Rossano (Calabria). Codex Purpureus Rossanensis. The Entry into Jerusalem. Sixth century

betoken the Classical influence. The place in which the manuscript was illuminated would thus appear to have been where both of the major trends in art were present, and it is tempting to suggest Constantinople itself, for the work is on the whole of very high quality, and heralds the complete fusion of styles which was brought about in the capital more than in any other place. The late fifth or early sixth century would seem the most likely date.[4]

298 Archiepiscopal Library, Rossano (Calabria). Codex Purpureus Rossanensis. Christ before Pilate. Sixth century

On a somewhat more monumental scale again is the Codex Purpureus Rossanensis, now preserved at Rossano in southern Italy. It is to be assigned to much the same date as the Vienna Genesis. Here the illustrations occupy a larger portion of the page than in the Vienna Genesis, the figures are more elegant, and the style is rather closer to the fully fledged Byzantine. The frontispiece to the table of canons, for example, is a superb piece of abstract composition, thoroughly Byzantine in feeling. But there are Eastern elements in the iconography, which have led some writers to attribute the volume to Anatolia. Syria seems in this case less likely; Constantinople is possible; indeed, it is perhaps more probable as a home than Anatolia. As Bianco Bandinelli has pointed out, the production of these great books was an extremely elaborate and expensive business, and they are likely to have been made only in some major centre. The finished character of the work is admirably shown in the scene of our Lord's Entry into Jerusalem. It is interesting to find the iconography of the scene so developed at so early a date; it underwent substantially very little change for the next thousand years.

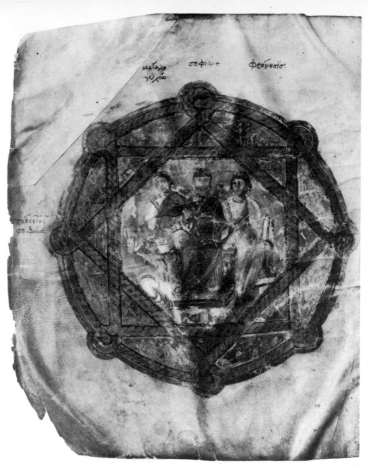

299 Austrian National Library, Vienna. *Natural History* of Dioscorides.
Vindobon Cod. Med. Graec. I. Anicia Juliana. 512

Secular manuscripts of this age, though in general hardly as rich
as the Rossanensis or the Vienna Genesis, were nevertheless both
numerous and important. An early Virgil in the Vatican (V. lat.
3867) contains miniatures rather akin to those of the Vienna Genesis,
and shows antique miniature art at its best. Dioscorides' *Natural
History* was much used, and copies usually contained numerous
entertaining and often beautiful illuminations. There is an important

330

300 Vatican Museum, Rome. Cosmography of Cosmas Indicopleustes. V. Gr. 699. St Paul on the road to Damascus. Ninth century

example at Vienna bearing a portrait of Anicia Juliana on f. 6, which was executed in Constantinople shortly before 512 (Vindobon. Med. Graec. 1). Another favourite book was the Travels of Cosmas Indicopleustes, which was first written in Egypt in the sixth century. The oldest example now extant is that in the Vatican (V. Gr. 699); it is probably to be assigned to the ninth century. The figures are shown in rather formal attitudes, and the conception is essentially monumental, but the faces are powerful and expressive and show nothing of the more elegant mannerism of the eleventh century. The scenes are shown in several tableaux, one above the other, yet within the same borders, and there is often a very abstract quality about them which is essentially Byzantine. An eleventh-century copy in the Sinai monastery for example contains a most expressive abstract composition depicting the movement of the heavens round the earth.

One other important manuscript which must be mentioned takes the form of a roll and not a codex. It is the famous Joshua Rotulus in the Vatican (V. Palat. Gr. 431). It is a long roll, with illustrations in tinted line interpolated in the text. At one time it was held that this roll represented the survival of a particular narrative style of art, where the record was depicted as a continuous series of scenes; the prototypes for such an arrangement are to be found on the great columns of Rome, like Trajan's column, where the story is arranged round the column in a spiral. The roll was thus regarded as the type example of what is called the continuous style. Views as to the actual date of the manuscript have varied; the seventh century was the most usually favoured, but it was generally agreed that the illustrations must have followed an archetype perhaps as early as the second century.[5] More recently, however, Weitzmann has assigned the roll to the tenth century, regarding it as due to the Classical revival sponsored by Constantine Porphyrogenitus (913–59). He also

301 Vatican Museum, Rome. The Joshua Roll. V. Palat. Gr. 431. Judgement scene. Tenth century

302 Vatican Museum, Rome. The Joshua Roll. V. Palat. Gr. 431. Joshua and
the two spies. Tenth century

believes that, far from representing an original continuous model,
the illustrations were actually copied from a paged book, and that
bridge-pieces were put in to give the appearance of a continuous
panorama.[6] Weitzmann's arguments are very persuasive, though
perhaps not wholly convincing, and whatever date is assigned to the
manuscript, it seems likely that it reproduces fairly closely some
earlier model. The importance of the continuous style, where a background opening up like a panorama was common to a whole series
of different scenes, was very considerable in early Christian art; it
influenced wall paintings and mosaics as well as manuscripts, and
the Joshua Roll must still be regarded as the most effective example
of the style that has come down to us.

In the Iconoclast period books with full-page illustrations were
naturally as severely proscribed as were representational wall paintings and mosaics, but small line drawings in the margins continued
to be done in a good many biblical texts, more especially copies of
the Psalms, and topical matter was often included in the illustrations;
the wicked were, for example, sometimes depicted as icon lovers. Old
Testament scenes were also sometimes illustrated on a small scale
without backgrounds. Architectural and geometric compositions
were also popular at this time, and an extra care was probably

333

303 Bibliothèque Nationale, Paris. Homilies of Gregory of Nazianzus. Cod. Gr. 510. The Transfiguration. 880–8

lavished on them because figural art was impossible. They were used extensively to frame the titles and canons, and similar non-representational compositions were also sometimes included in copies of the Gospels in place of the usual portraits of the evangelists. Lively animals and birds were often included in these compositions.

304 Bibliothèque Nationale, Paris. Homilies of Gregory of Nazianzus. Cod. Gr. 510. Vision of Ezekiel. 880–8

Almost immediately after the raising of the Iconoclast ban, figural art came back with renewed vigour. Perhaps because the tradition had been broken, there seems to have been an immediate return to Hellenistic models, and this is to be seen especially clearly in a

305 Bibliothèque Nationale, Paris. The Paris Psalter. Cod. Gr. 139. Moses on
Mount Sinai. Ninth century

magnificent copy of the Homilies of Gregory of Nazianzus in the
Bibliothèque Nationale (Gr. 510), which was executed for the
Emperor Basil I between 867 and 886. It contains an amazing wealth
of illustrations, by several different hands, and in several different
styles, and these serve to illustrate the situation in which art found
itself at the time. Some of the pages are thus purely Iconoclast,
bearing symbolical leaved crosses, and no more; others show a
medley of scenes in the narrative style like that of the Cappadocian
wall paintings; others again bear magnificent figures of completely

336

307 Royal Library, Copenhagen. Manuscript No. 6; the Book of Job, the Book
of the Prophets and others. King Solomon with a prophet. Tenth century

Hellenistic type. A page showing the Vision of Ezekiel may be noted.
The first type of page must have been done by artists who had
worked in Iconoclast times, who were familiar with this formalist
style; pages of the second type were perhaps done by monks called
in from Cappadocia to set the ball of narrative figural art rolling
once more; those of the third type were by masters of the capital,
who had perhaps been trained during Iconoclast times on work of a
secular character, and who turned to Hellenistic models as a matter
of course, the secular art always having tended to follow that trend;

338

308 Vatican Museum, Rome. Psalter. V. Palat. Gr. 381. King David between
Sophia and Prophetess. Thirteenth to fourteenth century

the very Hellenistic character of secular floor mosaics of the fifth and
sixth centuries from Antioch and Constantinople[7] is in marked
contrast to the essentially Byzantine style which had already established itself in mosaics of a religious character even before the time
of Justinian.

Probably of much the same date as the magnificent Paris 510,
though it has sometimes been assigned to the seventh century,[8] is
another manuscript in the Bibliothèque Nationale, usually known as
the Paris Psalter (Gr. 139). It also contains magnificent illuminations

339

309 Vatican Museum, Rome. Bible of Leo Patricius. Reg. Gr. I. David annointed king. Tenth century

of Hellenistic type; the page showing David composing the Psalms may be noted. The personification of melody is copied from a Hellenistic picture of the goddess Io, and the style is thoroughly

310 Laurentian Library, Florence. Commentary on the Great Prophets. Plut.
V. 9. The Prophet Jeremiah pointing to Christ. Eleventh century

antique. A number of other Psalters, with full-page illustrations,
show work of the same basically Hellenistic style, though it is not
always as much to the fore as here. They are usually known as the
'Aristocratic' Psalters. Among the most important is one in the
Marcian Library at Venice (Marcian Gr. 17), which was made for
Basil II (976–1025). There is another of much the same date in the
Vatican (V. Palat. Gr. 381), which is perhaps rather more antique in
style than that of Basil II, but the latter has a grandeur about it

341

311 British Museum, London. Psalter, Add. 19352. David annointed king. 1066

which is unequalled, and it is certainly one of the finest mid-Byzantine manuscripts that have come down to us.

In opposition to the 'Aristocratic' Psalters, with their full-page illustrations, was another group, which had small-scale illustrations in the margins only. They carried on the traditions of Iconoclast

312 Historical Museum, Moscow. The Khludov Psalter. 'The Kings of the Earth set themselves . . .' (Psalm 2, verse 2). Nativity (Psalm 2, verse 7). Ninth century

times. The Khludov Psalter at Moscow is probably the most important of them, and though its illustrations are no more than hasty line drawings in the margins, they are often very effective. Another example of the type is in the British Museum (Add. 19352); it was

313 Topkapi Saray Library, Istanbul. Octateuch, Cod. 8. Moses on Mount Sinai. Twelfth century

executed at Constantinople in 1066, and is especially important because its date and the locality where it was written and illustrated are known. The marginal illustrations were in some cases added subsequently, and took the form of a sort of commentary upon the text.

In addition to Psalters of these two types, numerous other forms of biblical manuscripts were habitually illustrated from the ninth century onwards. Most usual, perhaps, were the Octateuchs, or volumes comprising the first eight books of the Old Testament. Their illustrations were often numerous, though not always very elaborate.

τⲁⲓⲟ ⳑⲓ μⲟ ⲣⲁⲓⲟ δ κ ⲉ ⲓ ⲣⲁ ⲓ ⲟ ⳑ δ μ ⳑ ⲟ ⲧ ⲓ ⲟ μ ⲁ μ ⳑ ⲓ ⲟ ⳑ δ ⲣ μ δ μ ⲟ ⲟ ⲓ δ
ⳑ ⲁ ⲁ μⲓ · δ μⲧ ⳑ ⲓ ⲱ ⲙ ⲱ δ ⲣ ⲟ ⲱ ⲙ ⲭ ⲱ ⲣ ⲁ ⲩ · ⳑ ⲁ ⲓ μ ⲁ μ ⲧ δ ⲓ ⲟ ⲁ μ δ μ ⲟ ⲟ
ⲁ ⲓ ⲁ μ μ ⲁ ⲓ ⲱ ⲟ λ ⲁ ⲓ · ⲉ ⲓ ⲱ δ κ ⲁ ⲓ ⲟ ⲩ ⲧ ⲟ · ⲁ μ ⲁ ⲓ δ λ ⲉ ⲓ ⲁ μ ⲣ ⲟ μ δ ⳑ ⲁ

314 Vatican Museum, Rome. Menologion of Basil II Bulgaroktonos. V. Gr.
1613. Adoration. 979–84

Frequently they belong to a tradition similar to that followed by the
illustrator of the famous Joshua Roll. But the frontispiece of one of
the finest, the Smyrna Octateuch, which was unfortunately destroyed
in the great fire of Smyrna shortly after the First World War, was of
a more elaborate type; it depicted the Ancient of Days holding the
world, in a style heralding that of Blake. Popular again were volumes
concerned with the lives and dicta of the saints. Such was the
Menologion, where the exploits of the saints were recorded in the
order of the ecclesiastical calendar, or the Homilies, wherein their
writings were preserved. Of the copies of the former the Menologion

345

315 Bibliothèque Nationale, Paris. Homilies of St John Chrysostom. Coislin 79. King Nicephorus Botaneiates between St John Chrysostom and the Archangel Michael. 1078–81

of Basil II (976–1025) in the Vatican (V. Gr. 1613) is probably the finest; it was illustrated by eight different artists with as many as 430 illustrations. Each painter recorded his name in the margin beside each picture. The painters seem to have constituted a school, working under the direction of a single master. Individual differences of

346

316 Bibliothèque Nationale, Paris. Homilies of the monk James of Kokkinobaphos. Cod. Gr. 1208. The Ascension. Twelfth century

style are apparent, but it is not easy to tie down the personalities
exactly, for the differences of style in the models that were followed
also had a role to play, and it is for that reason that each of the eight
painters does not seem to show complete uniformity in his work.[9]

The Homilies of the various saints often contain, in addition to the

347

miniatures depicting religious scenes, a portrait of the patron for whom the book was produced. Thus a copy of the Homilies of St John Chrysostom in Paris (Bibl. Nat., Coislin 79), which was executed for Nicephorus III (1078–81), contains no less than four repetitions of the Emperor's portrait; one shows him between St John Chrysostom and the Archangel Michael. Examples of the Homilies of the monk James of Kokkinobaphos in the Vatican (V. Gr. 1162) and at Paris (Bibl. Nat. Gr. 1208) contain fine frontispieces depicting the Church of the Holy Apostles at Constantinople, which are of great interest because of their subject-matter, but the chief importance of these illustrations probably lies in the interpretation of them and of the text arrived at by Bréhier.[10] According to him the text reproduces the words of an old religious dialogue play, and he regards the miniatures as virtually sketches for the scenes before which the play was enacted. Further research on the lines instituted here by Bréhier has led to the identification of other dramas and scenes. The Akathistos hymn, for example, with its twenty-four episodes from the life of the Virgin, probably had such an origin, and Madame Cottas has studied in detail a further drama of the Passion of Christ, and has pointed out the considerable influence that it exercised not only on manuscript illustration, but also on the development of wall painting.[11] Further investigations along the same lines are likely to produce not only interesting information about the development of Byzantine painting, but also about the history of the whole European theatre.

More important than all these, Psalters, Homilies, and so on, however, were the illustrated copies of the Gospels, of which there were two more or less equally important forms, the Tetraevangelia, or four Gospels, and the Evangelistria, or liturgical Gospels, where the text was arranged in the order of the daily lessons. Practically all of the former contained portraits of the evangelists at the commencements of their respective Gospels, following the old Hellenistic custom of including a portrait of the author at the beginning of his work. These portraits exhibit considerable differences, not only in style and colouring, but also in iconography. Particular arrangements of the figures were probably associated with different regions. In the more old-fashioned ones the evangelists are shown standing, and they have the appearance of ancient philosophers; those in a copy of the Gospels at Paris, dating from 964 (Bibl. Nat. Gr. 70) may be cited. It has been suggested that the standing variant is to be asso-

317 Bibliothèque Nationale, Paris. Evangelistria. F. 75. Cod. Gr. 74. Herod promises the head of John the Baptist to the daughter of Herodias; the beheading of the Baptist. Mid eleventh century

ciated with Egypt.[12] More often, however, the figures are seated, but here again there are variants, and the side-face position has been assigned to Asia Minor and the frontal to Italy. Any very definite association of type and locality is, however, as yet premature.

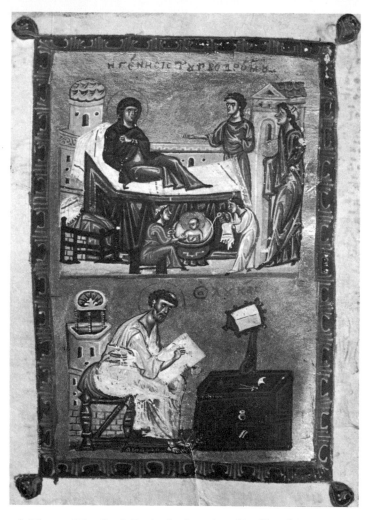

318 Library of the Greek Patriarchs, Jerusalem. Homilies of St Gregory of
Nazianzus. Manuscript No. A.T. 14. Birth of the Virgin, and the Evangelist
Luke. Eleventh century

In addition to the portraits of the evangelists, the more elaborate
copies of both types of Gospels sometimes also contain portraits of
patrons at the outset, and illustrations of the more important scenes
of our Lord's life throughout the text, either occupying a whole page,

319 Bibliothèque Nationale, Paris. Evangelistria. Cod. Gr. 70. The Evangelist St Matthew. 964

as in a fine Gospels in the Vatican (V. Urbin., Gr. 2), or added in the margin, as in a copy in the Bibliothèque Nationale (Gr. 115). Such scenes are more often present in the liturgical Gospels, where they precede the lessons for the days with which they have to do or are interspersed in the text, as in another copy in Paris (Bibl. Nat. Gr. 74). This manuscript, which belongs to the eleventh century, boasts as many as 372 small miniatures in a vivid, sprightly style, suggestive almost of Gothic art. The Nativity is thus, for example, frequently included before the reading for Christmas Day, the Anastasis before the reading for Easter Sunday, and so on. The style and iconography of these illustrations is closely parallel to that of the wall paintings of similar date, and the small-scale illustrations doubtless often served as the models from which the larger works were done. In the later manuscripts, indeed, it is possible to distinguish two distinct manners, which correspond with the Macedonian and Cretan schools of painting.

In general the work of the middle period of Byzantine art is distinguished by a lavish use of gold, both for backgrounds and for picking out the highlights on costumes. Jewels are freely imitated on the costumes; the colours are rarely naturalistic, being more often bright and daring; invariably, however, they are extremely effective. Elaborate borders were frequently introduced, but purely ornamental work did not play the same role as in manuscripts of the Hibernian and Northumbrian schools. The art may be described as essentially an urban one; there is little that is idyllic or naturalistic about it, and taken as a whole, the manuscripts of eleventh-century date show a more Oriental than Hellenistic spirit. The Eastern influence was not so much due to an inheritance from the past, but was often a contemporary one; it is to be seen concretely in the presence of Kufic script in the ornament as well as in the absence of Hellenistic naturalism in the drawing and the colouring.

Manuscripts of the fourteenth century, a period which saw such wonderful work in wall paintings and in mosaics, were generally not as rich as those of the middle period, but a few are of outstanding importance, notably one executed for John Cantacuzenos (1347-55) which is now in the Bibliothèque Nationale at Paris (Gr. 1242). The Transfiguration is a very lovely picture, grand in conception, and monumental in style, more comparable to an icon than to a miniature. But the majority of manuscripts of the age were small in size, and paper was as often employed as the parchment which had been wellnigh universal before. Perhaps the most distinctive feature about them was a growing interest in portraiture, for not only were imperial patrons frequently depicted, but other persons also, who seem to have been drawn from actual life. One of the most interesting is that of the

320 Bibliothèque Nationale, Paris. Manuscript of John VI Cantacuzenos. Cod.
Gr. 1242. The Transfiguration. 1347–54

353

321 Bodleian Library, Oxford. Manuscript: the Lincoln College Typicon. Emperor Constantinos Comnenos and Euphrosyne Dukaina Palaiologina. 1399–1400

322 Bibliothèque Nationale, Paris. Hippocrates Manuscript. Cod. Gr. 2144.
The High Admiral Apocaucos. *c.* 1342

323 British Museum, London. Curzon Gospels. The Bulgarian Czars Ivan
Alexander and Ivan Sisman. Fourteenth century

High Admiral Apocaucos on the title-page of a copy of Hippocrates
in the Bibliothèque Nationale (Gr. 2144). He sits on a wooden chair,
with a reading-desk beside him; his costume is of the finest woven
silk, of a type of which a number of actual examples are known in

museums and treasuries in the West; the work is in general spontaneous and expressive. The Lincoln College Typicon, now in the Bodleian at Oxford, contains as many as ten full-page portraits of members of the imperial family; all are quite effective, in a 'primitive' style

Throughout the twelfth, thirteenth, and fourteenth centuries a number of manuscripts were written and illustrated in the Balkans as well as in the Greek portions of the Byzantine world; the most important were those done in Bulgaria, with miniatures of essentially Byzantine type, but with texts in Old Bulgar. One, in the Vatican, dated to between 1356 and 1362, contains a translation from the Greek of the historical writings of Constantine Manasses; another, in the British Museum, is known as the Curzon Gospels. These Balkan manuscripts are little known, but on the whole they are of no more than secondary importance. More numerous were manuscripts in Armenian, of which a considerable number has come down to us. The paintings in them are often very crude, but they have considerable importance from the iconographical point of view. In the main the style was Oriental, though in the eleventh century Constantinopolitan models appear to have been copied to some extent, and the influence of these models survived into the twelfth; indeed, the Western style was at this time re-fused with the Eastern, to bring about something in the nature of an Armenian renaissance. In Georgia, work was less ambitious, for though quite a large number of fine manuscripts were produced, their style was directly modelled on the Byzantine, and whereas in wall and icon painting the Georgian manner was distinctive, in manuscript illumination it was derivative, though the work was well done.

The history of Byzantine panel painting was a long one, but it was not really until the twelfth century that this particular branch of art assumed the very great importance that is to be associated with it in later times. It may be that much early material has perished; it may be that in the rich and prosperous days of the Empire such sumptuous products as embossed metal, enamel, or mosaic took the place of panels, except in the poorer houses or churches; it may be that the production of panels was not taken very seriously until the iconostasis or screen between the body of the church and the sanctuary had been fully developed from the open-work balustrade of early times. It became, by the fourteenth century, a massive wooden structure, taken up entirely with the support of icons. Whatever the reason, there are few panels of early date in existence today which show really first-class work.

The origin of the art, so far as technique is concerned, is to be traced back to the tomb paintings of Graeco-Roman Egypt. These paintings were done with a tempera or similar medium, on a gesso ground, the gesso usually being rubbed into canvas, which was in turn attached to a panel. Presumably the canvas was there owing to conservatism, since canvas had formed an intrinsic part of the original mummy wrapping. Whatever the reason for this double backing, the system was retained in the Byzantine world right down to comparatively recent times as an essential part of the technique of icon painting. Another technique known in Egypt, the encaustic, where the colours were made of wax which was manipulated with a hot rod in place of a brush, survived only for a short time, and a few examples in the monastery of St Catherine on Mount Sinai and at Kiev are exceptions rather than typical products. They are to be dated to the seventh and eighth centuries. There are very large numbers of icons in the monastery of St Catherine in other tech-

324 Benaki Museum, Athens. Portrait from Fayoum, Egypt. Third century

niques, many of them of really outstanding quality; especially fine is a sixth-century one of St Peter.

The earliest paintings on panel that were produced outside Egypt date back to the sixth century. The best known is probably a small wooden casket from the Sancta Sanctorum at the Lateran, and

325 St Catherine's monastery, Mount Sinai. Icon. St Peter with Christ, St Stephen and the Virgin. Seventh century

326 Berlin Museum. Panel from Baouit. A Bishop. Sixth to seventh century

now in the Vatican Museum at Rome. It bears on the lid a number
of New Testament scenes, with the Crucifixion at the centre; both
the style and the iconography are Eastern, and it has been suggested
that the painting was done in Palestine, and brought back by some
pilgrim; each of these scenes probably bears witness to some shrine
that he had visited. The figures are squat, and the style is primitive.
More important is a much larger panel of the Madonna, from San
Francesco Romana in Rome, which has recently been brought to
light from under a number of subsequent layers of repaint.[1] The date
of the original has been disputed, but it may be as early as the sixth
century, and can hardly be later than the seventh. The style in this
case is not Eastern; the painting seems rather to herald the work of
the twelfth century in Italy, and it is to be classed as a monument of
Italian rather than of Byzantine art. A few other panels, of somewhat
uncertain date, complete the collection of pre-Iconoclast material.

In the Iconoclast period large religious paintings on panel were of
course excluded. But it may be suggested that small icons which
could be easily hidden were used at this time by those who did not

327 St Catherine's monastery, Mount Sinai. Icon. Madonna and Child, with
St Theodore and St George. Seventh century

wish to court displeasure, but who had at the same time a faith in
religious pictures. Indeed, the great popularity of the icon in the
home, which today characterizes the whole Orthodox world, be it

328 St Francesco Romana, Rome. Madonna. Seventh century

Slav or Greek, may perhaps date from this time, icons being kept at home when they were not permitted to be seen in public. It is also possible that some of the icons preserved in the monastery of St Catherine on Mount Sinai were done at this time, the ban not having been enforced so far from the capital.[2]

329 Tretiakov Gallery, Moscow. Icon from Constantinople. Our Lady of
Vladimir. *c.* 1130

330 Tretiakov Gallery, Moscow. Head of the Virgin from an icon of the Annunciation. Twelfth century

Icons of the Second Golden Age of Byzantine art, from the ninth to the twelfth century, are still not very numerous. A few panels survive in various places in Italy, but their style, like that of the Madonna from San Francesco Romana, is Italian rather than Byzantine, even if they are in what the Italians call the *maniera*

331 Tretiakov Gallery, Moscow. Icon of the Jaroslavl school. Our Lady of
Tolga. Fourteenth century

332 Helen Stathatos Collection, Athens. Italo-Byzantine icon. Madonna and Child. Fifteenth century

byzantina. More important are those in Russia, most of which have been brought to light owing to an active policy of cleaning the renowned icons which was inaugurated shortly before, and continued after, the Revolution. Some of these icons, like one with the Anastasis now in the Hermitage, were actually importations from Constantinople; others were painted by Greeks working in Russia; others again were purely Russian products, in the Byzantine manner. The most important of them is a panel of outstanding quality known as 'Our Lady of Vladimir', which was probably painted in Constantinople about 1125 and taken to Russia soon after.[3] It represents the Virgin of Tenderness, where the child's cheek is pressed in affection against that of his mother. Icons of 'Our Lady of Tolga' and of St Demetrius, also preserved in Russia, are again of twelfth-century date, and show the grandeur and superb quality of Byzantine work of the period, though they are perhaps rather less intimate and delicate in feeling than 'Our Lady of Vladimir', where the blend of austere reticence and passionate tenderness is carried to an almost incredible degree.

With the thirteenth century, panel painting seems to have increased in importance throughout the Orthodox world. Before that date panels were usually confined to single figures, such as Christ, the Virgin, or a particular saint; from the thirteenth century onwards scenes began to be depicted also, and as time went on the actual scenes selected, as well as the number of figures shown in each scene, began to increase, until, in the fifteenth century, all kinds of obscure subjects were treated. But at first only a few principal scenes of the New Testament were shown, the number selected being determined by some external association. Thus in early times seven scenes were usually chosen, the number being suggested by the days of creation. Later ten were chosen, because of the number of the beatitudes, and from the fourteenth century twelve was the more usual figure, on the basis of the number of the Apostles. The scenes selected almost invariably included the Annunciation, the Nativity, the Presentation, the Baptism, the Transfiguration, the Entry into Jerusalem, the Crucifixion, the Resurrection, the Ascension, and Pentecost. To make this number up to twelve, two other scenes were selected, their nature being determined by circumstances. Thus if the church in which the icon was to stand was dedicated to the Virgin, the Visitation and the Dormition (Assumption) would be added; if the patron were our Lord, choice was made from the Incredulity of

333 Hermitage Museum, Leningrad. Icon. The Anastasis. Twelfth century

Thomas, the Descent from the Cross, or, most frequently, the Raising of Lazarus. If further scenes were required, as in later times they often were, they were selected from the Miracles of Christ, from the Old Testament, or from the lives of particular saints and martyrs. Often icons of particular saints were surrounded by borders, wherein were depicted, in a series of miniatures, scenes from the life of the saint concerned.

The schools of icon painting were numerous, for each locality, in later times at least, boasted its own particular mannerisms, and these seem to have been more marked in panel painting than they were in wall painting. Again, panels tended to be more unworldly in character than the wall paintings, for whereas the wall painting was there primarily to record the Bible story on the walls of the church, the icon often tended to become almost a cult image, imbued with a semi-miraculous power in and for itself. As a result of this belief, the painter of icons tended to be less concerned with reality or nature than was the wall painter or mosaicist. Perspective and anatomy were often less regarded, colouring tended to be symbolic rather than realistic; the aim was to carry the spectator away from the affairs of this world rather than to reproduce it before him. Like the liturgy, the icon repeated certain well-known forms, and its merit lay in the quality of the repetition, not in any search for originality. As with a well-known play of Shakespeare, familiarity led to more profound appreciation, not to weariness.

Icon painting thus tended to embody the opposite aim to that which was before the painters of Renaissance Italy, and their technique was equally distinct. The icon painter thus laid on highlights in bright colours where a Western painter would shade; there were no attempts at chiaroscuro; colours were used as an intrinsic part of the composition. Western art, again, makes use of everyday figures to express a religious content, whereas the figures of the icon are not of every day; they are themselves fundamentally religious, of the other world rather than of this, the aim being to exalt the spirit to a higher plane. They make no appeal to sentiment, being concerned with the life of the mind rather than the life of the body. The aesthetic basis of the art is thus distinct, and it cannot be appreciated unless the normal canons of the Western world are cast aside. In fact, the outlook is probably closer to that of Far Eastern art, where the 'handed down model' was regarded as of outstanding importance, and where there was the same stress on the spiritual as

370

334 Pushkin Museum, Moscow. Icon. The Dormition. Fourteenth century

opposed to the mundane.[4] It is even possible that Chinese painting
may have exercised a more or less direct influence on the development
of the Byzantine panel-painting style, for the same conventions
seem to have been frequently adopted in both.[5] But to anyone who

comes to the icon with Eastern canons in mind, or who comes with an open judgement, the great power of the good work is at once apparent. It is, perhaps, an austere art, and it is something to which we are unaccustomed. But, like much of the art of today, which is not easy to understand at first glance, its significance lies below the surface; it is an art of the spirit rather than of the flesh, and must be approached from that point of view.

The distinction of schools is no easy matter, for the study of icon painting is still in its infancy, and a very great deal still remains to be

335 Byzantine Museum, Athens. Icon from Agios Nikolaos, Salonica. The Crucifixion. Fourteenth century

336 Tretiakov Gallery, Moscow. Icon. The Transfiguration. Attributed to
Theophanes the Greek. Fourteenth century

learnt. It would seem, however, that a particularly delicate, polished
manner distinguished the capital, and several icons survive from the
thirteenth century which were probably painted there, even if they
found their way to other places at a subsequent date. Most important
are some large panels from the Church of St Clement at Ochrida in

Macedonia; the most lovely shows the Virgin and Child on one side and the Annunciation on the other. There are similar icons at Dečani, in Serbia.[6] Others exist in churches in Greece, and a striking Ascension at Nicosia in Cyprus may also be noted, though it is of the fifteenth rather than the fourteenth century. By far the greatest

337 Macedonian State Collection, Skoplje. Icon from St Clement, Ochrida. Serbia. The Annunciation. Early fourteenth century

338 Tretiakov Gallery, Moscow. Icon of the Moscow school. The Annunciation. Fourteenth century

number of examples, however, have now found their way into museums, more especially the Benaki and the Byzantine Museums at Athens, the Hermitage at Leningrad, and the Pushkin Museum and the Tretiakov Gallery at Moscow. There are also a few examples in private collections. A fine Dormition of the Virgin of the fourteenth century in the Pushkin Museum at Moscow may be noted,

339 Byzantine Museum, Athens. Icon from Agios Nikolaos, Salonica. The
Hodeghetria. Fourteenth century

while a Baptism, once in the possession of Mr Stanley Casson, shows
the continuance of the style into the fifteenth century. As has already
been noted, more cleaning had until recently been done in Russia
than elsewhere, and this has served to disclose a good deal of
fourteenth- and fifteenth-century material of high quality. The most
important collection is that in the monastery of St Catherine on

340 The monastery church, Dečani (Serbia). Icon. The Virgin and Child. Fourteenth century

Mount Sinai. Its study is now in hand, and Professor Weitzmann has isolated an independent school working in Syria in the thirteenth century.[7]

A few Greeks were still working in Russia at the end of the
fourteenth century, notably Theophanes the Greek, whose name is
best known in connexion with wall paintings at Novgorod (1378)
and Moscow (1405). His icons illustrate the difference of manner
between panels and wall paintings, for several that can be assigned
to him have survived and are now preserved in the Tretiakov Gallery

341 Byzantine Museum, Athens. Icon. The Prophet Elijah. Seventeenth century

342 Benaki Museum, Athens. Byzantine icon. Abraham's Hospitality. Late fourteenth century

343 Benaki Museum, Athens. The Anastasis. Icon of Michael Damaskenos. Second half sixteenth century

at Moscow; they are more severe and more elegant than his works on a larger scale. Also, perhaps, they are more Russian, Russian work being more feminine in character than Byzantine at this date,

344 Cathedral of the Annunciation, Kremlin, Moscow. Icon by a pupil of
Theophanes. The Archangel Michael. 1405

345 Tretiakov Gallery, Moscow. Icon, school of Rublev. Christ enthroned.
Fifteenth century

and at the same time perhaps even more lovely. Nowhere is this to be
seen to a more marked degree than in the work of the great painter
Andrew Rublev (*c*. 1370–*c*. 1430), who worked with Theophanes in
Moscow. His Old Testament Trinity, painted about 1410, is a work
of the most subtle and enchanting beauty, and represents the highest
peak of Russian panel painting. It is to be distinguished from a
Byzantine work by the delicate pastel shades of the colouring, by the
subtle, swaying figures, with long necks and tall shoulders, and by

346 Russian Museum, Leningrad. Icon. The golden headed angel. Twelfth
century

a generally more rhythmical composition. These features are primarily national, and serve to distinguish Russian from Byzantine or
Greek work. But within Russia itself further distinctions on a stylistic
basis also serve to separate a number of local schools one from the
other. The most important were those of Novgorod, flourishing from
the thirteenth to the mid fifteenth century, Pskov, flourishing in the
fifteenth and sixteenth centuries, Suzdal, from the thirteenth to the

347 Tretiakov Gallery, Moscow. Icon by Andrew Rublev. The Old Testament
Trinity. *c.* 1410

fifteenth century, Vladimir, from the thirteenth to the fourteenth
century, and Moscow, from the early fifteenth century until the
eclipse of the old manner at the end of the seventeenth century, as
a result of the Westernizing reforms of Peter the Great. A late school,
the Stroganov, which developed out of that of Moscow, was more of
local importance.

Icons of the fifteenth and sixteenth centuries are naturally very much more numerous than those of earlier date, and many were still of high quality, though mass production had to some extent already set in. In Greece the greatest number are to be associated with the Cretan school, which was essentially a panel-painting style. The earliest paintings in Crete itself belong to the beginning of the fourteenth century; an artist by the name of Pagomenos who was working there between 1314 and 1328 may be noted. He, and other painters in the island, seem to have developed a rather meticulous manner, characterized by great precision and by a marked use of bright highlights, between this time and the decoration of the Peribleptos at Mistra (c. 1350), and soon after a distinctive Cretan iconography began to develop also. But it is not easy to say exactly how much of the manner that later came to be known as Cretan was due to native artists and how much to the school of Mistra.[8] It has also been suggested that Venetian influence was important, but recent evidence suggests that the influence was probably more in the opposite direction, for in their earlier work such painters as Giovanni Bellini employed at times a very icon-like manner. At a later date, on the other hand, Venice undoubtedly influenced the development of the Cretan school, and the sixteenth-century paintings of southern Greece and the islands often show concrete instances of Venetian influence. For instance, the habit of signing icons with the painter's name was probably adopted from Italy, and it became usual at this time; at an earlier date the majority of the icons that we know were anonymous. Of the numerous artists whose names we know, the most important was probably Michael Damaskenos.

Quite distinct from the Cretan school proper is one which was termed Graeco-Italian by Kondakov, Likhachev, and others. To it are to be assigned the works of a number of Greeks who worked in Italy, such as Emanuel Zanfurnari, who lived in the later sixteenth and earlier seventeenth centuries; he painted a fine icon of the death of St Ephraim Syrus, of which there is one version in the Vatican; another formerly in the Northwick Collection in Gloucestershire may be of rather earlier date. Another important work of this group is the reliquary of Cardinal Bessarion in the Accademia at Venice, which is dated to 1443.[9] The school is characterized by a rather more sombre colouring than that of the Cretan proper, and by a generally softer touch. In addition shading was at times used to effect modelling, and the highlights were much less marked, so that the general

Ὁ Ἀρχ(άγγελος) ΜΙΧΑ(ὴλ) Ταξιάρχη(ς)

Byzantine Museum, Athens. Icon. The Archangel Michael with sceptre and globe. Probably from Constantinople. Fourteenth century

348 Greek Institute for Byzantine and Post-Byzantine Studies, Venice. Icon. Nativity. Sixteenth century

effect was less ethereal, and a more direct appeal was made by way of sentiment.

In addition to these wider groups, the Cretan and the Graeco-Italian, local schools are also to be distinguished. Thus one may be associated with Mount Athos, another with the more easterly Greek

349 Hiristos Church, Princes Island (Büyük Ada), Istanbul. Icon. The Crucifixion. Eighteenth century

350 Accademia, Venice. Reliquary of Cardinal Bessarion. Crucifixion and
scenes of the Passion. Fifteenth century

islands, another with Cyprus, and so on. On Athos, in addition to an iconography of Eastern extraction and to that affection for obscure subject-matter which always seems to be associated with a monastic community, a love of minute, profuse decoration seems to have been to the fore, the colours were bright and decorative, and eyes were usually shown as small black pin-heads. The work of the more easterly islands shows a preference for light colours, such as pale blue and pink. That of Cyprus is much more Latinized, shading being more popular than the use of bright highlights; figures of kneeling donors in semi-European costumes are often included. In Bulgaria, again, a national manner seems to have been arrived at by the fifteenth century, if not before, the most characteristic feature being the use of a black background. Later we see a number of local schools in that country, which can be distinguished without very great difficulty.[10] Similar schools existed in Serbia, though as yet little has been done to distinguish them. At Venice and along the Adriatic coast another school was at work, the paintings of which show a complete mingling of Venetian and Byzantine elements. The most usual subject was the Virgin and Child. The backgrounds of these Madonnas are gilt, and are also often decorated with scroll patterns through the gold. The features of the Madonnas are carefully modelled, and a direct appeal is made to sentiment. This may best be termed the Adriatic school.

The study of Byzantine stone sculpture is still very much in its infancy, and it is only of very recent years that sufficient material has become available to permit anything like a comprehensive survey. Excavations and explorations in the Near East, more especially since the First World War, have, however, filled the museums of Constantinople, Athens, Sofia, and elsewhere, and there is today enough material available to show that stone sculpture was, anyhow until the eleventh or twelfth century, a great deal more important than was at one time imagined, and even if figural work gave place to a great extent to ornamental, the ornamental work was often by no means of negligible artistic quality. It remains, however, for much of this material to be published in easily accessible form, and no satisfactory monograph on Byzantine stone sculpture has as yet been produced.

The stylistic changes which came about in this art between the fourth and seventh centuries were perhaps more marked than those in any other, and the distinction between a truly Roman and a truly Byzantine piece of sculpture is very marked indeed. A change had actually set in in Roman work well before Christianization, and we can trace its course by way of such monuments as the arch of Galerius at Salonica (298), the arch of Constantine at Rome, and the base of the column of Theodosios at Constantinople (390). But the change of style was not by any means uniform all over the Empire, for at Rome it was much slower, and portrait sculpture continued in the old strain almost until the sixth century, whereas in the East it was rapid and all-embracing. The survival of the Roman style of portraiture into Byzantine times is illustrated by a number of monuments, notably the colossal statue of Valentinian I at Barletta (364–74). A similar statue depicting Justinian stood at Constantinople, but it does not survive. The large imperial sarcophagi of

351 St Mark's, Venice. Two porphyry groups. Tetrarchs. Early fourth century

352 Archaeological Museum, Istanbul. Stone sculpture. From the neighbourhood of Sinope. Fifth or sixth century

porphyry, now in the Vatican and on the terrace of the Archaeological Museum at Constantinople, are again Romanizing works,
though it is likely that they were carved in Egypt, since the material
came from there, and there is evidence to suggest that sculpture was
more often moved in a finished state than in the raw in ancient times.
But it seems more likely that such carvings as these, which are in a very
Classical manner, were done either in Rome or Constantinople than

353-4 Obelisk of Theodosios, Istanbul. Reliefs on the base. *c.* 390

355 Archaeological Museum, Istanbul. The Sarigüzel sarcophagus. Fifth
century

in the Nile valley, where a more Oriental style seems to have pre-
dominated. Certain other sculptures in porphyry, such as the figures
of tetrarchs built into St Mark's at Venice, or two similar figures in
the Vatican, are in a non-idealistic, primitive style, with large
heads, staring eyes and dumpy proportions. Such work was done in
Syria and Palestine, and the style passed from there to Egypt even
before the adoption of Christianity as the official religion; later it
played an important role in the development of Coptic art.[1]

In other work of the fourth century the Hellenic element was most
to the fore, as for example in a sarcophagus from Constantinople
known as the Sarigüzel sarcophagus. The figure subjects that adorn
the sides of a group of sarcophagi from Asia Minor, known as the
Sidamarra or Lydian sarcophagi, are more Hellenistic.[2] There is a
particularly famous example in the Berlin Museum bearing a figure
of Christ, which has frequently been illustrated. The ornamental
work is, on the other hand, quite un-Classical, for it avoids naturalism and modelling, and seeks its effect through contrasting light and
shade. The vine and acanthus scrolls which form the basis of this
decoration are, in fact, treated as stylized, formal ornament, rather
than as variants upon naturalistic forms.

It has sometimes been argued that this type of sculpture was
adopted purely as the result of the evolution of Roman mannerisms,
but it is more probable that it came about owing to the influence of
a distinct artistic comprehension, which had its birth in the East, and
penetrated to Anatolia early in the Christian era.[3] From the sixth

century onwards, in any case, figural reliefs of Hellenistic type, and ornamental work which is basically non-representational in conception, appear together side by side all over the Byzantine world. Capitals, cornices, and other architectural works in stone were, however, more often decorated with non-representational motifs, while pulpits, closure slabs, and so forth were often adorned with figures. An ambo from Salonica, which is now in the Archaeological Museum at Istanbul, shows the blend of the two manners in the sixth century. The blend is shown also in a type of capital which was particularly popular in the fourth and fifth centuries, and which is

356 State Museum, Berlin. Early Christian and Byzantine Collections. Marble sarcophagus from Sidamarra. Fourth century

357 Archaeological Museum, Istanbul. Detail of ambo from Salonica. Virgin and Child. Sixth century

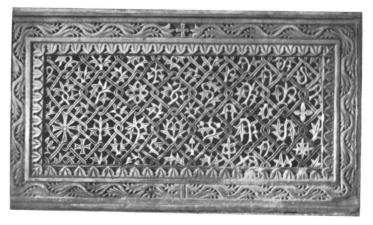

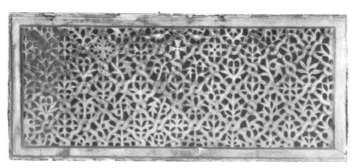

358–60 National Museum, Ravenna. Marble parapet panels from San Vitale.
Sixth century

361 St Mark's Venice. Marble. Capital in apse. Eleventh century

362 Baouit (Egypt). Parapet panels with stumps of columns. Sixth to seventh century

usually known as the Theodosian. Here the Classical volutes and the acanthus decoration of Classical art are retained, but they are treated in a completely non-Classical manner. The change of idea and style is accompanied also by a technical change, the drill being used almost to the exclusion of the chisel; it was better suited to produce the silhouette effect which was desired, whereas the chisel was essentially an implement designed to achieve modelling.

Another distinctive feature of fifth- and early-sixth-century work is a flat, cold style of figural sculpture, not unlike that practised in Palmyrene work some three centuries earlier, or in an interesting group of funeral stelae from Altyn Tash in Asia Minor, which are to be assigned to the first century A.D.[4] A head from Ephesus, now at Vienna, is in much the same style. One at Milan, probably of Theodora, is also not wholly in a classical style. While its association with Theodora is uncertain, there is reason to support its attribution to the age of Justinian. More usual than such free-standing sculptures, however, were slabs with a decoration in bas-relief. Examples are quite numerous, especially in the Museum of Antiquities at Istanbul; a slab bearing the Archangel Gabriel at Antalia may be cited. Some date it to the sixth century; others have assigned it to the eleventh, but this dating is certainly too late, though now that the true character of the art of the period immediately after Iconoclasm is coming to be recognized, a date in the ninth century would not be impossible. The same style is to the fore in capitals in the Constantinople Museum, where animals take the place of the Classical volutes. They are to be assigned to the sixth century, a date at which a great many elaborate variations on the Classical theme of the capital were being made, though the decorations were more often ornamental than figural.

In contrast to such very polished and finished carvings, others of a coarser, more rough and ready style may be cited, such as some reliefs from the Church of the Studios at Constantinople, which are to be assigned to the fifth century. One shows the Entry into Jerusalem. There is a similar relief in the Museum of Antiquities showing the Sacrifice of Abraham, and another at Berlin, bearing St Peter. These were probably done at Constantinople, but the carver was in close touch with the Syrian style of work. Yet the Syrian style was capable of producing very effective, if not elegant, results, and the two front columns of the ciborium in St Mark's at Venice are the most outstanding examples. They date from the fifth century, though they were probably brought to St Mark's from Syria only at a later date.[5]

If figural work was executed at several centres and in a number of different styles in and around the age of Justinian, purely ornamental work was even more universal. It is to be seen at its best, perhaps, in Constantinople itself, for example in the capitals of Sancta Sophia, where the motifs are all treated very formally, even

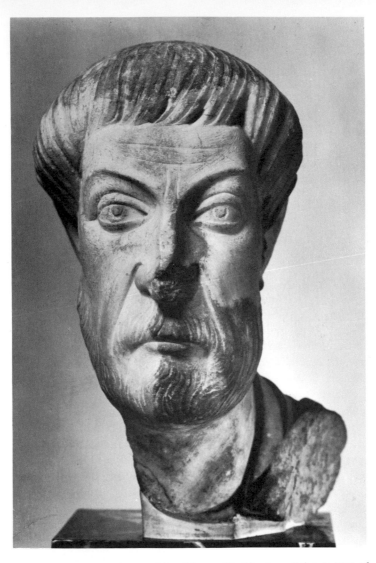

363 Museum of the History of Art, Vienna. Marble, from Ephesus. Bust of
Eutropios. Fifth century

if they are basically naturalistic. The undercutting of the ornament,
the formalistic feeling, and the 'all-over' character of the decoration
are all essentially Eastern, but Classical forms, like the volutes at the

364 Archaeological Museum, Istanbul. Limestone relief from St John of Studios. The Entry into Jerusalem. Fifth century

corners, often survive, and in other types the Classical acanthus remains as the basis of the decoration, though it has undergone changes. Its most popular variant was known as the wind-blown acanthus; there are fine examples of the type at Salonica, Ravenna, and elsewhere. Indeed, the examples from different areas are sometimes so closely akin that it seems likely that all were carved in a common centre, and were exported in a finished state to the various sites in which they were used. The plates serve to illustrate not only the changes of style and the types of decoration, but also the changes of form that came about as a result of the development of the Byzantine architectural style; the impost capital, where the Classical volutes survive below, but where an extensive surface to support a brick arch has been provided above, is especially noteworthy. The main centre of production for such things was Marmora Island, where the principal quarries were situated. Often capitals imported from there were copied in far distant places. In San Vitale at Ravenna, for example, the capitals are imports from the Marmora, whereas the imposts above them were carved locally; their workmanship is very much coarser. But this does not mean that good work was restricted to the Marmora alone. Sometimes that done

365–6 St Mark's, Venice. Alabaster. Ciborium columns. Fifth century

elsewhere was of a very high standard, as for example in the sarco-phagi of Ravenna, like that of Archbishop Theodore. The Arch-bishop died in 691, and the sarcophagus was perhaps carved for him, though the practice of re-employing good sarcophagi was by no means unknown, and the best are probably to be assigned to the later fifth and earlier sixth centuries, rather than to the seventh; it was at the earlier period that Ravenna was most prosperous, and then that the finest of its mosaics were set up.

The various styles of sculpture which had been evolved by the sixth century continued in use in the seventh, and recent research suggests that quite a lot of work was also done in Iconoclast times; the closure slabs bearing a decoration of purely geometric motifs or of single crosses, which are common in Greece and at Constanti-nople, were probably in many cases produced at that time, and there was probably a revival in post-Iconoclast times; a fine slab in the British Museum is probably to be assigned to the tenth century. At the close of the period figural work probably began to blossom anew with the same vigour as in miniature painting. With the eleventh century a more formal style developed, where the lines were severe and abstract, and where naturalistic modelling gave place to rhyth-mic composition. The finest example of this style is a fragmentary slab, bearing the Virgin Orans, from the Church of the Mangana at Constantinople, and now in the Museum of Antiquities. The church was founded by Constantine Monomachos between 1048 and 1054, and the slab is probably to be assigned to the same date. There are a number of similar slabs in the same museum, in St Mark's at Venice, at Ravenna, and elsewhere, but none is as fine as that from the Mangana. Archangels, saints, and sometimes imperial figures were also depicted on slabs in a similar way. It is, however, often very hard to date examples, and there has been dispute as to whether a fragmentary ciborium arch from the Church of St Mary Panachrantos at Constantinople should be assigned to the sixth or a later century; the work has now been shown to be as late as the fourteenth, thanks to the discovery of related sculptures in the Church of St Mary Pammakaristos (Fetiye Camii).

In addition to figural subjects, animals and birds of Oriental type and geometric patterns were also carved. The former seem to have been especially popular in Greece; they were also used in Italy. Such slabs would appear often to have been copied from textiles imported from Persia or elsewhere in the Islamic world, and purely Islamic

367-8 Mausoleum of Galla Placidia, Ravenna. Two marble sarcophagi. Fifth century

369 Archaeological Museum, Antalia (Anatolia). Archangel Gabriel. Sixth century

motifs like the Kufic script were sometimes copied as well. Indeed, Kufic letters, often not properly understood, but used simply as an ornamental motif, were frequently used as the borders of sculptured slabs. A whole series of such slabs, mostly of tenth-century date, is built into the walls of a church at Athens known as the Little Metropolis. For some reason the Oriental influence was much more marked in Greece than elsewhere; at Constantinople, though animal and bird motifs occur, they savour more of the old models known and used by the early Christians than of the textiles of eighth- and ninth-century Persia.

Slabs of these various types were usually carved in low relief, but other techniques were also known, even if they were less common.

370 Archaeological Museum, Istanbul. Part of a ciborium arch from St Mary Panachrantos, Constantinople. Thirteenth or fourteenth century

Thus the ground was sometimes completely cut away, leaving the design as an open-work pattern, or it was cut away rather roughly and the incised area was filled in with coloured paste or coloured stones, to produce what may best be termed incrustation work. The former technique was seldom practised after the sixth century; the

371 Archaeological Museum, Istanbul. Fragment of
statue of an emperor. Eleventh century

372 Archaeological Museum, Istanbul. Marble relief from the Mangana
Church in Constantinople. The Virgin. Eleventh century

373 Archaeological Museum, Istanbul. Marble incrustation work.
St Eudoxia. Eleventh century

latter was probably most common in the tenth and eleventh. A number of examples, now in the Constantinople Museum, were found during excavations in St Mary Panachrantos; the finest of them bears a standing figure of St Eudoxia, the incrustation being in coloured marbles and bone.

Low-relief work akin to that usual between the ninth and twelfth centuries was produced also in Palaeologue times, but the relief tended to become lower as time went on, till eventually a system which was little more than engraving supplanted that of carving proper. Technically speaking, such work had reached the extreme of decadence, and the results cannot lay claim to great artistic merit. Yet they are, nevertheless, sometimes not without charm, as in the case of a seated figure of Christ of the fourteenth or early fifteenth century in the Metropolis at Mistra. But this decline of technique was not universal, and some very unusual carvings of the thirteenth century above the south door of the Church of Sancta Sophia at Trebizond are in high relief and are also quite well done. They depict scenes from Genesis, the iconography being of the Eastern rather than the fully fledged Byzantine family. It is possible that the

374 Byzantine Museum, Athens. Coloured marble inlay. Three Apostles. From Vlatadon monastery, Salonica. Eleventh century

375 Cluny Museum, Paris. Marble capital from a church in Athens. Twelfth century

376 Museum of the History of Art, Vienna. Marble relief.
St Panteleimon. Thirteenth century

377 Church, Achthamar (Armenia). Relief on the outer wall. 915–21

378 Mistra Museum, Mistra (Peloponnese). Marble sculpture. Christ
enthroned. Fifteenth century

413

sculptors were to some extent inspired from Armenia, where stone carving of a rather formal type flourished from the tenth till the fourteenth centuries; the most important examples are the reliefs showing Old Testament scenes and animals of Persian type that adorn the whole exterior of the church on the island of Achthamar in Lake Van (915-21).[6]

Ornamental as opposed to figural work in this last age changed in a rather similar way, for it tended to become more profuse and more minute; sometimes the sculptured slabs look almost like ornamental drawings on the page of a book. Islamic motifs came to be employed more and more frequently, including geometric and interlacing patterns and Kufic script. Some quite attractive slabs bearing ornament of this type are preserved in the Byzantine Museum at Athens; others are to be seen in various places in Greece and the Balkans; the most striking are perhaps those built into a church at Volo in Thessaly.[7] Designs which obviously spring from the same models appear on contemporary textiles and ceramics.

Sculpture in Wood

Though it was probably important, sculpture in wood of early date is now practically unknown to us, owing to the fragile nature of the material, which has prevented its preservation except in the driest of climates, like that of Egypt. There Coptic woodwork has survived in quite considerable quantities, though it is outside the scope of this volume. In the Byzantine world itself wood was certainly important for doors, and probably also for iconostases, though the development of these on a large scale did not come about till the middle period. Of the early doors in wood, the most important that have survived are those of Sta Sabina in Rome, which were set up in 432. They are divided up into small panels, bearing biblical scenes. The iconography is of the Eastern family, but it is not certain whether the doors were carved in Syria or in Rome by Eastern craftsmen.[8] That the majority of doors of this type have long since perished is suggested by the pitiable state of such a fine late example as that in the Church of the Nativity at Bethlehem, which dates from 1227. A few doors, in a more or less damaged condition, do, however, survive in Greece and the Balkans. Most important are those of the Church of St Nicholas at Ochrida in Yugoslavia, of the first quarter of the fourteenth century, which bear figure subjects, or those at Olympiotissa in Thessaly, dated 1305, which bear geometric designs. There

414

379 Sta Sabina, Rome. Detail of the wooden doors. Christ changing the water into wine. 432

are examples of fifteenth-century date in quite a number of the museums of the Balkans, notably at Bucharest.

From the post-Byzantine period very much more survives, for wood was by then extensively used for iconostases, episcopal thrones and similar pieces of ecclesiastical furniture. Some of this woodwork is finely carved in a rather rococo style. Often the carving was subsequently gilt; a characteristic example of an iconostasis of early eighteenth-century date from a church in Cyprus is now preserved in

380 Sta Sabina, Rome. The wooden doors. 432

381 Sta Sabina, Rome. Detail from the wooden doors. Christ. 432

the Victoria and Albert Museum. Small crosses in sandalwood were also frequently carved in a very minute style from late Palaeologue times onwards; the majority, however, belong to post-Byzantine times, that is to say, they date from after the fall of Constantinople in 1453 and are to be classed as examples of 'peasant' art. They are often attractive, but are not to be compared with the magnificent carvings in ivory of imperial days. Mount Athos was an important centre of production of such things.

Free-standing sculpture in wood, as we know it in the Western world, was never usual in Byzantine art, where the painted panel

382 Monastery of Zographou, Mount Athos. Detail of a wooden altar canopy.
Eighteenth century

took the place that was occupied by the cult statue in the Renaissance or Gothic world. A tall figure of a saint at Ochrida, which
dates from the fourteenth century, is practically the only example
that is known on a large scale; and it is almost as much Romanesque
as it is Byzantine; small figures or reliefs in wood were, however,
more common, but they are to be classed alongside the ivories, rather
than as pieces of monumental sculpture.

Byzantine ivories can most conveniently be considered under two divisions, an early and a late. In the early division a number of definite groups can be distinguished, determined both according to the nature of the object and upon stylistic grounds, but it is by no means easy to be sure of the provenance of more than a few of the individual examples. In the second division there is far less deviation from the mean, for a clearly marked Byzantine style dominated all the work. The nature of the objects, again, is much more uniform, for small plaques bearing Christ, the Virgin, or saints were wellnigh universal, except for an important group of caskets, most of which are adorned with secular subjects.

In a study of the early ivories, a good many centres, or possible centres, of production have to be taken into account. Work was certainly done at Rome, both before and after the adoption of Christianity, and the lovely diptych of the Symmachi and Nicomachi, carved to celebrate a marriage between these two families, is no doubt to be assigned there. Though it is to be dated to the fifth century, it shows no sign of the influence of the realist style. It is now divided between the Victoria and Albert and the Cluny Museums. When once the capital was transferred there, Constantinople must also have become a centre of production. Ivories were perhaps carved in northern Italy; Milan has been noted as the home of a distinctive school and work was probably done at Ravenna. The Brescia casket, of the mid fourth century, may again probably be assigned to Rome or Milan. A group has also been associated with Provence.[1] But the evidence goes to show that there were two centres which were more important, namely Alexandria and Antioch. Work in both was at first of a definitely Hellenistic character, but as time progressed Syrian 'realism' gradually exercised a more and more marked effect, especially at Antioch, and by the fourth century ivories associated with that city can be distinguished by their forceful style, whereas those of Alexandria remained more idealistic in conception. Indeed, an essentially Classical style, where elegance and delicacy were the dominating factors, survived there until the sixth century. In the rest of Egypt, however, the realist style of Syria was adopted at an earlier date, so it is not always possible to say that all 'realist' work should be assigned to Antioch.

A few of the ivories that survive may be fairly definitely attributed to one or other of these cities. An ivory bearing the Dioscorides and Europa at Trieste is thus clearly Alexandrine, while the famous Pyxis at Berlin was probably carved at Antioch. It is probably to be dated

383 Museo Civico, Brescia. Ivory casket. Fourth century

384 British Museum, London. Ivory pyxis with scenes from the life of St Menas.
Sixth century

to the fifth century. The large heads and accentuated expressions are
typical of all that Syria stood for in art at this time. There is a good
deal of the same realism in a number of other ivories. Panels with
personifications of Rome and Constantinople at Vienna, one at
Berlin bearing Apollo, or one at Ravenna bearing Apollo and
Daphne, may be noted. They are to be dated to the sixth rather than
the fifth century, and by that time Alexandria had become to some
extent permeated with the Syrian style, so that it is hard to say
whether they were carved at Alexandria or Antioch; the fact that a
number of such ivories bear Classical subjects rather favours the
former city, which was an outpost of Hellenism with regard to
subject-matter as well as to style.

The full flowering of the Hellenistic style is to be seen in the large
series of panels attached to the throne of Maximian at Ravenna,

385–6 Ivory diptych. Fifth century. Leaf of the Nicomachi. Cluny Museum, Paris. Leaf of the Symmachi. Victoria and Albert Museum, London

which is probably the best known of all early Christian ivories. There has been a great deal of discussion as to where the panels were carved; Alexandria was at one time regarded as most likely; more

387 National Museum, Ravenna. Ivory throne of Archbishop Maximianus.
Early sixth century

recently opinion has veered in favour of Constantinople. It was
apparently made for Maximianus, archbishop of Ravenna from 545
till 556, and though some authorities consider that the plaques of

388 State Museums, Berlin. Wing of ivory diptych. Christ between Peter and
Paul. Sixth century

389 Cluny Museum, Paris. Ivory panel. St Paul. Syrian. Sixth century

which it is composed were actually carved about half a century earlier, there is really little reason to dispute the supposition that the carving was done at the same time that the throne was made. Four hands are to be distinguished, but there is no reason to suppose that they did not all belong to the same locality.[2] There are several other ivories which are more markedly Eastern, notably two book covers in the Public Library at Erivan in Armenia and one in the Bibliothèque Nationale, two panels bearing Gospel scenes in the

390 National Museum, Ravenna. Ivory from the throne of Archbishop Maximianus. John the Baptist with the four Evangelists. Early sixth century

425

391 The Cathedral, Milan. Treasury. Ivory diptych with scenes from the life of
Christ. Ninth century

Fitzwilliam Museum at Cambridge, a panel with the Baptism and
one bearing St Menas in the British Museum, and a plaque bearing
St Paul in the Cluny Museum. It is probable that all these were
carved in the same place: Syria or Palestine, Antioch, Alexandria,
and Constantinople have all been suggested as possible homes by
different authorities, and the case for Alexandria has probably been
put forward with the greatest weight of evidence.[3] But some of the

392 Bibliothèque Nationale, Paris. Ivory book cover with scenes after the
Resurrection. Carolingian. Ninth century

panels of the Ravenna throne show fairly close resemblance to the Consular diptychs done at Constantinople and there are quite substantial grounds for assigning them to the same place; and those at Erivan are very Oriental. All that can be said for certain is that the Syrian realist style and the spirit of Hellenism were mingled to a very considerable degree.

Though Antioch and Alexandria were perhaps the most important centres of ivory carving until the fifth century, the countries of which they were respectively the most important towns were also centres of production, and distinct Syro-Palestinian and Egyptian schools may be distinguished; in both cases the work lacks the polish and finish which the great cities were able to give. Egyptian work was characterized by a rather florid naturalism and by very full designs; by the sixth century its products had become easily distinguishable, being rather coarse and essentially provincial. Though not without merit, these works can hardly rank with what was done in Alexandria. Syro-Palestinian work also had a provincial flavour, though on the whole the carvers there seem to have been in closer touch with Antioch than were those of Egypt with Alexandria. Owing to the importance of Palestine as a centre of pilgrim traffic and to the ease with which ivories could be transported, it is probable that the works of this school exercised a very considerable influence both in Italy and at Constantinople. Jerusalem was probably the centre of the school. A diptych with Passion scenes at Milan, of the later fifth century, a panel with the Ascension at Munich, another with the two Marys in the Trivulzio Collection at Milan, and panels from a casket with scenes of the Passion in the British Museum have been assigned to this group. Some authorities believe that much of the carving was actually done in Rome or even in Milan, probably by Palestinian residents.[4] There was a considerable Palestinian colony there as early as the fifth century, and ivory carvers almost certainly moved about a good deal; nevertheless, the reasons for assigning these ivories to Palestine rather than to Rome or Milan are not very clear.

Rather more 'Eastern' in style is the work of a second Syro-Palestinian school, which has by some been associated with Edessa. A panel, originally probably a book cover, in the British Museum which bears the Nativity below and the Adoration above, is typical of the group. Vertical perspective – that is, the placing of figures one above the other in the same plane, rather than behind one another in different planes – the enlargement of the principal figures out of

393 Bavarian National Museum, Munich. Ivory panel. The three women at the Sepulchre and the Ascension. Fifth century

394 National Museum, Ravenna. Ivory triptych from Murano. Central leaf.
Middle: Christ with saints and three youths in the furnace. *Left:* Healing
of the blind and possessed. *Right:* Raising of Lazarus and healing of lame.
Below: Story of Jonah. Fifth or sixth century

all comparison to the others, a great accentuation of the heads, and
a general uncouthness are the characteristic features. Such ivories as
one showing our Lord between St Peter and St Paul from Murano,
and now at Ravenna, one with the Adoration in the John Rylands
Library at Manchester, or the Daniel pyxis in the British Museum,
are to be assigned to the group, and there are similar panels at Paris,
Bologna, and Moscow.

Oriental elements are also present in the group assigned by Baldwin
Smith to Provence and by other authorities to Milan, Antioch, or

395 Cabinet des Médailles, Paris. Wing of the ivory diptych of Consul
Magnus. 578

Asia Minor. A book cover at Milan, casket panels in the Victoria and Albert Museum, two panels of a diptych, one at Berlin and one at Nevers, and a pyxis at Rouen are the most important examples. Though Baldwin Smith's case for Provence is well supported, Milan would seem a more probable centre, if only because it was a more important place, near to the centre of civilization, and not in an outlying area like Provence, where one would expect to find something more provincial. Moreover, it is known that ivory carvers worked at Milan, and if their work was distinctive stylistically, this seems the most likely group to be associated with the city. Strzygowski's assignment to Asia Minor is less probable.[5]

Another important group of early ivories is determined primarily on the basis of shape and function rather than probable locality, namely the Consular diptychs. About fifty of these are known, and they extend from the beginning of the fifth century till the abolition of the Consulate in 541. Only six of the surviving diptychs were made for Rome; the others are connected with Constantinople. There has, however, been a good deal of debate as to where they were made. The style of the earlier ones is distinctly Roman, and serves to illustrate the continuance of imperial art at the new capital, but there are also often marked Oriental or Hellenistic affinities. Some of the later diptychs are more purely Byzantine, and herald the style of religious plaques of the sixth and seventh centuries. The diptych of Probus (406), now at Aosta, is thus essentially Roman in style, feeling, and appearance; leaves in the name of Anastasius, Justinian, and others are definitely associated with Constantinople, as are the imperial diptychs, like the leaf with the Empress Ariadne at Florence, while a leaf of the fifth or sixth century bearing the Archangel Michael in the British Museum shows the delicate, polished manner and the superb quality typical of the best Byzantine work. The features that characterize it are those that constitute the hall-mark of the capital, and this ivory, above any other, serves as proof that the art of Constantinople was not merely an eclectic art, as some writers have suggested. Alexandrine, Antiochene, and Roman traits appear, yet even if the features characteristic of one of these are uppermost in certain individual examples, the subtle blending of influences that the majority shows is a more important factor. This blending had not always gone as far in ivory carving by the sixth century as it had in major sculpture or mosaic, but the Byzantine manner had nevertheless been established and was ready to burst

396 Museo Nazionale del Bargello, Florence. Ivory.
The Empress Ariadne. *c.* 500

forth into flower. For these reasons it may be suggested that Constantinople was the centre in which the ivories of this group were carved, though it is probable that the actual carvers came from different centres; some were certainly from Syria, and others probably from Rome. In addition to the diptychs, a few other ivories are

397 Louvre, Paris. Wing of ivory diptych. Barberini Ivory. *c.* 500

398 British Museum, London.
Ivory. The Archangel Michael.
Sixth century

probably to be included in this Constantinopolitan group, notably the important composite panel in the Louvre known as the Barberini Ivory. It bears the figure of a mounted emperor, who is probably to be identified as Anastasius; it is to be dated to about 500.

From the seventh century onwards it was in Constantinople and the immediate dependencies of the capital, such as Salonica, that the most important work was done, for Alexandria and Antioch had passed under Moslem control, while Italy was suffering difficulties owing to the attacks of the Goths. This narrowing of the geographical sphere of the art was accompanied by a narrowing of the actual output, for certain forms which were quite common in the earlier period fell out of use. Most important of these were the pyxis, and the composite ivory, made up of a number of separate panels fitted together. Acanthus and similar floral borders also tended to become less usual. Single panels, diptychs, and triptychs, indeed, became practically the only objects that were carved for the church; an interesting ivory at Trier depicting a procession conveying relics to a church may serve as an example. In the secular sphere rectangular caskets and horns are the only things of which there are more than a few individual examples.

399 The Cathedral, Trier (Germany). Ivory. Procession with relics. Sixth or seventh century

400 Cluny Museum, Paris. Ivory casket. Battle scenes. Tenth century

The rectangular caskets form a very important group, for not only are their designs very diversified, but they are also usually of very high quality. The majority of the decorations are of a secular character, the themes being taken from Classical mythology, and because of this it was at one time suggested that all were produced during the Iconoclast period. This, however, is improbable, for there are other caskets bearing religious themes which are not only well-nigh identical in technique, but which also have the same very characteristic form of border, made up of a series of rosettes; so typical are these, indeed, that they have led to the whole group being

401 Museo Nazionale del Bargello, Florence. Ivory casket. St John the Baptist, St John Chrysostom, the Virgin and Christ. Twelfth century

437

termed 'the rosette casket group'. Further, the style and quality of workmanship is akin to what was being done in other arts, most notably miniature painting, in the ninth century. There is, in fact, every reason to assign the group to the ninth and tenth centuries and to regard the ivories as yet another manifestation of the revival of art at the time.[6] The earlier examples are in general the finest; the later ones, where religious themes predominate, are rather more stereotyped. Those bearing secular decorations were probably employed as marriage caskets, those with religious themes were more probably used to contain particular relics or treasures in the churches. They were nearly all made at Constantinople, for the caskets are obviously mostly of a single group and of so rich a character that no society but the most civilized and prosperous could possibly have been responsible for their production. For this reason suggestions put forward by some writers that they are to be associated with Italy or the Adriatic coast may be disregarded.

The most famous and probably the most beautiful example of the group is the Veroli casket in the Victoria and Albert Museum, which we would assign to the tenth century. The relief is high, the plastic feeling marked, and the composition is superbly balanced and free, while the work is of the very highest quality. A rather similar casket in the Cluny Museum must be of much the same date. The characteristic rosette borders appear on both, as they do on a casket in the National Museum at Florence composed of small panels bearing the busts of evangelists and apostles; this may be rather later in date. An unusual casket at Troyes is without the rosette borders, and its carvings are in a rather more monumental style; they represent mounted warriors at the sides and fantastic birds of rather Chinese type at the ends. The ends were probably inspired by an Eastern model, the sides by a textile, and there are two or three textiles of rather similar character, notably that at Mozac showing a mounted emperor, which may be compared with it. Grabar has suggested that the casket and the textiles alike should be assigned to the Iconoclast period,[7] but this is hardly probable. Whatever the date, both serve as an additional pointer to the marked degree of Eastern influence that had penetrated at that time.

Another casket of unusual form, for it is twelve-sided with a pyramidal top, attests links in the opposite direction, for Dalton regards it as a Western work which translates East Christian ideals into a new language. It is now preserved at Sens. Byzantine influence

402–4 Victoria and Albert Museum, London. Ivory. The Veroli casket. Tenth
century

439

405-6 Cathedral treasury, Troyes. Cover and front of ivory casket. Two emperors before a city, whose gates are opening. *Below:* Lion hunt. Eleventh century

had penetrated to the West in a series of waves from the ninth century onwards, and it may well be that we have to do here with something carved in the West in a Byzantine style; the form, which is unique in the Byzantine area, supports this supposition, but it is impossible to be sure. Nor is it easy to date the casket; the tenth, eleventh, and twelfth centuries have all been suggested; the twelfth century seems the most likely.

Another group of ivories determined by form is made up of the oliphants or carved tusks, which appeared first in the Iconoclast period. They often bear rather Oriental motifs, suggesting links with

Persia, though on a few of them there are circus scenes and one has a religious decoration. Decorations similar to those on the majority, namely animals and beasts set in a network of circles, are also known on ivories which were carved in Spain and Sicily, and it is not always easy to distinguish the Islamic from the Byzantine examples. Indeed, the things seem to have been carved in a number of centres, for patrons of all faiths. Furthermore, the Eastern examples were imitated in the West, though the carving in this case usually shows

407-8 Hessisches Landesmuseum, Darmstadt (Germany). Panels from ivory casket with mythological scenes. Tenth century

a rather forced manner which attests the fact that they were copies. It has been suggested that the decoration affords a clue as to the use for which the horns were intended; those with circus scenes were thus for use in the circus, those with religious scenes were dedicated to eccesiastical usage, and those with an animal decoration were intended for the chase. This is possible, for such horns in the West were sometimes given to churches – witness the horn of Ulph at York – and the fact that the majority bear animal motifs supports the obvious conclusion that the majority of them were most often used in the hunting field.

It is, however, in the religious ivories of the period that the Byzantine genius appears in its highest and most characteristic form. Some may perhaps to our ideas be somewhat aloof in feeling, and their ornament rather stereotyped in appearance, but even these have grace and beauty when one becomes familiar with their idiom, and others tell at once by the superb delicacy of the carving, the lovely proportions of the figures, the profound feeling which must have inspired them. Indeed, they have the same sublime quality as that of the best of the paintings and mosaics of the time. Their stylistic development was closely linked with that of painting, and at times it is possible to date the paintings by comparison with ivories or vice versa. The most characteristic feature about them, probably, is the nature of the figures with their slight and elongated proportions. They stand isolated on a plain flat ground, with their names cut, usually in very beautiful lettering, on either side of the heads. They give an astonishing impression of a general detachment from life and the things of every day, and evoke a deeply spiritual atmosphere. From the traces of colour which remain on some of them it seems likely that they were quite often coloured. This was the case with much medieval art, though today one questions whether the results can have been as beautiful as those achieved by the monochrome surfaces which we know. The subjects are invariably religious, either single figures of our Lord or the Virgin, groups of saints, one or more scenes from the Bible story, and sometimes the coronation of one of the emperors by Christ. The backs are often adorned with formal designs, such as a cross, springing up from a frame of acanthus leaves. The iconography of the figures and scenes is identical with that of contemporary painting. The large majority of them must have been carved in Constantinople.

The problem of dating these later ivories is not always easy. A few,

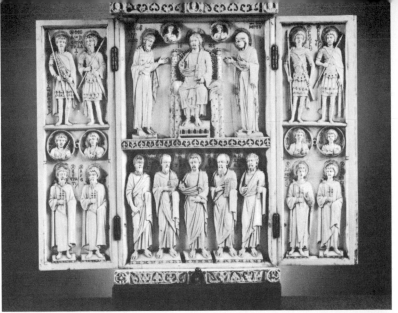

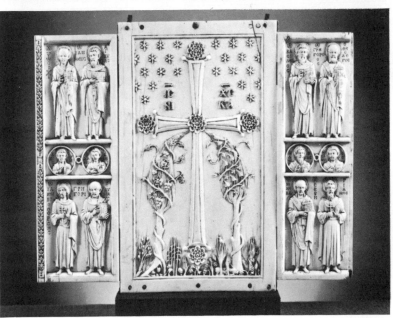

409–10 Louvre, Paris. Ivory. The Harbaville Triptych. *Above:* Front; The Deesis and saints. *Below:* Back; Triumphal Cross in Paradise and saints. Tenth century

however, can be dated on the basis of external evidence, and these serve as landmarks in a more general study. Thus one at Berlin, showing the coronation of Leo VI, can be assigned to the year in which he was crowned, that is, 886. It is, however, rather coarse, and is certainly not one of the finest ivories of the age. Of higher quality is a plaque at Moscow showing the coronation of Constantine VII, which dates from 944; a similar one in the Bibliothèque Nationale

411 Museum of Fine Art, Moscow. Ivory plaque from Etchmiadzin. Christ crowning Emperor Constantine Porphyrogenetos. 944

412 Benaki Museum, Athens. Right wing of ivory triptych with Archangel Gabriel. Tenth century

444

ІС ХС

РѠМАNОС
ΒΛСΙΛЄΥС
РѠМΑΙѠN

ЄΥΔΟΚΙΛ
ΒΛСΙΛΙС
РѠМΑΙѠN

413 Cabinet des Médailles, Paris. Ivory. Crowning of Emperor Romanos and his Empress Eudoxia. Probably 959

shows the coronation of the emperor Romanos and his consort Eudoxia. It has sometimes been associated with Romanos IV (1068–71) and sometimes with Romanos II, who was crowned in 959. If it

445

414 Victoria and Albert Museum, London. Ivory. Christ as Pantocrator. Ninth century

be compared with paintings, the latter seems the more probable. A fine triptych in the Palazzo Venezia at Rome is akin. There is a similar triptych in the Vatican, which must be of much the same date, and another in the Louvre, known as the Harbaville triptych. This is by far the finest of the three, for it shows an elegance and delicacy which are absent in the others. All are in the polished, elegant style typical of the Court school. A distinct group, where the faces are rounder and the figures less elegant, has been termed the Nicephorus group by Goldschmidt and Weitzmann; the most important example is an ivory in the Church of St Francis at Cortona, with the name of Nicephorus Phocas (963–9).

446

415 Bodleian Library, Oxford. Ivory. Christ enthroned. Tenth century

A few other ivories can also be dated fairly exactly on stylistic grounds. Thus a panel bearing the head and shoulders of Christ in the Victoria and Albert Museum is probably to be assigned to the ninth or early tenth century, on the basis of its forceful, vigorous manner, as is a rather less superb plaque bearing the Archangel Gabriel in the Tyler Collection. An ivory in the Vatican showing the Nativity is close in style to the Menologion of Basil II (976–1025), and can be assigned to much the same date. A number of plaques showing the figure of Christ can be attributed to earlier or later dates on the basis of the respective degree of strength or elegance in their conception. Thus one in the Louvre is probably of the tenth century, one in the Bodleian is probably rather later, and a third in the Victoria and Albert Museum belongs rather to the eleventh or early twelfth century. A panel bearing the figure of St John at Liverpool, and an especially lovely one with the Virgin, full length, at Utrecht, are later eleventh century, for it was then that the particular combination of grace and elegance, dignity and strength which they show was arrived at. A statuette of the Virgin in the Victoria and Albert Museum may be compared to the Utrecht Madonna; it is practically the only example of free-standing sculpture on a small scale that is known. To much the same date are to be assigned a number of triptych leaves bearing full-length figures of saints in various collections, notably one at Dresden, one at Vienna, and one at Venice. All are probably by the same hand.[8] Other plaques which are to be assigned to the eleventh century bear scenes as opposed to single figures. One of the most important, in the Victoria and Albert Museum, bears the Nativity, the Transfiguration, the Raising of Lazarus, the Marys at the Tomb, and Christ with the Marys in the Garden. Others are at Berlin, with the Entry into Jerusalem, and at Dresden, with the two Marys and the Anastasis. To the twelfth rather than the eleventh century is to be assigned an ivory bearing the Baptist in the centre and SS. Philip, Stephen, Andrew, and Thomas at the four corners, in the Victoria and Albert Museum. It is a fine example of the exquisite delicacy of the best later work. Numerous other plaques exist in other collections, though it is impossible to call attention to them here. A panel with the Forty Martyrs at Berlin may be even later.

In addition to this sumptuous work in ivory, quite a lot of carving was done in other materials, especially in later times. Thus plaques of bone with geometric patterns or stylized animals and birds upon

416 Victoria and Albert Museum, London. Ivory. St John the Baptist with
St Philip, St Stephen, St Andrew and St Thomas. Eleventh century

417 Archiepiscopal Museum, Utrecht. Middle section of ivory triptych. The Virgin Hodeghetria. Eleventh century

418 Liverpool Museum. Ivory. John the Baptist. Eleventh century
419 Victoria and Albert Museum, London. Ivory. The Virgin Hodeghetria.
Tenth century

451

OIAΓΙΟΙΤΕCCΑΡΑΚΟΝΤΑ

421 State Museums, Berlin. Ivory plaque. The Forty Martyrs of Sebaste.
Twelfth to thirteenth century

them, rather like those on the closure slabs of marble, were made
from the eleventh century onwards; they were used mainly for
attaching to wooden caskets. They seem to have been most usual in
Palaeologue times, when the expense of ivory precluded its use at all

420 Victoria and Albert Museum, London. Ivory plaque
with scenes from the New Testament. Twelfth century

453

generally. Morse, or walrus tusk, was also occasionally used in later times, especially for small crosses for attachment to necklaces; it was probably imported from the West. In post-Byzantine times, too, a good deal of carving was done in bone and in hard woods like box, minute scenes and small figures being favoured. Such carvings were often upon small crosses, which were framed in elaborate metal mounts; they were used upon altars all over Greece, Russia, and the Balkans. Though the work is often extremely skilful and very delicate, such products are most generally to be described as craft rather than art.

Of greater importance than the work on wood or bone was that on gems, such as amethyst, or in soft stones, such as steatite, which seems to have come into fashion in the tenth century. Quite large 'icons', bearing a number of scenes or figures, were made, as well as small plaques intended as pendants. Much of this carving was rather stereotyped and poor, but there are in existence a few steatites which can rank with the best of the ivories, and many were probably at one time distinguished by a delicacy of execution which can no longer be appreciated, owing to the softness of the material, which suffers very easily from attrition. One of the earliest and finest carvings in this material is a small head of an emperor in the Museum at Berlin (Dahlem), which is to be assigned to the tenth or early eleventh century. To the eleventh century belongs a fine plaque with the Archangel Michael at Fiesole: the relief is high and the style vigorous. Probably of the same date is a very fine steatite bearing St Theodore Stratelates in the Chersonese Museum,[9] while a large one bearing the twelve feasts in the cathedral at Toledo is probably twelfth century. A smaller panel with the same subject in the monastery of Vatopedi on Mount Athos is perhaps to be assigned to early Palaeologue times. There is also a particularly fine plaque bearing St George in the same monastery. Slightly later again is another rendering of the twelve feasts from the Church of St Clement at Ochrida. Other examples in public and private collections are too numerous to mention individually, though those in the British Museum and the Louvre may be noted as the collections are easily accessible.

Occasionally artificial compositions or pastes were also used in imitation of steatite or some more precious material like lapis-lazuli. A fine figure of Christ in actual lapis, with initial lettering in gold inlay, formerly in the treasure of the Abbey of St Denys, is now in

422 Museo Bandini, Fiesole. Green steatite, gilded. *c.* 1100

the Louvre. It is probably to be dated to the eleventh century. In addition small precious stones were also engraved, usually with busts of Christ or the Virgin, and rock-crystal was cut into ewers, with

423 Cathedral Museum, Toledo. Steatite. The Twelve Feasts of the Church.
Twelfth century

animals or birds as decoration; it is not always easy to distinguish
the Byzantine examples from those done for Islamic patrons in
Fatimid Egypt.

Metal was extensively used in the Byzantine world, in very early times for statues, until the sixth or seventh century for vessels, mainly for secular usage, and from then onwards for vessels, plaques, book covers, and so forth, the majority of which were ecclesiastical in character. The early statues, like that of Valentinian at Bari, are essentially Roman rather than Byzantine, and they do not concern us here; they are, moreover, to be classed as sculpture rather than metal work. The vessels, on the other hand, are often as much Byzantine as Roman, and are of considerable importance. They can conveniently be grouped together, all being of silver, with ornament in relief, and all being apparently fairly universally employed in the richer circles. They were transported long distances, either for purposes of trade or as loot, so that the locality in which specimens have been found has little connexion with that in which they were originally made. Thus Byzantine, as well as Sasanian, silver plate has been discovered in Russia, where it was probably used as a means of barter to obtain furs; it has been discovered in Spain, and it has been discovered in Britain. The style of decoration on these finds, notably those in the Hermitage at Leningrad and the Palace of Arms at Moscow,[1] is basically Hellenistic, but it is probable that even as early as the fourth century Oriental elements had begun to creep in. Alexandria and Antioch were both no doubt centres of manufacture, and to take example from the other arts, one would expect to find a greater degree of Oriental influence in objects made at the latter place than in those made at the former. For example, on a silver disk at Madrid, which was made for the emperor Theodosios, the same enlarged heads and clumsy proportions are apparent as on the stone base of the Theodosios obelisk at Constantinople, and these characteristics have already been noted as savouring of the Syrian style. The base was, however, probably carved at

457

Constantinople, and it is possible that the disk, like a similar one of Justinian, now at Leningrad, was also made in the capital; their association with ruling emperors makes this supposition likely. Purely Syrian work is, however, to be seen in the scenes in low relief which decorate a group of small flasks or ampullae which were acquired by pilgrims in the Holy Land in early times and taken home as containers for holy oil or Jordan water. A large collection of them is preserved in the Cathedral Treasury at Monza.

Of the famous hordes of silver treasure one of the best known is that found on the Esquiline Hill in Rome, now in the British Museum. It has by some been attributed to Alexandria, but Rome is more likely, and the same is true of the Traprain treasure at Edinburgh. Famous treasures from Lampsacus in Asia Minor and from several sites in Cyprus were at one time assigned to Antioch, but more recent study suggests that Constantinople is more likely, partly on stylistic grounds and partly because many of the vessels bear control stamps or 'hall-marks' in the imperial name, and there

424 British Museum, London. Silver Shrine of Secundus and Projects, from the Esquiline treasure. *c.* 380

is reason to believe that the use of these was restricted to the imperial workshops at the capital. The decorations were frequently very Classical in character, and non-Christian themes were in use even as late as the seventh century. The earlier decorations were usually in high relief and stood out like sculptures; one of the best examples is the famous amphora from Concesti now in the Hermitage. In the

425 Hermitage Museum, Leningrad. The Concesti amphora. Silver-gilt. Fifth century

426 Hermitage Museum, Leningrad. Silver dish of Bishop Paternus. 518

later examples the relief was lower and the work more stylized, as
on a dish in the Hermitage with a stamp in the name of Heraclius
(610–41) on the base. Engraving was often used in association with
relief work, as on the lovely dish of Paternus in the Hermitage,
dating from *c.* 518, and niello was also employed to enliven the
designs, as on a superb dish in the Archaeological Museum at
Constantinople bearing a figure which has been identified as the
Personification of India. Two patens, with the Communion of the
Apostles, one at Constantinople and one at Washington, are to be
assigned to the reign of Justin II (565–78); the control stamps suggest
Constantinople, but the style is suggestive of Syria.[2]

460

Of a more elaborate character so far as technique is concerned is the famous chalice discovered near Antioch in 1910, where there is an open-work decoration in silver above a silver core. Its date and even its authenticity have been much disputed, but the general consensus of opinion now regards it as genuine. It is probably to be assigned to the fourth century; it is certainly not the chalice used by our Lord at the Last Supper, as was at one time suggested. A second chalice and one or more book covers were brought to light at the

427 Archaeological Museum, Istanbul. Silver plate with the Personification of India. Sixth century

461

428 Archaeological Museum, Istanbul. Silver paten with the Communion of
the Apostles. Detail. 565–78

same time, and the fact that they are obviously of the fourth or early
fifth century supports a similar date for the chalice itself.

Church plate of silver, with decoration in relief or engraved,
gradually superseded that with secular motifs, and vessels of the type
appear to have remained in use until Iconoclast times, very little
change being effected in their appearance. In Iconoclast times silver
was probably still produced, and a number of chalices bearing simple
inscriptions or crosses only, notably one at Dumbarton Oaks, are
perhaps to be assigned to that time. But with the ninth century a new
fashion for extremely ornate ecclesiastical vessels came into vogue.
Metal cores were adorned with a superficial decoration of precious
stones and enamels, or with filigree work in gold. Precious or semi-
precious stones were also used to form the bodies of vessels, and
were themselves decorated with metal or other stones, and crystal
was employed and adorned in the same way. The results, of which
a rich collection is preserved in St Mark's at Venice, were magnificent, but perhaps rather barbarous. The vessels are astonishingly

429 Cathedral treasury, Halberstadt (Germany). Silver-gilt paten; the Crucifixion. Eleventh century

430 The treasury, St Mark's, Venice. Alabaster paten with cloisonné enamel of Christ at centre and precious stones round rim. Eleventh century

431 Monastery of Vatopedi, Mount Athos. Chalice of Manuel Cantacuzenos. 1349-81

impressive in their richness, but though they often almost stagger the observer, they fail to move his subtler aesthetic emotions, for it is their richness rather than their intrinsic beauty that tells. A great eight-lobed paten at Halberstadt, where the decoration is in relief only, is, on purely aesthetic grounds, more impressive. And a six-lobed alabaster paten in St Mark's may also be noted, for it is subtle and delicate, and lacks the rather garish appeal of some of the other treasures that are preserved there. It has a jewelled border and an enamel of Christ at the centre, but the simple loveliness of the plain stone ground is really more impressive than the ornate detail. Things like these were mostly made in the tenth and eleventh centuries, a period at which the appellation sumptuous, which has sometimes been applied to Byzantine art as a whole, was especially fitting. But fine ecclesiastical vessels continued to be made till the end, and a chalice bearing the name of Manuel Cantacuzenos (1349-81) in the monastery of Vatopedi on Mount Athos may be noted.

More significant, if less ornate, than the ecclesiastical vessels was the work in relief of the middle period. On a large scale the most important objects were the great bronze doors which were set up in

432 San Michele, Monte Sant'Angelo. Do
sanctuary. Inlaid bronze. 1276

most of the more considerable churches. Many have since been melted down for one reason or another, but a few survive, notably at the western and southern entrances of Sancta Sophia at Constantinople; the latter bearing inscriptions in the name of the emperors Theophilus and Michael, were set up in 840. Clavijo records that another pair of great doors of silver gilt were taken by Tamerlane from Bursa and erected outside the tent of his favourite wife at Samarkand.[3] It is probable that they were made of thin metal plates mounted on a wooden core, like those that cover tie-beams of the seventh century in the Dome of the Rock at Jerusalem.[4] Another technique in use was what is now called Damascene work, which was probably introduced to the Byzantine from the Islamic world. From Byzantium it passed to the West, and a number of fine doors of the eleventh century in Italy bear decoration in this technique as well as in cast bronze or repoussé relief. Some of these Italian doors were made locally, while others were imported from Byzantium. Of the latter the most important are probably those at Monte Sant' Angelo, which were made at Constantinople in 1076. The doors of this period frequently bear religious scenes, akin to those to be seen

433 Victoria and Albert Museum, London. Bronze triptych. Virgin and Child. St Gregory of Nazianzus and St John Chrysostom. Twelfth century

434 St Peter's chapel of Relics, Rome. Cross of Justin II. 575

in the paintings or mosaics so far as iconography is concerned. At a later date geometric patterns, under Islamic influence, began to supersede the figural ones, and from the twelfth century onwards these were wellnigh universal. Some fine bronze doors bearing such patterns are preserved in the monastery of the Lavra on Mount Athos.

Small-size panels bearing cast figures, akin to those on the doors, were also made; one of the best known is a triptych in the Victoria and Albert Museum, which may be assigned to the twelfth century. But for such small-scale things the repoussé technique was more usually employed. Here the metal is thin, and the design is beaten

467

435 Monastery of the Lavra, Mount Athos. Cover of Nicephorus Phocas
Bible. Silver-gilt with precious stones. *c.* 970

out from the back, either freehand, or into some sort of matrix.
Bronze, copper, silver, and gold were all employed; the baser metals
were usually gilt on the completion of the work. The earliest small-
scale example in this technique is probably a cross in St Peter's at
Rome, presented by Justin II (565–78). Crosses at Ravenna and elsewhere are of only slightly later date. Reliquaries which are probably
to be assigned to the sixth century formerly existed at Jaucourt, near
Troyes in France, and at Brescia and Alba Fucense in Italy.

In the middle period of Byzantine art the repoussé technique
became especially popular for the decoration of plaques intended

436 Victoria and Albert Museum, London. Copper-gilt. Madonna and Child. Eleventh century

for attachment to book covers, icons, or reliquaries, since the thin metal was better preserved when attached to a backing of wood, and was sufficiently light not to make the objects to which it was attached unduly heavy. Examples are numerous from the tenth century onwards, and production continued certainly throughout, and probably even after, the Palaeologue period, though coarser metals by then usually superseded the more precious ones. A few examples are dated, either by inscriptions upon them or by the fact that they can be associated with special individuals. In this category is the lovely cover of the Bible of Nicephorus Phocas (963–9) in the monastery of the Lavra on Mount Athos. It bears the standing figure of Christ. Small plaques of cloisonné enamel have here also been added to indicate details such as the cushion on which our Lord stands. A fine plaque bearing the Deesis, that is, Christ between the Virgin and St John, which is perhaps about a century later, is preserved in the John Rylands Library at Manchester, and there is a very fine and unusually large figure of the Virgin, standing full length, in the Victoria and Albert Museum. It has, unfortunately, been regilt, but the actual repoussé work is delicate; it is to be assigned to the eleventh century. The richest collection of examples, as in the case of ecclesiastical vessels, however, is that in the treasury of St Mark's at Venice. A fine book cover and an artophorion, or reliquary in the form of a church for containing the Eucharistic bread, may be noted. Of the examples of later date the repoussé covers of icons formerly in the Church of St Clement at Ochrida are interesting, and there are numerous similar icon covers in the museums of Greece and the Balkans, dating from the thirteenth century onwards. On these the decoration is usually of geometric patterns, scrolls, and similar stylized floral motifs; the figural subjects practically ceased after the twelfth century.

A particularly interesting group of metal work with repoussé decoration is made up of the staurotheques or reliquaries of flat rectangular form, intended to contain fragments of the True Cross. The fragment itself was usually inserted into an opening at the centre, in the form of a double-armed cross. Cloisonné enamel plaques or precious stones set in cabochon mounts were often added to the repoussé metal, for the most lavish and sumptuous workmanship was invariably employed for this especially sacred form of object. There are examples in quite a number of museums and treasuries; the most important is perhaps that which is preserved at Esztergom in Hungary. It is probably to be dated to the eleventh century. A simpler staurotheque, now at Urbino and formerly at Murano, may also be noted because it is not well known. Other examples can be seen in the Louvre, in the Palazzo Venezia at Rome, or in the treasury of St Mark's at Venice.

437 Archaeological Museum, Istanbul. Ear-rings. Gold with precious stones. Sixth century

Works in repoussé metal were probably extensively exported from Byzantium. Even before the twelfth century the traffic in relics had been important, and an interest in such things was probably spurred on as a result of the treasures that were brought back by crusaders. When relics were sold they were frequently first suitably enshrined in cases of metal; when they were sent as presents, as they frequently were, they were wellnigh invariably elaborately mounted. Large numbers of precious objects thus reached the West even before the looting of Constantinople in 1204, and these, as well as others brought back by the looters, were not only preserved in churches, but were also copied locally, especially in Italy. Some fine plaques of a basically Byzantine appearance are thus actually Western rather than Byzantine works. A book cover, bearing saintly figures, in the treasury of St Mark's at Venice is of this category, as is a finer one bearing the figure of Christ seated before an oval glory.

A very distinct category of metal object is constituted by works of very small scale for the adornment of the person. Finger rings of gold, silver, copper, and bronze, with engraved figures or inscriptions, or serving as mounts for engraved gems, were thus common from the earliest times. Constantinople was probably the main centre

438 The monastery of Fonte Avellana, Pesaro. Silver-gilt reliquary of the True Cross. Twelfth century

of manufacture, but they were probably also produced in every large town. Monograms or symbols of a religious character constituted the most usual form of ornament. Ear-rings, brooches, and necklaces were also made, and these sometimes show extremely fine workman-

439 Christian Museum, Esztergom. Reliquary of the True Cross. Eleventh
century

ship. But only a few examples have come down to us, since such things were not usually placed in the tombs as they were in pagan times, and being small and valuable they have suffered more than larger objects at the hands of thieves and looters. Gold work, filigree, and especially *orfèvrerie cloisonnée*, where gems or pastes are set in little frames or clasps, were the techniques most favoured by the rich. Such things took the place of cameos, which were made only in the first period. In general, however, we know less about Byzantine jewellery than we do of pagan, and to judge from paintings and other forms of reproduction, it was not as important in the secular world of Eastern Christendom as it was in the West. Ritual and imperial costumes were, it is true, loaded with precious metals, stones, and even enamels, but in everyday life such things were not so universally employed. More important were pendant crosses, used to contain a relic, or valued for themselves alone, as religious symbols. In fact, the nature of the jewellery serves to bear out the essentially religious background of the whole of Byzantine life, even in the most luxury-loving and ostentatious periods.

Into a separate class again fall the coins. Though the impressive portraiture of the Roman or the superb miniature sculpture of the Greek coinage is completely lacking, the East Christian coinage has a charm of its own, and it was certainly not completely stereotyped as has sometimes been suggested. The imperial portraits, though they followed a very strict convention, were often full of life and spirit, and the subjects on the reverse of the coins, which were generally of a religious character, often showed considerable delicacy of feeling and execution. Byzantine coins, indeed, are invariably interesting, and quite often beautiful, and they deserve some attention from the art historian in and for themselves, even if they are not to be classed as one of the most important products of the age from the artistic point of view. Seals, which were often closely similar to the coins, were usually made of lead, on to which a design or inscription was impressed by some form of die. The documents, vessels, or whatever it may have been that they were intended to seal, were tied with strings which were passed through a hole in the centre of the lead plaque before the design was impressed upon it. Usually such seals bear a religious figure – Christ, the Virgin, or some saint – upon one face, and an inscription or complicated monogram upon the other. The decipherment of these monograms furnishes a number of intriguing problems.

474

12 Enamels

The art of enamelling was no new one when the Byzantine Empire was born, superb examples having been produced in Egypt, in the western part of the Roman Empire, and in the East. In the first centuries of its existence, however, the new culture seems to have been responsible for nothing very strikingly original in this art, though literary evidence suggests that enamelling of a sort was done there from the fourth century onwards. An ear-ring in the Louvre is perhaps to be assigned to this period, and a clasp forming part of an ivory binding in Milan Cathedral was made, according to Kondakov, before the days of Justinian. It is of light green and red enamels, which in places turn to violet or emerald-green. Of the treasures in enamel which were presented by Justinian to his foundation of Sancta Sophia nothing has survived, though a few enamels preserved in Western museums and treasuries may be of the same date. The most important of them is a reliquary supposedly presented by Justin II to the Abbey of St Radegonde at Poitiers; its appearance suggests that it should actually be assigned to a later date.

Most of the earlier enamels and certainly all those from the West at this time were executed in the technique known as champlevé, where a metal ground of some thickness, usually of copper or bronze, was cut out to form small fields or partitions, into which the enamel was run. The technique which was to become so characteristic of the Byzantine world, however, was distinct, in that the ground was usually of gold, and the fields for the enamel pigment were formed of thin gold bands, which were soldered to the background. These gold bands take the place as it were of the pencil lines of a drawing, and as they could be bent about with ease, they permitted of considerable subtlety of design. The depth of the partitions formed by these bands constitutes, according to Kondakov, a valuable criterion for dating. In the eleventh century one millimetre was apparently the

440 Victoria and Albert Museum, London. Gold and cloisonné enamel. The so-called Beresford Hope Cross. Front and rear sides. Perhaps sixth century

usual height, while by the thirteenth century the partitions had increased to about two millimetres. The nature of the colours also changed with the progress of time; before the ninth century they were thus dark and lacking in variety, translucent emerald-greens, deep blues, and purples predominating. Purple was often used for the hair at this time, while the flesh tints were waxen or greenish. In the tenth century pure bright colours replaced the darker ones of earlier times, sky- and turquoise-blues, violet, and bright purple being usual, with pinkish flesh tints. There was, however, a tendency towards a greater degree of opaqueness, which was accentuated with the eleventh century. At the same time the figures tended to become flatter, the cloisons increased in number, and the whole conception became much more linear. With the twelfth century white and turquoise-blue became the predominating colours, light-coloured shades and red being used only very sparingly. At the same time

441 The treasury, St Mark's, Venice. From Constantinople. Silver-gi Reliquary of the True Cross with cloisonné enamel and precious stone Tenth century

there was a tendency to an increase in size and a rather coarser treatment. In the thirteenth century copper often replaced gold for the ground, and white lettering was introduced as a characteristic feature. Towards the end of the century, also, the colours usually became very misty, and of a more vitreous consistency. The tones were varied, deep blue, bright yellow, red, and vermilion all being usual, but in spite of this variety the work of this late age was coarse and somehow lacked freshness. Further, it may be noted that the best drawing and drapery was associated with the work of the tenth century, while in the eleventh it was usually on a small scale and very delicate.

A few enamels of decorative character are perhaps to be assigned to Iconoclast times, but it was only with the later ninth and early tenth century that this art became really important. Some dispute has raged with regard to the dating of a reliquary cross in the Victoria and Albert Museum, known as the Beresford Hope cross, which is generally accepted as one of the earliest examples that have come down to us. Some would assign it to pre-Iconoclast times, and perhaps even to the sixth century; others believe that it belongs to the ninth century. The developed iconography supports the latter assumption, though it does not completely preclude an earlier date. Technical details also support it, though not conclusively. A rather similar but larger cross in the Vatican, on the other hand, is more likely to be pre-Iconoclast, for it was presented to the Sancta Sanctorum by Pope Paschal I (817–24) while the Iconoclast ban was still in force in the East. Alternatively it may have been made in Italy in the early ninth or late eighth century, perhaps by a Greek refugee. It is far larger than other crosses of the type, being some nine inches long, as opposed to three or four, and there is reason to believe that size was a characteristic of Italian work in this technique. A monumental plaque bearing Christ Pantocrator in the Palazzo Venezia at Rome, which is more than two feet high, may be compared, in this respect of size, though it is not to be dated before 1100; it is probably of Italian workmanship. The Beresford Hope cross is, on the other hand, almost certainly Constantinopolitan.

With the tenth century documentation comes to our aid, for enamels are sometimes mentioned in the records in connexion with the names of Constantine Porphyrogenitus (911–59) and Basil II (976–1025). Constantinople was certainly the chief source of manufacture throughout the tenth century, though with the twelfth, Sicily

442 State Museums, Berlin. St Demetrius. Enamels on gold. Eleventh century

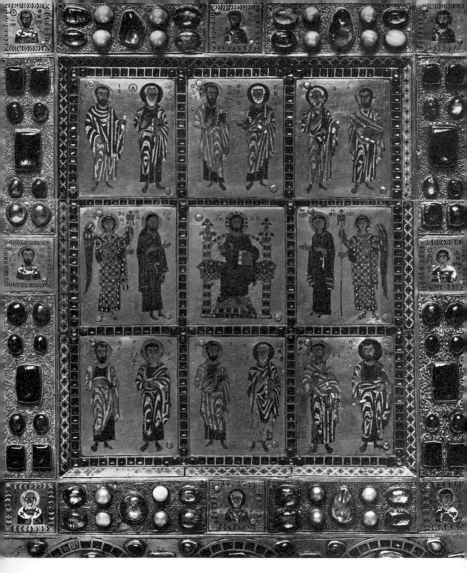

443 Cathedral treasury, Limburg-an-der-Lahn (Germany). Staurotheque from
Constantinople. Silver-gilt with cloisonné enamel. Tenth century

444–5 St Mark's, Venice. Two panels of the Pala d'Oro. Cloison
enamel and precious stones. Twelfth to fourteenth centur

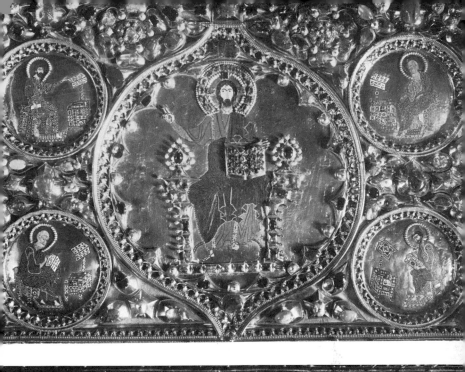

had become a centre of production, and good work was also done in Georgia. Of the enamels that survive a few happily are dated. Such are a paten and a chalice, with the name of Romanos I Lecapenos (919–44) and a medallion in the name of the Empress Zoe (1028–50), all in St Mark's. The enamels of the Nicephorus Phocas Bible cover in the Lavra on Mount Athos, which must belong to about 965, may also be noted, as well as the Limburg reliquary, which bears an inscription in the names of Constantine and Romanos (919–44). A famous crown in the Budapest Museum bears enamels representing Constantine Monomachos (1042–54), the Empress Zoe, and her sister Theophano; the figures of dancing girls of rather Oriental character which form a part of its decoration are particularly enchanting. They are paralleled on a plaque in the Victoria and Albert Museum, but the authenticity of this has recently been questioned.[1] The enamels on the royal crown of Hungary are also probably to be regarded as Byzantine. One bears a portrait of the Emperor Constantine Ducas (1059–67) and another that of Geza I of Hungary (1074–7), so it was probably made up of plaques of slightly different dates.[2] A portrait of the Emperor Michael Ducas (1071–8) which is closely akin appears on an icon from Khakuli in Georgia; he and his Georgian wife Mary are shown being crowned by Christ, and there are numerous other enamels on it, some of them Byzantine and some Georgian. A fine cross at Copenhagen is again probably Byzantine, though it was found in the tomb of the local Queen Dagmar, who died in 1212.

Many more enamels must be dated on stylistic grounds only, and there are crosses to hold relics, small plaques for attachment to book bindings or icons, medallions of small size, which were sewn on to the imperial costumes, or even quite large objects like processional crosses in quite a number of treasuries, museums, or collections. Some of the finest are probably those in the Pierpont Morgan Collection in America, but the lovely enamels on the Esztergom reliquary in Hungary may be noted, and there is a very superb cross of considerable size, decorated with enamels on both faces, in the treasury of Cosenza Cathedral. By far the richest collection, however, is in the treasury of St Mark's, where there is work of the finest quality, of every size and of all dates from the ninth to the thirteenth centuries. A Crucifixion forming part of a book cover is perhaps one of the finest. A large number of enamels of different dates and varying sizes and quality are also made up into a screen known as the

446-7 National Museum, Budapest. Enamels from the crown of Emperor
Constantine IX Monomachos. *c.* 1042-54

Pala d'Oro in the church itself. In all there are eighty-six enamels upon this screen, some of them showing scenes from the Feasts of the Church. The screen was originally made for Doge Orseoli in 976, but was restored between 1102 and 1107, when some of the enamels were added. Some of the later additions were probably made in Italy. It was again restored in 1345.

After the twelfth century or, indeed, even before that date, it is not always easy to distinguish Italian from Constantinopolitan products, for the quality of workmanship had declined in the East, and the original models were followed closely in a number of different workshops in Italy and even in Germany. In general, however, the examples made in Italy tend to be rather more fussy and they often bear inscriptions in Latin instead of Greek. The German ones are more Romanesque in style. As already stated, Georgia was probably also a centre of manufacture. There again Byzantine models were copied, and some of the enamels which survive in Georgia today are actually products of Constantinopolitan workshops. Those which adorn a cross, itself Georgian, in the monastery of Nicorzminda afford an example. But others were made locally, and quite considerable numbers of them were preserved in various churches throughout the country, anyhow until 1917; many of them are now in the museum at Tbilisi (Tiflis), where there is a collection of outstanding importance. A number of enamels were purchased and published in Russia before the Revolution as Georgian works, though they have subsequently been shown to be forgeries.

The production of enamels of a rather coarse type continued in Greece and the Balkans long after the fall of the actual Empire. Of these late works some liturgical fans at Serres in Macedonia, which are to be assigned to the sixteenth century, are perhaps the most important. But there are small crosses and other objects of similar workmanship in many collections, notably in the Benaki Museum at Athens. Most of these are in the champlevé and not the cloisonné technique.

13 Textiles

Textiles constitute a very important branch of Byzantine art, not only because of their own intrinsic merits, but also because of the very considerable role that they played as models for sculptors and even painters. They could be easily transported from region to region, and it was without doubt by means of the textiles that a great many motifs of decoration were introduced, more especially from the Islamic world. The design of a great eagle with spread wings, for example, which we see on a piece of pottery of the ninth century or thereabouts which is now in the writer's possession, is close to that of such a stuff as the magnificent silk at Auxerre, while the rosettes that appear as the distinctive feature of the group of ivory caskets known as the Rosette caskets again reproduce a motif properly belonging to textiles. Many of the Consular diptychs of fourth- and fifth-century date also depict textiles, though in this case a whole stuff is shown as part of a costume; it is not just one of its decorative motifs that is reproduced in another material. A similar instance of the reproduction of a complete stuff occurs on the well-known relief of the Sasanian king Chosroes II (590–628) at Taq-i-Bostan in Persia, and it is above anything else thanks to such instances as these that certain stuffs can be associated with certain areas or periods. Were it not for these guides, the assignation of the actual materials to Persia, Syria, or Byzantium and the dating of them even to the nearest century would be in many cases an almost impossible problem, owing to the ease with which textiles could be transported and the way in which the motifs were retained, thanks to innate conservatism.

Indeed, were it not for these concrete reproductions in stone or some other solid material our knowledge of such fragile things as textiles in early times would be but very one-sided, for it is only from Egypt that any really extensive quantity of examples has come down to us. There textiles were invariably employed for burial purposes; they were manufactured on a large scale, and in addition the dry soil served to preserve them in a way unparalleled elsewhere. There is in fact a wealth of material dating from the earliest times down to about the eighth century A.D. from there, which quite eclipses the few very tattered examples from elsewhere. Much of the Egyptian work is definitely Hellenistic in design, and Greeks as well as Egyptians seem to have been employed as designers. Three main styles may be distinguished in Christian times, the Graeco-Roman, in vogue from the third to the fifth centuries, the Transitional style, from the fifth to the sixth, and the Coptic from the sixth onwards, for work which was Coptic in character continued to be executed even after the Islamic conquest of Egypt in the seventh century, though the conquest was responsible for bringing to the land a mass of new motifs and ideas, most of which stemmed from Persia. The Islamic work concerns us only in so far as the motifs which were proper to it were taken over by Byzantine weavers. The Coptic style, again, was a local one, without serious repercussions in Byzantium. But the situation with regard to the earlier styles is different, for Egypt was then a very vital part of the Empire, and the textiles which were produced there were in many cases just as much Byzantine as were the ivory carvings of Alexandria.

During the first few centuries of the Byzantine era linen and wool were the most common materials, the linen forming the ground and the wool the decoration. Tapestry weaving or embroidery were the most usual techniques, though looped weaving was also employed to give greater thickness to the costumes.[1] Figure subjects, such as pagan deities, mythological scenes, animals and fish, or purely geometrical patterns, formed the usual decorations. A thin, line-drawing style, with simple colouring, was characteristic. With the fifth and sixth centuries considerable elaboration took place. Flowers and baskets of fruit began to play a dominant role in the decorations, Christian symbols, such as the XP cross, were often introduced, even into pagan scenes, and purely Christian scenes also began to appear. The colouring tended to be rather brighter than in the preceding centuries, and techniques were more diverse. For example, dyed stuffs, where the design was drawn out in a 'resist' before the material was dipped, became common, and stuffs with an elaborate woven pattern probably became more usual than embroideries.

In addition to the elaboration of techniques, the actual material began to change at this time, thanks to the introduction of silk. The first silks with a woven pattern were quite small, and took the form of panels for attachment to costumes, and the designs were in two colours only, a pale pattern on a dark, usually a purple, ground. But soon other colours were introduced, and by the middle of the sixth century silk weavings of considerable elaboration were being executed. Some of those that survive are undoubtedly to be assigned to Egypt; they usually bear designs of considerable elaboration, but on a small scale. Others were produced in other parts of the Near East, more especially in Syria, Mesopotamia, and Persia, and it is in attempting to identify the examples that survive with particular centres of manufacture that the first real problems are encountered.

A good many different theories have been propounded. Strzygowski, for example, held that practically all the figured silks with designs on a large scale should be assigned to Persia, where the silk-weaving industry had certainly been established at quite an early date, though practically no examples have come down to us owing to their destruction in the damp climate of the region. Von Falke, on the other hand, thought that Persia learnt to make figured silks only in the time of Shapur, thanks to the introduction of Greek and Egyptian weavers after the campaigns of 355 to 360. In his view Egypt was always a more important centre, and even if many of the designs of the larger silks were of a Persian type, it was, he thinks, the Egyptians who developed the techniques and learnt to produce these designs on a large scale. Other authorities hold that neither Egypt nor Persia was the prime centre, but that the honour should be assigned to Syria, and the discovery at Palmyra of stuffs which are distinct in style from both those of Persia and those of Egypt serves to support this view. Further, there is evidence too that Antioch was an important centre of manufacture anyhow by the fifth century.[2]

Whichever of these theories is correct, the evidence suggests that the first actual Byzantine weavers, that is, the men working at Constantinople, and not in some outlying portion of the Empire, learnt a great deal as regards technique from Egypt, even if many of the motifs, notably the addorsed and confronted beasts, the fantastic animals, and the horsemen in pairs, with the sacred 'hom' between them, were ultimately of Persian origin. The Persian designs probably penetrated to Egypt at the same time that they penetrated to Byzantium; anyhow, in both areas, and in Syria as well, these Persianizing motifs had been generally adopted by the sixth century. That they

448 Capella Sancta Sanctorum, Rome. Silk. The Annunciation. Seventh or
eighth century

should have travelled westwards in such great profusion is not
surprising, for the cultivation of silk was an Eastern monopoly, and
all the actual material was brought to the West by way of Persia until
about 552, when legend records that two monks of Khotan sold the
secret of cultivation to the emissaries of Justinian. What is interesting
is that Chinese designs were so seldom copied, and even if the
material was all brought from there, it was often towards Persia that
the Chinese weavers looked for inspiration in this respect. Nor did
the weavers of Persia and the Near East learn very much with regard
to technique, for the manner of weaving in China was in many ways
quite distinct from that of Hither Asia.

The purely pagan textiles that are to be assigned to Egypt may be
passed over briefly, even though the Hellenistic motifs of their
decoration survived in the Byzantine world for many centuries.
Attention may, however, be called to a few, such as the fine Triumph
of Dionysios in the Louvre, of the fourth century, with decoration in
the dyed technique, the woven linen showing marine monsters and

449 Cluny Museum, Paris. Silk. Quadriga. Eighth to ninth century

Nereids at Dumbarton Oaks, Washington, of the fourth or fifth century, or the linen showing a seated divinity, of the sixth century in the same collection.[3] Of Egyptian manufacture, but of Christian character, is a printed stuff of the fifth or sixth century, in the Royal Scottish Museum at Edinburgh, showing the Hetoimasia or Preparation of the Throne. To Egypt again is to be attributed an important linen textile in the Rockefeller Collection, which bears a bearded military saint, probably St Theodore; on the basis of similarities which it shows to the seated divinity at Dumbarton Oaks, Peirce and Tyler date this textile to the last quarter of the fifth century.[4] But the figure is so strikingly Byzantine in appearance, and shows so complete a fusion of the Semitic and Hellenistic trends, that it is tempting to assign the textile to Constantinople and to a date around the seventh century. A final decision will become possible only when more comparative material from outside Egypt has been discovered.

As opposed to the predominantly pagan character of much of the Egyptian work, a superb silk in the Vatican may be mentioned which

489

shows scenes that are purely and completely Christian, namely the Annunciation and the Nativity, repeated over the stuff in a series of medallions. The colours are green, gold-brown, and white, and the ground gold; the technique is particularly accomplished. Von Falke regarded it as of Alexandrine workmanship, but the style and iconography are so characteristic of the developing Byzantine art that it is tempting to suggest instead the imperial looms of Constantinople. It must date from the seventh or eighth century. Oriental influence is to be discerned here in the bejewelled throne on which the Madonna sits, and though some authorities consider that the framing of the scenes in circles is a Hellenistic feature, others regard such arrangements as essentially Persian. They are probably correct, for Hellenistic art preferred to devote a whole panel to each scene, and to produce it on a large scale, rather than as a part of an elaborate repeat pattern. Similar circles are used on another fine silk of the eighth century, where the motif is a four-horse chariot or quadriga. The chariot is in gold, and the design is greenish purple. Portions of the stuff can be seen in the Cathedral treasury at Aachen and the Cluny Museum at Paris. The disposition of the design of this textile is much more Hellenistic, though the capital city of Constantinople also seems the most likely home.

As time progressed the use of circles to frame the different figural compositions became more and more popular, and at the same time new motifs penetrated from the east, and the workshops of Constantinople, Persia, Syria, and Egypt had, so far as decorative stuffs were concerned, a more or less common repertory. But it would seem that at Constantinople a more monumental manner was developed, the designs showing no hint of finickiness, and the colour schemes being always grand and impressive. Sometimes inscriptions in Greek were added, but these were on a small scale, and were there as records rather than as decoration, as were the Kufic inscriptions in the Islamic world, where lettering constituted an essential part of the design, or at times even the only one. Certain other factors also help to distinguish the products of Constantinople at this time. Thus the royal workshops there held a monopoly of the imperial purple, and the most grandiose stuffs were probably woven nowhere else. Further, with the Islamic conquests of Syria and Egypt just before the middle of the seventh century, the possibility of competition from these centres came to an end, for though work continued in them, it was done to suit the demands of Islamic and not of Byzantine patrons,

450 Cathedral treasury, Aachen. Elephants in medallions. Silk. *c.* 1000

so that Christian, and to a great extent even figural motifs, were in the main precluded.

With the beginnings of Iconoclasm, however, the factors governing the production of textiles at Constantinople changed once more, for the figural style which had been developed so gloriously till then

451 Siegburg. Silk. Lions with an inscription of the emperors Romanos I
Lakapenos and Christopheros. Formerly in St Michael's Abbey, Siegburg.
920–51

was stopped. Decorative motifs, similar to those which satisfied
Moslem patrons, were called for, and as a result it becomes once
more hard to distinguish between the products of the different
centres. A good deal of finished work also seems to have been
imported from the Islamic world at this time, and some of it was
probably copied by the Constantinopolitan weavers.

With the close of Iconoclasm Christian motifs once more began to
appear, but the decorative style, introduced originally as a result of
the dominance of a particular religious dogma, continued to survive
because of a change in taste, and no great textiles bearing Bible
scenes like that in the Vatican referred to above have survived.
Rather the Byzantine workshops set their hall-mark on their products
by a new majesty of design, and the great eagle stuff at Auxerre is
proved to be Byzantine not so much because of the adoption of the
eagle as an essentially Byzantine motif as because of the nature of
the design, the eagle being repeated over the surface in great un-
framed panels, and not in a series of small-scale medallions, linked
together to form an elaborate repeat pattern. There is another fine
eagle stuff at Bressanone. An important stuff with a decoration of
elephants in medallions from the tomb of Charlemagne, which is still

452 St Eusebius, Auxerre. Grave cloth of St Germain. Silk with eagles. Tenth century

453 Hofburg treasury, Vienna. Embroidered coronation cloak of Roger II, from Palermo. 1133–4

preserved at Aachen, bears an inscription stating that it was made in the imperial workshops at Constantinople. It was probably put into the tomb when it was opened in the Ottonian period, and must date from the end of the tenth century. It is fairly close in style to stuffs of which there are pieces at Siegburg and Düsseldorf, which bear inscriptions in Greek stating that they were made for Romanos and Christopher (921–31) and Basil II and Constantine VIII (976–1025) respectively.

The Second Golden Age seems to have been one when textile weaving was at its height in the capital, and the value which was then set upon stuffs is illustrated by a passage in the document known as the Chronicle of Nestor, where it is stated that the emperor John Tzimisces (969–76) hoped that a rich present of gold and textiles would serve to prevent Sviatoslav of Russia from invading Byzantine territory.[5] And it was textiles that were sent as the most honourable form of present to the emperors of the West when embassies were dispatched to present compliments or negotiate some treaty. It was, in fact, in this way that many of the textiles now preserved in the cathedral treasuries of the West came to the area, though others were probably sent along with the relics of saints, which had already become a most cherished form of import. The stuffs with eagles as their motif of decoration, like those at Berlin, were probably mainly sent as presents from the imperial looms, and served as secular gifts; others, with more orientalizing designs, like that known as the shroud of St Siviard at Sens, which were eventually used for the burial of sainted bishops, may perhaps originally have been sent with relics. Some of them came from Islamic, some from Byzantine looms, and the authorities are by no means agreed as to which of them exactly should be assigned to which source.

It was, however, on the royal looms at Constantinople that most of the best work was produced until the eleventh century. By then, if not before, a number of other centres in the Byzantine world had begun to become important also. Of these the most flourishing were in Cyprus and at Thebes and Corinth in Greece. And in the twelfth century weavers were transported from these two towns in Greece to develop the textile industry in Sicily, which soon became extremely flourishing. The Sicilian looms were responsible for some excellent work, done to oblige both Christian and Moslem patrons. One of the most notable products is the superb embroidery in the Schatzkammer at Vienna known as the coronation mantle of King Roger;

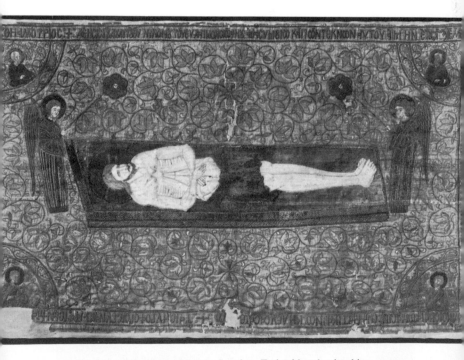

454 Victoria and Albert Museum, London. Embroidered epitaphion. 1407

it is dated to 1134. Confronted eagles, together with gryphons back to back, constitute the motifs that occupy medallions on another fine stuff which is also perhaps to be assigned to Sicily; it is now at Sens, and is known as the shroud of St Potentien. An interesting banner, bearing a figure of St Michael, and the date 1141, now preserved in the monastery of Santa Croce at Avellana, is also perhaps to be assigned to Sicily, as is a fine textile with doves from the tomb of an archbishop of Canterbury. An embroidered cape at Metz, usually known as the mantle of Charlemagne, is perhaps also to be assigned to Sicily. Its pattern reproduces the favourite eagle motif.

Many of these stuffs, more especially those bearing large-scale animal motifs, were originally intended as hangings in the secular buildings, and the Great Palace of the Byzantine emperors at Constantinople must have been richly adorned with them. Some may perhaps also have been used in churches, but after the Iconoclast

455 Castell'Arquato. Embroidery in gold thread on purple silk. Communion of the Apostles. Fourteenth century

456 Putna monastery, Rumania. Embroidery of the time of Stephen the Great. The Annunciation. 1457–1504

period these doubtless often bore religious scenes, like a textile which has now disappeared, though a description survives, which the Emperor Michael III (842–67) sent as a present to Pope Nicholas I; it bore figures of Christ and the Apostles, and must almost have commemorated the reintroduction of figured religious stuffs after the

457 Benaki Museum, Athens. Embroidered manipulum. Angel. Sixteenth century

lifting of the Iconoclast ban. One would think that only the stuffs with motifs on a fairly modest scale would have been in general use for costumes, but the dresses which are shown in the paintings suggest that often even those bearing the more majestic designs were employed in this way, especially in later times. The High Admiral Apocaucos, who forms the subject of a well-known miniature dating from about 1340, is thus clothed in a magnificent silk ornamented with immense medallions.

In addition to the woven patterns, royal costumes were also profusely adorned with precious stones or even small medallions of enamel, which were sewn on to the textile ground; the dress of Manuel I Comnenos (1143–80) was described by a contemporary writer as being like a meadow covered with flowers. Hangings also seem to have been adorned in this way at times, and both hangings and dresses were probably also decorated with embroidery, though we know little of this art before the Palaeologue period. From the thirteenth century onwards, however, this technique was developed in a very particular manner for the decoration of ecclesiastical vestments and altar cloths, more especially those used on Good Friday, on which the body of our Lord was depicted; they were known as

498

epitaphioi. One of the finest examples, dated to 1407, is preserved in the Victoria and Albert Museum, but there are specimens of slightly later date in a number of museums and treasuries, more especially those on Mount Athos. There are also many rich treasuries containing fine embroidered vestments in Rumania. These stuffs are decorated very heavily and thickly, with the aid of metal threads and semi-precious stones, and though the technique was effective for religious usage, it would have been unsuitable for any secular purpose. The lovely embroideries which were produced on the mainland, and more especially in the islands of Greece, in the seventeenth, eighteenth, and nineteenth centuries as bridal dowries and for similar purposes are quite distinct, and owe much more to the inspiration of the woven silks of the Turkish period than they do to any survival of old Byzantine ideas.

458 Benaki Museum, Athens. Embroidered epitaphion. Sixteenth century

But little Byzantine glass has come down to us, and of that which has, the great majority of examples are of early date. The pottery that we know, and a very great number of different types and techniques were in common use, is all of comparatively late date, practically all of it belonging to the great middle period of Byzantine art. It is thus only when the two techniques are studied consecutively that a complete picture of the type of table vessel used in the Byzantine world can be obtained. The majority of the glass vessels are of a very particular type, known usually by the name of *fonde d'oro*, because the bases were adorned with a decoration of figures executed in gold-leaf, and mounted between two layers of glass fused together in the furnace. The bases of the vessels being double, and the sides often only of one layer of glass, it is usually only the bases that have been preserved, but though few complete examples are known, there is enough evidence to show that most vessels were of quite simple form, being either fairly flat, like dishes, or with wide bodies like big wine glasses, with broad bases instead of a stem. The decoration of the bases usually consisted of human figures shown in groups, akin in appearance to those which we see on the Consular diptychs. Smaller figures, such as orants or animals in little medallions, were sometimes added on the sides, and these medallions have often split away from the vessel and have been preserved singly. There is a good representative collection of such glasses in the British Museum, and there are specimens in most public collections, though by far the largest number is preserved in the Vatican. It was probably in Rome that most of them were made, though Alexandria was also a centre of manufacture. Nothing that has so far been found can be associated with Constantinople.

Another type of glass vessel that was fairly usual in early times was the small bottle or flask to hold perfume or holy water. Such bottles intended for the latter usage often bear a small cross in relief on the side or below the base by way of decoration. The majority were manufactured in Syria and Palestine or in Egypt, and date from the third to the sixth centuries. They were principally used by pilgrims, and in consequence found their way to a large number of places outside those countries. These simple forms continued in use, however, until quite late times, and a group of tall, thin-necked perfume flasks may be distinguished, which were probably made at Constantinople in the Middle period. Allied to them in technique is

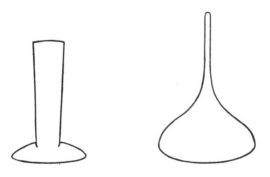

459–60 Glass vessel and perfume bottle. Twelfth century

another group, with tall body, rather like a big test-tube, but widening out at the base to form a support. Such vessels may perhaps have been used for drinking, and they too have been found in association with pottery and other finds of tenth to twelfth century date. A fat, beaker-shaped glass with lid in the Vatican may also be noted here. It dates from about 1075, and serves to show that thin blown glasses of more elaborate forms, but otherwise akin to the perfume flasks, were also made in the Middle period. Apart from a very few examples such as these, practically nothing has been unearthed in the excavation of Byzantine sites at Constantinople, in Greece, in Asia Minor, or in the Balkans, with the exception of tiny fragments. These are of no interest from the artistic point of view, and in the present state of our knowledge are even of little help to the expert.

If anything more elaborate or more ambitious be sought, it is, however, necessary to turn the gaze towards Egypt, and to the centuries before the Moslem conquest. It would seem that the manufacture of all the types of glass known in Egypt in dynastic and in Roman times continued there until the Middle Ages. Fine examples of blown glass, of polychrome glass, and of glasses with elaborate moulded or engraved decorations that survive are thus probably to be assigned there. A fine bowl with moulded decoration, discovered near Cologne, and published by Peirce and Tyler,[1] is thus to be attributed to Egypt, as is a glass with engraved decoration in the Stora Collection, where the subject is a quadriga or four-horse chariot. It is probably to be assigned to the fifth century, though the design is closely similar to that on a textile of about 800 from Aachen now in the Cluny Museum at Paris.

Some glass vessels from the region of Kerch in the Crimea, notably a paten of the sixth century bearing the figure and initials of Christ, are probably to be regarded as importations from Syria, which had also been the centre of an important glass-making industry since pre-Christian times, and some glasses of a red colour from the same area are also probably to be assigned to Syria. They bear embossed ornamentation.[2] After the Moslem conquest Syria seems to have continued as a centre of manufacture, not only in the service of Moslem patrons, but also for export, and some of the lovely glasses with enamelled decoration in several colours were apparently made for others than Moslems. Thus a beaker of blue glass, with a painted decoration of birds in medallions, which is now in the Tyler Collection,[3] shows close affinities with the well-known Islamic glass of Syria of the ninth century.

Of vessels which can be termed Byzantine in the narrower sense of the term, that is to say vessels which were actually made at Constantinople, in Greece, or in Asia Minor after the sixth century, we know practically nothing. It is, however, recorded that there were Jewish glass-workers in Constantinople from the sixth century onwards, and lamps of glass which were probably made locally are described as forming a part of the treasure of Sancta Sophia in 563. They were probably not unlike the lamps that have been discovered at Jerash and elsewhere, that is to say, conical in form, or like an inverted bell. They were small in size, and were used together in large numbers in a polycandelion or chandelier.[4]

It is also recorded that glass was made at Salonica in the tenth century, and there are some flasks and bottles from there and other sites in Greece in the Byzantine Museum at Athens. Some lamps of clear greenish glass in the treasury of St Mark's are akin. They were certainly brought to Venice amongst other treasures when Constantinople was sacked by members of the Fourth Crusade in 1204. They are of fairly elaborate form, for they were intended to be used individually, and not merely as oil-containers in a chandelier. Such glass lamps usually appear to have been mounted in gold or silver, and these mounts were also often of very elaborate workmanship. They are to be assigned to the tenth and eleventh centuries, and usually bear a moulded ornament consisting of a dot surrounded by one or more circles.[5] A fine glass vessel mounted as a reliquary in the cathedral treasury at Halberstadt bears the same characteristic ornament; it is probably to be assigned to Constantinople. A jug, with long wide neck, handle and lid, in the Grüneisen Collection is also of Comnene date, though its provenance is uncertain.[6] An extremely ornate bowl of red glass in the treasury of St Mark's, which has usually been regarded as Byzantine work of the tenth or eleventh century on account of the antique style of its decoration, has been associated with Corinth. It has also been suggested that it should be assigned to some Western workshop, and it may also be later in date. Wherever it was made, it is by no means a typical piece.[7]

Another group is made up of bowls and other vessels of very thick glass, with moulded decorations in high relief. There are examples in the treasury of St Mark's and elsewhere.[8] The motifs are usually animals of rather Oriental character, akin in appearance to those which are so usual on the textiles, and the glasses show a relationship also to the superb rock-crystals of Fatimid Egypt. Indeed, one such glass, formerly in the collection of Mr W. H. Buckley, would appear to have been made in the same place as the crystals, and many of the crystals found their way into the treasuries of cathedrals and churches at a very early stage in their careers, even if they were not at times made for Christian patrons. Mr Buckley believes that they may have been made in Mesopotamia or even Persia, as well as in Egypt.[9] Finally, a recent discovery made in the Church of the Pantocrator in Constantinople shows that polychrome stained glass with decorations painted on it was in use as window glass in the Byzantine capital.[10]

If glass vessels which are to be assigned to between the fourth and eighth centuries are comparatively usual, examples of glazed pottery from these centuries are extremely rare. So far as we can tell, it may be stated that pottery of Roman type, either unglazed, or of red ware with a deep green glaze, and with a moulded or impressed decoration, was still made, but few examples that can be dated on archaeological grounds have come to light. Whether Samian ware was manufactured by the Byzantines is uncertain, but fragments have appeared on Byzantine sites from time to time. A highly polished red ware closely akin to it was, however, used in Mesopotamia, in Sasanian, and apparently also in early Islamic times, and this may have been copied from a ware in use in the Byzantine world at the period. Somewhat similar wares were used in Egypt, and the Copts developed a fine painted but unglazed pottery of their own, the best examples of which are to be assigned to the seventh century. Small unglazed lamps of Roman form and pilgrim flasks with an impressed decoration like those found in such numbers at the shrine of St Menas were also common, and it would seem that after about the eighth century the lamps, though of the same form, were more often glazed than not. But of more elaborate glazed potteries, forerunners of those which become so very important after the ninth century, practically nothing is known. The only important example is a bowl in the British Museum, known as the bowl of Constantine. It bears a figure of Christ, under a very thick opaque glaze, and though the iconography of the figure is essentially Byzantine, the technique is completely Egyptian, and the bowl must be assigned to that country, and perhaps to the sixth century.[11]

From the ninth century onwards, on the other hand, a considerable variety of types of pottery with glazed decorations began to appear, some of them showing close relationships with wares known in the Islamic world, but others of a very individual character. The main groups may be mentioned in turn. The earliest appears to be a class where the bodies were of fine white paste, and where the glazes were laid directly upon them, without any intermediary slip. The glazes themselves turn to a pale greenish yellow after firing. Sometimes the

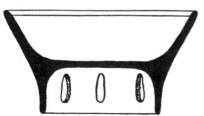

461 Constantinople. Chafing dish. Ninth to tenth century

462 Vignier Collection. Aquamanile. Eleventh century

vessels remained otherwise unadorned, sometimes inscriptions or simple designs were scratched into the paste while it was soft, and sometimes more elaborate designs were impressed upon the inside of the base of the vessel with a mould. An example of the latter type shows an eagle with spread wings. It is interesting to compare it with the well-known Auxerre textile, which is to be dated to the early eleventh century. The two must be of much the same date. Vessels bearing these stamped decorations were usually of simple form, namely plates or bowls, but similar pastes and glazes were also used for more elaborate shapes, such as jugs, fruit-stands, or chafing dishes. The latter have been found in quite large numbers in excavations at Constantinople, and consist of bowls standing on a very high base, perforated with holes. Some form of lamp was put under the base, air penetrating to it through the holes; it served to keep warm food in the dish above it. An example from Constantinople is illustrated in Figure 461, and an elaborate jug in the form of an aquamanile is shown in Figure 462. Here engraving and relief have been used to effect the decoration. It was formerly in the Vignier Collection in Paris. The glaze is of a deeper green than is usual in vessels of the group, but heavy deep green glazes seem to have been in fairly common use, and attention may be drawn to two very fine pots of drum shape, one in the Victoria and Albert Museum and one in the writer's possession. Here the glaze is very dark green indeed, and the decoration has been incised into the paste. It could hardly be more simple, but also, hardly, more effective. A group where small blobs of clay were pressed on to the body to form the decoration may also be noted here, for the glazes overlying them are the same. 'Petal ware' seems the best name by which to designate this group. It has its prototypes both in second-century Roman art and in Parthian Mesopotamia, and pottery of closely similar type was made in medieval times in Britain.

Another important early group, with similar white body, is distinguished by a painted decoration above it, often in several colours. Quite often the colours were put on very thickly, so that they stand up underneath a transparent over-glaze in quite high relief; it would seem that the height of the relief serves to some extent as an indication of date, the relief being higher in later examples, whereas in the earlier ones the pigments were thin. In addition they were probably less colourful, palish browns and greens being most usual. By the tenth century, if not before, deep brown, deep green, blue, black, bright yellow, tomato-red, gold, and perhaps also silver were in general use, and though gold and silver never seem to have been used together, the other colours have all been found in association on the most elaborate examples. Vessels of various forms, especially bowls and handled cups, like tea-cups, were made, and in addition the technique was especially favoured for the decoration of plaques or tiles. Sometimes these were quite small, about one inch across, and flat in section, and sometimes they were about four inches broad and perhaps ten inches long and curved in section, the designs being on some on the convex and on some on the concave side. The sections were fitted together to form frames for icons or to mark the extremities of wall niches and so on. A third type of plaque was square, and in addition to floral motifs these plaques also often bore portraits of saints or other human figures. In one famous example, found at Patleina in Bulgaria, a number of square tiles, each bearing the portion of a figure, fit together to form a composite whole, with the head and shoulders of St Theodore. A large collection of such tiles, said to have been found near Constantinople, is preserved in the Walters Art Gallery of Baltimore.

Examples of this ware have come from Corinth and elsewhere in Greece, from Russia, from Constantinople, and from Preslav and Patleina in Bulgaria. At both the latter places tiles were found *in situ*, and near Preslav actual kilns have also been excavated. The

463 Archaeological Museum, Istanbul. Revetment plaques Polychrome ware. Tenth century

technique is so individual a one that it may be concluded that it was invented in one centre, whence it was introduced to the others. At present, however, it is impossible to say where this centre was. It may have been in Bulgaria, but the technique is so elaborate, and the group savours so much of being produced under the most lavish and exclusive patronage, that Constantinople seems in some ways a more probable home. The question must for a time remain in the balance. The nature of the designs does not help, for they are very varied, and include not only figures, which in general follow the normal rules of Byzantine iconography, but also animals and leaf motifs of an essentially Oriental type, and geometric motifs which stem from a purely Hellenistic source; the latter motifs are most often found on examples from Constantinople, though the motifs of Oriental origin were by no means excluded from the capital. This is undoubtedly the

464 Corinth Museum. Base of bowl with praying woman. Polychrome ware. Twelfth century

465 Patleina, Bulgaria. Ceramic icon. St Theodore. Ninth to tenth century

grandest and most exclusive group of Byzantine pottery, and shows the genius of the Byzantine potter in its most original and individual form.

It would seem that potteries of these two main groups, both characterized by their white bodies, were in general use from the eighth century onwards. With the eleventh century, if not before, wares of another important type also began to become popular, and by the fourteenth century they had almost completely replaced those of the former group. They are distinguished primarily by their red bodies. Unlike the first group, which is essentially of Byzantine style and technique, the second group was one widely distributed over the whole Near East, and examples in the Byzantine world must originally have been inspired from the Islamic area, and more especially from Persia. This type of pottery is usually known by the name graffito. The bodies are of red clay, as opposed to the white sandy pastes of the former type, they were invariably covered with a white slip under the glaze, and the decoration was done by removing this slip, either in thin lines with a narrow pointed instrument, or in wider areas, with some form of spatula, before the glazes were added, so that they took on a different hue where they overlaid the body from that where they overlaid the slip. The glazes were sometimes monochrome, and sometimes of several colours, the colours usually being employed to stress the form of the graffito design, though they never followed its outline exactly, as in a coloured drawing.

A number of distinct groups of this family of pottery can be distinguished in the Byzantine world, some of them spread all over it, and others restricted to particular areas. Of the latter the most important is a group where large portions of the slip were removed with a spatula, so that the design was left in reserve. In Constantinople, and, so far as we can tell, nowhere else, these designs took the form of very precise geometrical patterns or of monograms, under a monochrome glaze, which turns to cream or pale yellow over the slip and to brown or black where it overlies the body. Elsewhere the geometric patterns do not occur, but animals and sometimes even human figures seem to have served as the themes for the decoration. Examples from Corinth, Athens, Salonica, and elsewhere may be cited. On the whole, however, it would seem that line drawing was more usual in Greece and the Balkans, and round about the twelfth century a distinctive group with very delicate line drawings appears to have been in fairly general use; some of the finest examples come from Sparta. This type of ware was also in use at Constantinople. Floral motifs, birds, and animals were the usual subjects, but occasionally the direct influence of Islamic art is to be seen in the use of Kufic script to form a decorative border around the rim of the dish or bowl. One of the finest examples with such a decoration, in the Kaiser Friedrich Museum at Berlin, comes from Miletus; it is probably to be assigned to the eleventh century.

As time progressed, the line drawing and the incised techniques tended to merge, and when this took place, additional colours,

466 Corinth Museum. Bowl with stylized bird. Graffito ware. Twelfth century

notably deep brown and green, were used for the glazes. Fine bowls
of this style, very Persian in appearance both with regard to technique and to design, have been found on most Byzantine sites all
over the Near East. Particular types of vessel or forms of decoration
appear to have been developed in particular regions. Thus rather
wide bowls, of fine proportions, seem to have characterized Greece,
while in Cyprus the bowls were usually smaller and deeper, and were
often placed at the tops of very high bases, like inverted beakers. In
Cyprus the designs also very frequently included sketchily drawn
human figures; elsewhere birds, and especially animals, were more
usual.

By the twelfth century the use of two or more colours in the glazes
had become wellnigh universal, and new types had begun to appear,
where the graffito was omitted, and where coloured glazes only
were used. They were thin, runny, glazes, quite distinct from the

thick, upstanding, underglaze pigments usual on vessels of the poly-chrome group of earlier times. Though the results achieved with the aid of these runny colours were often quite attractive, really fine work was unusual, and the drawing, or rather the painting, was poor and sketchy. The decorators copied and recopied old motifs, till the original purport of the design was often forgotten; quite often, for example, bowls bear a decoration which can only represent a bird's wing; the birds themselves have been omitted. Sometimes, again, the designs had no representational basis, as in a group which may be termed marbled ware, where the colours were put on and the bowl was then shaken, so that the colours ran together to produce a design like the marbled endpaper of a book. This technique was developed only in very late Byzantine times, and vessels decorated in this way are more often early Turkish than Byzantine. Another group, which bears a carefully drawn decoration of floral or angular patterns in deep blue over a white slip, is represented by finds from Constanti-nople and Asia Minor, more especially Miletus. It is probably to be associated with Seljuk rather than Byzantine culture, though the frequency of examples in excavations at Constantinople suggests that the type of ware was made there and not merely imported.[12]

There has already been occasion to note the Oriental affinities of much Byzantine art from the eighth century onwards, and these affinities become especially obvious as a result of a study of the ceramics. But the originality of the Byzantine genius is none the less apparent, and recent discoveries show that Byzantine pottery, of which hardly anything at all was known four or five decades ago, is worthy to be considered alongside the more familiar potteries produced for Islamic patrons in Egypt, Syria, or Persia. At present, however, much of our information has to be gathered from a study of fragments, and complete examples are conspicuous by their rarity. Further, only one kiln site, in Bulgaria, has so far been discovered. The field is now ripe for a more universal and more extensive study of this very important subject, and researches cannot fail to produce results of the very first importance.

An entertaining story is recorded by Persian historians that in the time of Shapur the Great (309–79) a Byzantine artist came to Persia to make a portrait of the Emperor. The portrait was drawn, and the artist took a copy of it back with him to Constantinople, where it was used as the subject of decoration of some gold plates in the palace. Some years later Shapur came to the Byzantine capital in disguise; he succeeded in penetrating into the palace during a feast, but one of the guards, remarking his likeness to the portraits on the gold plates, called attention to the fact. The disguised Shapur was taken before the Byzantine Emperor; he confessed his identity and was thrown into jail, whence he soon afterwards contrived to escape. The legend is one of long standing in Persia, and even if it is not to be regarded as strictly true, it serves as an excellent illustration of the freedom of communication between the Persian and Byzantine empires, and in all probability presents a truer picture of the actual state of relationships between the two powers than do the long lists of skirmishes and battles that took place until the rise of Islam put an end to Sasanian rule in Persia.

There are, indeed, many concrete instances of cultural contacts between Byzantium and Persia: there was a very active trade between the two empires, and so far as art was concerned there seems to have been an almost uninterrupted give and take between them, Byzantine influence in Persia being wellnigh as important as Persian influence in Byzantium. A few instances of Byzantine influence in Persia may be cited. It is, for example, recorded by Firdausi that Shapur I (241–72) entrusted a Byzantine architect with the building of a great bridge across the River Karun at Shustar. The bridge survives to this day, though one cannot say positively that it is a Byzantine work, for there was much in Sasanian building that came from the Hellenistic world. Nevertheless, its nature is in accordance with the demands which the King set upon the architect, for it was to be like a cord stretched across the river. The castle at Khawarnaq near Hira in Mesopotamia was again supposed to have been built by a Byzantine architect from Constantinople, and an architect from Constantinople was also believed to have directed the construction of the great Sasanian palace at Ctesiphon. Much of the palace survives to this day, and its workmanship is Eastern rather than Western in style. But even if this is the case, the repeated allusion to Byzantine builders is not without significance, and there are many elements in Sasanian construction which attest the influence of the Roman and Byzantine world. In the converse direction, the immense importance which must be assigned to Eastern elements in the development of the Byzantine architectural style serve as even weightier evidence of the contacts, even if we are not prepared to accept the whole of Strzygowski's Eastern thesis as gospel.

Unfortunately we know but little of the minor arts of Sasanian Persia, and though occasional references in the texts to the skill of the artificers of 'Rum', that is, the Byzantine world, may be cited, concrete instances of their work in the Sasanian world are as yet lacking. With regard to influence in the opposite direction, on the other hand, there is a great deal of evidence. Thus the silks of Eastern Christendom were often of a completely Persian character, and the formal beast ornament which was so popular in the Byzantine world, on silks, on stone sculptures, and at times even on ivories, also stemmed from the East; it was probably first conceived in Mesopotamia, though it was taken over and extensively developed by the Sasanians. The peacock's feather motif, which appears so often in Byzantine mosaics and on sculptures, was probably first used by the Sasanians, and the earliest instance that is known is a capital at Taq-i-Bostan. Byzantine costumes, insignia, and jewellery often show similar Sasanian elements. For example, the two small peaks which top the head-dresses of the emperors on certain Byzantine coins or that of Theodora in the famous mosaic in San Vitale at Ravenna are no more than variants upon the double wings which were a normal part of the great Sasanian crowns; the crown of Chosroes II may be compared. The fibula that holds the chlamys on the shoulder of Byzantine imperial costume is again of Sasanian origin, and figures on the Theodosios base at Constantinople or that on the Barberini Ivory may be compared with those on the Sasanian rock reliefs. Even as late as the thirteenth century the Sasanian form

467–8 Crown of Chosroes II and plan of the Omayyad Palace, Mshatta

of crown was still being used by the emperors of Trebizond and the despots of Mistra.

The evidence regarding the intrusion of Sasanian elements in arts of a larger scale is no less striking. A portion of the Great Palace at Constantinople thus seems to have been in the form of a rectangle surrounded by a wall, in which were courts, like those of Sasanian palaces such as Sarvistan, and there was a building of completely Eastern appearance like Mshatta in the palace, which was known as the περσικος δόμος. Palaces which have been excavated at Aboba Pliska in Bulgaria show the direct influence of Sasanian models,[1] and in general links between the arts of those two areas seem to have been extremely close. Thus the little clay cylinders with one end glazed which were found inserted into the walls of churches at Tirnovo would seem to have been copied from the cones with inscribed ends which were used in Babylonia and Assyria, while Bulgarian metal work dating from between the ninth and the twelfth centuries was of markedly Sasanian type. Silver plates from various sources which have been published by Migeon may be cited,[2] as well as the famous treasure of Nagy Szent Miklos in Hungary, which has usually been claimed as Bulgarian work. Sasanian influence seems also to have been exercised on Byzantine silver, and a large dish from Carthage which was shown at the Byzantine Exhibition in Paris in 1931 (No. 388) bore a repoussé ornament of marked Sasanian character.

In addition to these links between the Byzantine and the Sasanian worlds, there were similar contacts between the arts of Byzantium

469 Convent of Vlatadon, Salonica. Leaved cross. Tenth century

and those of Mesopotamia and Syria, when once the Islamic conquests had embraced these lands. We still do not know very much about the artistic products of the various Christian sects which flourished as independent bodies in these areas, notably the Nestorians and the Monophysites, but one particular art motif which was extremely popular in the Byzantine world both before and, especially, during the Iconoclast period may be noted, namely the leaved cross. This motif consists of a cross with tall stem, from the base of which scrolls or leaves rise up to form a balancing pattern on either side. It appears to have been one of the most common motifs used by the Nestorian Christians, examples being known from Syria on the one hand to China on the other. It was, however, also used quite extensively in the Byzantine world, and so far as we can tell constituted one of the favourite forms of decoration for sculptures in Iconoclast times, and just after the close of that period we also see it in manuscript illustrations, like those of the superb copy of the Homilies of Gregory of Nazianzus in Paris (Bib. Nat. Gr. 510).[3]

Any influence that the Islamic world may have exercised on Byzantine art was naturally of comparatively late date, and at the outset contacts were in the opposite direction, for in the first centuries of its history the Islamic world boasted no art of its own. At the time of the rise of Mohammad, that is to say in the middle of the second quarter of the seventh century of the Christian era, the Arabs of Arabia were a wild and rather primitive people, with little religious faith and practically no religious instinct of a ritual kind. Christianity had passed over the northern part of the region, to be widely accepted in the more cultured parts of Mesopotamia, without affecting more than a few town-dwellers in Arabia itself. Mazdaism, the official religion of Sasanian Persia, had also been adopted in the larger towns of Mesopotamia, as well as to some extent by the more settled Arab tribes like the Ghassanids and the Lakhmids. The capital city of the latter, Hira, on the Euphrates, close to the present Kufa, was apparently more or less equally divided between Christians and Mazdeans,[4] and the latter religion also boasted adherents as far westward as Dura. But the real Arabs, the Bedouin, had never been converted to either faith, and they still adhered to the age-old primitive cults of the desert. In their principal towns, Mecca and Medina, the only developed religion which commanded a large number of followers was the Jewish.

If there was little religion in the life and thought of the tribes who were first responsible for the spread of Islam, there was still less of anything in the nature of a creative or even of a conservative instinct among them. Sumptuous foundations were soon to be laid, but existing monuments were thoughtlessly destroyed, and a characteristic of the race seemed as apparent at an early date as it did till recently, namely the inability to repair or keep in order any construction whatsoever, whether building, whose appeal was principally religious or aesthetic, or canal, the role of which was primarily utilitarian. If Iraq and parts of Arabia are today desert it is not only because of the ruthless destructions of a Hulagu or a Tamerlane, it is not only owing to inevitable climatic pulsations or the destruction of forests; the listlessness of the Arab race has wrought as much damage as any conquest, however destructive, and has caused as much desiccation as any lack of rainfall. This particular characteristic actually had an even wider effect, for it seems to have influenced practically the whole of Islam, and though the Persians in Achaemenid and Sasanian times appear to have been an energetic people in whom the preservative instinct was well developed, and whose creative artistic powers can never be disputed, they are today as careless of constructions as are the Arabs and wellnigh as destructive as were the ravaging Mongol hordes.

At the outset, Byzantine, Syrian, and Persian methods, motifs, and forms were taken over wholesale in order to effect the establishment of the individual culture which this new religious state demanded, and the first ruling dynasty of Islam, the Omayyad, with its capital at Damascus, adopted a culture which was essentially Syro-Byzantine. The rulers of the dynasty were, in fact, deliberately attempting to achieve something that was essentially foreign to their Arab heritage when they adopted a settled life in towns and when they constructed such great sanctuaries as the Dome of the Rock at Jerusalem or the Great Mosque at Damascus. The former was frankly designed to draw to it the pilgrim traffic from Mecca and Medina; the latter had originally been a Christian basilica, the reconstruction and adornment of which was a magnificent expression of the extravagant ostentation of its patron, the Caliph al-Walid. That the two were successful as religious institutions and that they were so admirable from the artistic point of view was due to three causes. First of these was the innate curiosity and the love of a gay and grand display in the mental make-up of the Arabs themselves, which led them to visit and admire the buildings so long as they were bright and fresh. The second was the long and accomplished tradition in Syria and the enterprising spirit of early Christendom which lived on there for some two centuries after the establishment of Islam. The third was the proximity of Byzantine culture, which was responsible to a great extent both for the conception and for the execution of the actual work. The conception of the plan of the Dome of the Rock would have been impossible, as Creswell has shown, without Byzantine and Christian Syrian prototypes,[5] while the decoration of these two buildings with mosaics would have been equally impossible had not extensive technical and ornamental experiments been made in the preceding centuries under the patronage of the Byzantine emperors.

Similar influences are to be traced in the minor arts, and Byzantine taste also exercised a very marked effect on Omayyad life. In this respect, however, it must be admitted that the results were not as auspicious as they were with regard to architecture and mosaic decoration. Today the inhabitants of Egypt are unaffected by the numerous germs which infect the water that they drink or the vegetables that they eat, whereas the European at once succumbs. In the seventh century the Byzantines were similarly able to support the luxuries and vices of their cities, whereas the Arabs, newcomers accustomed only to the severity of desert conditions, or at best to the somewhat insecure existence of the small towns along the fringe of the Red Sea, soon became victims of the new luxury, and drink and carousal on the one hand and plotting and intrigues on the other soon brought the majority of them to an untimely end. A rather similar victory was to be achieved by Byzantine luxury at a later date, when the austere Turks conquered the Empire and settled in Constantinople. The gradual decay which then set in continued for almost four centuries. In the Omayyad period the results were more rapid; after only about one hundred years of life the Omayyad dynasty crumbled and fell.

When they first appeared on the scene in Syria, however, the conquering Arabs were energetic enough, and the defeat of the Byzantine outposts and garrisons was an easy matter. The first Arab victory was that of 629, when the Byzantines were overcome by guile rather than force of arms not far from the Dead Sea. In 634 Byzantine dominion was further shaken by a second great Arab victory, which secured for them Damascus, and with it the overlordship of Syria. In 636 the Emperor Heraclius fled somewhat ingloriously to Constantinople, taking with him the True Cross from Jerusalem. After a brief respite he attempted to regain his losses, but the expedition was a failure, and with Syria assured the Moslems were soon able to overrun Mesopotamia, and so open a secure route to Persia and to further conquests in the heart of Asia. In 641 the conquest of Egypt was completed from Syria as a base. Advances were also made into the south of Asia Minor, as a result of which the Byzantine emperor was forced to send an ambassador to Syria to sue for peace. A truce was arranged for two years, and there is reason to believe that this respite of hostilities cost the Byzantines a fairly heavy indemnity. In spite of the peace, however, Armenia was lost to the Byzantines in the same year, owing to a local revolt engineered by the caliph Moawiyah, and soon afterwards Rhodes fell before the Moslem fleet, and the famous Colossus was sold to a Jewish merchant. Periodic invasions of the frontier of Asia Minor seem to have been continued even during the armistice, and they were soon to become an established custom. But in 672 a far more ambitious scheme was envisaged, namely an attack on Constantinople itself, by land and sea. But it met with complete failure, and the Moslems were forced as a result to submit to a peace which guaranteed a heavy tribute to the Byzantines.

History tells of many such truces as these, and they are of almost as great an interest to the historian of art as to the historian of events, for they were engineered by ambassadors from one power to the other, and these ambassadors always seem to have been received in a most friendly manner, in spite of political hostilities. What is especially important for us, however, is that they took with them a lavish supply of presents of an artistic character, and that in addition they were often called in by the Moslems to advise on problems of architecture or to criticize what had been done. A typical instance is recorded by one of the Arab historians, who notes that Moawiyah had just completed a new palace and had received therein a Byzantine envoy. After the political discussions were finished, the caliph asked the envoy his opinion of the building. He answered, 'The upper part will do for birds and the lower for rats.' No very diplomatic reply, it would seem! But the caliph treated it with respect, for he had the building pulled down and rebuilt, which shows the value that was set upon Byzantine taste and artistic judgement. At the same time the story offers an interesting sidelight on Moawiyah's character, for the tolerance and broadness of mind which did not take offence at so open a criticism was no common thing at this time, especially in a society of the type of that to which the caliph belonged.

But in spite of the friendly reception of the embassies, hostilities continued, and the increasing power of the Moslems and the outward push from the east are the most striking factors affecting the history of the period. The Byzantine Empire received a series of rude and often serious set-backs, but the rulers succeeded in weathering them, and their resistance is to be attributed to the quality and innate vigour of Byzantine culture as a whole rather than to any outstanding ability on the part of individual generals or any very brilliant action by the army. Indeed, such successes as were achieved were of a temporary character, and they never succeeded in staying the advancing tide of Islam to the same extent as did the respect and reverence in which Byzantine culture was held. We see this respect illustrated in Moawiyah's tolerance of the Byzantine ambassador's criticism of his palace; we see it in the tenor of much of Omayyad life; but most of all we see it in concrete form in the nature and character of the art and architecture favoured by Islamic patrons during the seventh and eighth centuries.

With the fall of the Omayyad dynasty and the transference of the capital to Mesopotamia in 750 the Byzantine heritage was to a great extent cast aside, and a new phase of the history of Islamic art and architecture opened, when Persian elements were to the fore. But if Byzantine culture ceased to exercise much influence, Byzantine power in Asia Minor was at the same time less threatened, for the Abbasid rulers were fully occupied with the organization of their own portion of the vast Moslem Empire, and any thoughts of further large-scale attacks on their part were banished from their minds. In spite of the essentially Persian character of Abbasid art and culture, however, a number of Byzantine elements nevertheless still penetrated. The early Abbasid army was thus organized on a Byzantine model, and the caliph Mansur even had a corps of fire-throwers, who were clothed in special fire-proof uniforms, and their fire must have been copied from the dreaded Greek fire of the Byzantine forces. Early Abbasid architecture, again, also owed something to Greek ideas, and the site of Baghdad was looked upon as especially favourable for the capital, for, in the words of Mansur's advisers, goods from Byzantine lands could be easily brought thither down the Tigris.[6] The Byzantine influence apparent in early Islamic book illustrations of the school usually known as the Mesopotamian was also very important, and there was a similar influence upon metal work, especially in the twelfth century. A large group of vessels with inlaid ornament, usually known under the general term of Mosul work, though it is now established that there were numerous other centres of manufacture also, thus quite often bear Christian subjects as a part of their decoration; the well-known bowl of St Louis in the Louvre and a famous enamelled dish in the Ferdinands Museum at Innsbruck may be cited as examples. The motif of a branch ending in an animal's head, which was at a rather later date frequently used for the decoration of carpets in Persia, can also be assigned to the Byzantine world; it was used there in sculpture before the eighth century, as for example on slabs at Ravenna.[7]

In the opposite direction Islamic influence on Byzantine art was perhaps even more extensive, and textiles and sculptures owed a particularly important debt to Moslem motifs. Thus certain floral forms, confronted animals, and birds, though ultimately of Sasanian origin, assumed in the Byzantine world from the ninth century a style which had been developed under Abbasid patronage, and the frequent use of Kufic script for decoration on Byzantine textiles, sculptures, and pots once more attests the closeness of the links that bound Constantinople, and even more Greece, to Mesopotamia and Persia. But widespread though these Eastern motifs and even techniques were, they were never copied slavishly; Byzantine art benefited from this outside source of inspiration, and affairs were characterized by a fruitful traffic in ideas occasioned by curiosity and love of the new, rather than by any sterility of imagination.

With the arrival of the Turks in western Asia in the eleventh century the old aggressive attitude, forgotten during the centuries of Abbasid rule, was once more revived, and from then onwards a series of new penetrations into Asia Minor began under the directing impulse of the Seljuk rulers. Indeed, the state of affairs which had characterized Omayyad days was in many ways renewed, and not only were there constant attacks by the Moslems, but also a renewed attention was paid to Byzantine models by Seljuk architects and decorators. Some Seljuk sculptures of the twelfth century which are preserved in the Museum at Konia may be cited in proof of this, for their style might almost be described as provincial Byzantine. A similar influence was exercised on the development of Seljuk thought and learning, for Greek mathematicians and philosophers were assembled by the Seljuk rulers at Konia, and some of the princes were even sent to Constantinople so that their education might be completed.

With the advent of the Ottoman Turks at the end of the thirteenth century this state of friendly intercourse, interspersed with periodic hostilities, was brought to an end, and a more severe and continued struggle for domination set in, which was punctuated by the fall of one Byzantine stronghold after another, until the final siege and capture of Constantinople in 1453. Yet even then, in spite of the fact that the Empire had come to an end, something of the great heritage of Byzantium was handed down to the new rulers on the Golden Horn, so that in the sixteenth and seventeenth centuries not only was court life dominated by a number of customs and ceremonies which were to a great extent Byzantine in character, but also architecture was affected by the inspiration of the plan which had first been used by the Byzantines in the construction of Justinian's great Cathedral of Sancta Sophia. Without this prototype, Ottoman religious architecture could never have taken on the form which makes a first view of Constantinople one of the most glorious aesthetic experiences that is possible today: without the prototype of Byzantine imperialism, the Turkish Sultanate would never have taken on that peculiar character which made it one of the ruling factors in European history until the nineteenth century.

The spread of Byzantine culture into regions beyond her permanent control was very considerable, for the whole of eastern Europe and western Asia were affected. Nowhere, however, was this influence more to the fore than in the Slavonic world, where the whole basis of culture was Byzantine, and where it was the Byzantine element that was important, rather than the variations upon it produced in the different localities. This basis existed in Bulgaria and Serbia, it existed in Rumania and Russia, and it was even present in many regions addicted to the Catholic rather than the Orthodox version of the Christian faith, though in such regions it had often become obscured by subsequent Western influences, so that its presence was not always clearly obvious.

Bulgaria and Serbia have already been alluded to, more especially in connexion with twelfth- and thirteenth-century developments in wall painting, since for long periods these regions had been under the direct control of the Byzantine capital, and the churches that were built there and the frescoes that were painted had in many cases been the works of Greek painters from Constantinople. Even when these countries became independent, Byzantine influence had remained supreme: artists were brought from Greek areas, and it was only at a comparatively late date that completely local styles began to become important in work which was of a sophisticated and not merely of a primitive character. Moreover, both these countries shared the same fate as the Greek portion of the Byzantine world – they fell under Turkish domination in the fifteenth century.

In Russia, on the other hand, developments ran along different lines, for, although a part of the land was conquered by Mongols, a part remained independent, and even the conquered area was subject for only a limited period. Before this subjection Christian art and culture had already taken on a national complexion; after it the various regions were at once firmly knit together to form a stable Orthodox empire, whose rulers regarded themselves first as the peers, and then, after the fall of Constantinople in 1453, as the legitimate and direct successors of the Byzantine emperors. In central Russia, indeed, a homogeneous civilization had flourished for some five centuries before the time of Peter the Great, and it was a land in which roads and watercourses afforded ready communication and made culture essentially universal. The nature of the land and the life led there prevented any possibility of that independent progress in one area or conservatism in another which characterized the more mountainous portions of the Orthodox world.

The story of Christian Russia concerns us closely. In the latter half of the tenth century Vladimir, prince of Kiev, succeeded in uniting under his rule the greater part of what is today southern and central Russia. It was a wild and lawless area, yet Vladimir's ambitions were more than those of a nomad conqueror. He aimed at founding in Russia a great empire with an advanced and distinctive civilization of its own, and he realized that to attempt to do this without a stable basis of organized religion was impossible. But what religion was he to choose? Islam, to the south and east, was a flourishing and virile faith; Orthodoxy to the south, offered a more mystic creed, better suited, perhaps, to Russian lines of thought, and it had already made considerable inroads into the region, thanks to Byzantine missionaries and the presence of Byzantine trading colonies in the Chersonese; Judaism was a religion hallowed by time; Catholicism in the West had all the attraction of novelty, and it offered temporal inducements which were extremely alluring, for Byzantium might prove to be an enemy as well as a friend, and in the West powerful alliances might be sought which would help to obviate the dangers. Choice was truly an embarrassment, yet a solution had to be found, and an early Slav manuscript known as the Chronicle of Nestor tells us that Vladimir sent forth envoys to the centre of each religion, with instructions to bring back a report on its merits and attractions. That of the envoys who visited Constantinople was so much the most impressive that Vladimir, who was no doubt guided also by the importance of the links already established with Byzantium, selected Orthodoxy as the official faith of his new Russia.[1] He not only based the religious teaching on that followed in the Byzantine world, but also set out to found the art of his new empire on the same basis. The degree to which Byzantine influence penetrated Russia in the next two centuries is striking proof of the appropriateness of the choice made by Vladimir. No other religion would have suited the Russians nearly so well, and no culture but the Byzantine could have provided such scope for development along national lines. Moreover, such other Slavonic countries as were to any degree civilized were already of the Orthodox faith, and were either closely allied to Byzantium or had derived their whole culture from there.

In 988 Orthodox Christianity became the official religion of Russia, and with the priests who went from Constantinople to baptize and preach the new religion there also travelled architects, mosaicists, and painters. A great work awaited them, for hitherto life in Russia had been conducted on a more or less nomad basis, and there were practically no local buildings or architectural styles that could be adopted to Christian usage. Hence at the outset practically every town of consequence was laid out to resemble Constantinople, each of them being given a Sancta Sophia, a palace, and a golden gate. This Byzantine character was especially marked at the capital, Kiev, where, in addition to the main buildings, the multiplicity of great churches that characterized Constantinople was also copied. The Church of the Dormition of the Virgin was thus founded by Vladimir in 989, the Cathedral of Sancta Sophia by Yaroslav in 1037, and the monastery of the Catacombs by Iziaslav in 1073. The churches were decorated with mosaics or paintings, the earliest of which, like the mosaics in Sancta Sophia, were completely Byzantine, differing from work produced in Constantinople or Greece even less than the churches themselves.[2] The inscriptions in the Sancta Sophia mosaics were thus in Greek letters, and the mosaics themselves are to be compared with those at Daphni and Hosios Lukas. A great Pantocrator in the dome, and a Virgin in the apse, with the Communion of the Apostles below still survive. Some paintings on a staircase, showing scenes from the Hippodrome, must also have been inspired from Byzantium, though their style was distinct, being closer to that of some of the more Oriental of the early manuscripts. Similar monuments were set up in a number of other towns; the cathedral at Chernigov, founded in 1031, may be cited as an example. Most of them have, however, been very much altered at subsequent dates.

The supremacy of Kiev was not long-lived, and in the late eleventh and twelfth centuries it was supplanted as a cultural and artistic capital by Novgorod and Vladimir. Novgorod was never the seat of a principality, and patronage there was exercised by the rich burghers and merchants; art consequently developed along more modest, but also more purely Russian, lines, and this was true both of the city and of the region which was primarily dependent upon it. Vladimir, on the other hand, was made the temporal capital by Andrew Bogoliubski when he sacked Kiev in 1109, and it remained a powerful city until its conquest by the Mongols in 1238. Patronage there was thus of a more despotic character, and there was less opportunity for the development of purely local styles and idioms. There was, however, something of a break with the past at Vladimir as well as at Novgorod, for it was towards Asia Minor and the Caucasus that Vladimir seems to have looked initially, rather than towards Constantinople, and the buildings of the area, with their tall proportions and carved external decoration, are more akin to the stone churches of the eastern part of the Byzantine world or of Armenia than they are to those of the Western world. This is especially the case in the Cathedral of the Dormition at Vladimir, founded in 1158, or in that of the famous church at Yuriev-Polskij, founded in 1230; the presence of extensive sculptured ornament at both places not only attests the influence of what was originally an Armenian idea, but also shows it in concrete form in the nature of many of the motifs that constitute the decoration. In addition to this influence, which may be regarded as basic, there also appear to have penetrated to the region certain elements from the Western world, and sculptures in one or two places are completely Romanesque in style. Had it not been for the Mongol invasion, some most interesting developments showing a mingling of Armenian, Western, and local influences would no doubt have taken place. As it was, when the Mongols were finally expelled in the fifteenth century, Moscow, the new capital and centre of Russia, looked for its culture and art to Novgorod, which had escaped the invasion, rather than to the Vladimir-Suzdal region, which had been overrun.

The beginnings of Novgorodian art were essentially Byzantine, for the Cathedral of Sancta Sophia there, founded in 1045, was almost as closely modelled upon Constantinopolitan architecture as were the early churches at Kiev. But the churches that followed it were more individual, and we can trace in them the evolution of a new style which was developed to suit the locality and which was influenced by the indigenous wooden architecture. Roofs were thus made more pointed, to prevent the snow from settling, bulbous domes replaced the more regular Byzantine ones, probably with the same utilitarian purpose in view, the height of buildings was increased, since the wooden architecture of the area had favoured tall buildings, and painted panels or icons came to play a more important part in the decoration of the interiors than wall paintings, which were of course ill suited to wooden walls. This evolution was naturally slow, and its stages can be perceived only when a considerable number of churches are studied; it was, however, wellnigh complete by the fifteenth century, both at Novgorod and at Pskov, where similar developments took place. Of the churches of Novgorod the following may be mentioned: St George (1119–30), St Theodore Stratelates (1360), and the Transfiguration (1374). In the region the most important buildings are the churches at Nereditsa (1198) and Kovalevo (1345).

Stylistic changes in painting were less marked than those that characterized architecture, for although the monumental style of the mid-Byzantine period, which had inspired the Kiev mosaics, was principally active only in the eleventh and twelfth centuries, the style of the Byzantine Renaissance made itself felt from the later twelfth century onwards. Indeed, the beginnings of that Renaissance are as manifest in wall paintings at Vladimir, notably in a great group of the Apostles in the Church of St Demetrius, dating from 1193, as they are in those at Nerez (1164), and its accomplishment in the early fourteenth century is as manifest in the work of Theophanes the Greek done in Russia as in the frescoes of the Church of the Chora (Kariye Camii) at Constantinople; it has even been suggested that Theophanes worked on these before he migrated from Byzantium to Russia, but their recent cleaning shows that they must date from some seventy years earlier.[3] In Russia Theophanes developed a very distinctive style, which is clearly to be seen in wall paintings done by him in the Church of the Transfiguration at Novgorod in 1378. It was thanks to the teaching of Greek immigrants like Theophanes that a sound foundation was established in Russian painting, and it was on this basis that local styles were founded, so that an intrinsically Russian manner had come into being anyhow by the end of the third quarter of the fourteenth century. The following monuments leading up to the establishment of the new style may be noted at Novgorod: Sancta Sophia (1108), figures of prophets and saints in the Cathedral of the Nativity of the Virgin (1125), and paintings in the Arkhazkaya Church (1189). Outside Novgorod the most important wall paintings are to be found at Nereditsa (1199), at Staraya

Ladoga (twelfth century), in the Church of St Michael at Shovorodsko (1360), in the Church of the Preobrazenia, Olenoe (1378), where there was work by Theophanes the Greek, and at Volotovo (1370–80), where the work is more purely Russian in style.[4]

Though Theophanes probably continued to work in the early fifteenth century, his style by then seems to have become more Russian in character, and a few icons which have been tentatively assigned to him are possessed of all the characteristics which distinguish Russian work from Greek from this time onwards, namely thin, sloping shoulders; delicate, almost effeminate, proportions; subtle colouring; great stress on rhythmical composition. And with Theophanes's death painters of Russian blood became more important than the Greek immigrants. Foremost among them was an artist of outstanding genius, Andrew Rublev, who was born about 1360 and died in 1430. His early life was spent as a lay brother in a monastery, where he worked as apprentice to an icon painter; early in the fifteenth century he was associated with Theophanes the Greek on wall paintings in the Cathedral of the Annunciation at Moscow (1405), and in 1408 he was working on frescoes in the Cathedral of the Dormition of the Virgin at Vladimir. It was, however, in his panels that Rublev's style was most developed. A few which can be definitely assigned to him are preserved; others have been associated with his name on stylistic grounds. The most famous is the superb panel of the Old Testament Trinity, which was painted about 1410 for the monastery of the Trinity and St Sergius near Moscow; it is now preserved in the Tretiakov Gallery at Moscow. It shows perhaps more clearly than any other icon the profound religious emotion which characterized Rublev's work, for it is in every essence a spiritual painting. The spiritual quality is endemic, not superimposed, and it is perhaps this character above any other that distinguishes the outlook of the Russian icon painter, or, for that matter, the Romanesque painter in the West, from that of the painters of the Italian Renaissance.

Though the names of Theophanes and Rublev have come down to us, the majority of painters remained anonymous, for the Church as a whole was still regarded as of greater importance than the individual. A great deal of work was, however, produced, and each city of consequence boasted a distinctive school of its own; the most important are those of Novgorod, Pskov, Tver, Suzdal, Vladimir, and Moscow. And if Novgorod was the most important of these at the beginning of the century, Moscow was certainly the main centre at its end. Once more an individual of outstanding importance has left his name for us; he was Denys, who did wall paintings in the Therapont monastery not far from Moscow, which are dated to 1500. His work is delicate and very delightful, but the tendency towards effeminacy, which was already apparent at the beginning of the fifteenth century, had progressed, and in Denys's work hints of decadence are already apparent. But in spite of this tendency towards charm rather than majesty, a great many paintings, especially icons, of real quality were still to be produced until the Westernizing reforms of Peter the Great in the seventeenth century set a term to the old religious art of Russia. After this time icons, though they were still produced in large numbers, ceased to represent the progressive and vital art of the nation; icon painting became a craft rather than an art, and the work which was produced was not of a character to awaken the interest of any but the expert or the student of ecclesiastical history.

So long, so flourishing, or so independent a history can hardly be traced in the arts of the other Slav lands, since over long periods the story of their art can only be considered together with that of Byzantium, and independent developments were on the whole short-lived. But brief résumés of the history of Bulgaria and Yugoslavia may be given here, for their early histories are distinct, and again, when their complete independence had been achieved, the arts of the two countries once more began to develop along individual lines.

The original Bulgars came to the Balkans from the region to the north of the Caspian and established themselves as an independent power in 679. An analysis of their culture at this time shows that two quite distinct elements can be distinguished, one eastern, or proto-Bulgar, and one Slavonic. The earliest monuments in the land were more closely linked with the former, and some palaces at the first Bulgar capital, Aboba Pliska, the rock reliefs at Madara, and some interesting pieces of metal work from various sites, all show the influence of Sasanian art. As time progressed, these proto-Bulgar elements became gradually submerged, first as a result of contacts with Byzantium, and later, because of the growth of the Slav spirit. Thus by the middle of the ninth century Eastern and Hellenistic elements in Bulgarian art were already more or less equally balanced, in spite of the fact that Christianity did not become the official religion until 864. The acceptance of the new religion naturally opened the country to a wave of Byzantine influence, and in the principal cities like Preslav in the central plain or Tirnovo near the River Danube churches were built along lines very closely similar to what was being done in Constantinople. And if these links were close under the first Bulgarian rulers, like Boris (853–88) and Simeon (893–927), they became even stronger after 1018, when Bulgaria became a Byzantine province.

From 1186 to 1393 Bulgaria was once more an independent kingdom, with its capital at Tirnovo, but the links with Constantinople remained strong. A number of churches were thus built at Tirnovo which were even more Constantinopolitan than those of the first Bulgarian empire, and the paintings within them were in many cases by Greek masters. Indeed, there was probably an influx of painters from Constantinople in the early thirteenth century, owing to the domination of that city by Latin rulers from 1204. The work of these Greeks was probably in the main confined to the larger centres and the more important churches, and it was just these churches that were destroyed when the Turks conquered the country. Small buildings in the more inaccessible places were more often spared, but their decorations had mostly been done by local craftsmen, so that though they are interesting as examples of local peasant art, they seldom contain work that is of real aesthetic importance. The good work was, however, not all destroyed, and attention may be called to paintings in several churches at Tirnovo, to those in the Church of St George at Sofia, and to those at Boiana. The latter church contains work of varied types, some of which is of outstanding excellence, and some of it less sophisticated but more Bulgarian; the best work dates from 1259.

As in Greece and the rest of the Balkans, the Turkish conquests of the second half of the fifteenth century put an end to independence, but not to Christianity, and small churches continued to be built and works of art produced until quite recent times; they became more and more Bulgarian and less and less Byzantine as time proceeded. But though much of this work is of interest in the story of the peasant arts of the Balkans, it falls outside the sphere of Byzantine art proper.

The history of art in Serbia, that is to say the Orthodox portion of the country which is today called Yugoslavia, followed a course closely similar to that of Bulgaria, though it does not go back nearly so far. In early days, indeed, we know but little of the region, which was a wild outpost rather than a centre of civilization. It was not until the ninth century that the country was Christianized, principally owing to the labours of two Greek monks, Constantine (Cyril) and Methodius, who entered the region from Salonica. In the tenth century a part of the country was for a time subject to Bulgaria; in the eleventh it was under Byzantine control, and only with the twelfth was national independence achieved, under the leadership of Stephen Nemanja. For the first century or so of Serbian independence, however, links with the Byzantine world remained close, Greek painters seem to have been more numerous than native ones, and there were close links with the Greek Church, especially with Mount Athos. Stephen Nemanja even retired there in his old age, to live as a monk in the monastery of Chilandari, which was founded by him as a Serbian institution; though he was also joined with the Byzantine emperor as the patron of more than one purely Greek monastery on the peninsula.

The growth of Serbia as an independent power in the thirteenth century was assisted by the advances of the Crusades which were harrying Byzantine power, and a number of powerful rulers such as Stephen II (1219–27) and Milutin (1257–1320) succeeded in widening the bounds of the Empire very considerably. Dushan, who came to the throne in 1331, even dreamed of founding a Graeco-Slav state with himself at the head, but he died at Adrianople in 1355 before his ability to carry out this ambitious project, which was to begin with the capture of Constantinople, was put to the test. All the rulers at this time were great builders, and they were responsible for the foundation and decoration of a large number of churches and monasteries. Their architecture, though fundamentally based on the Byzantine, was much influenced by local and Western traits, and Millet notes in addition certain Eastern elements which came from Asia Minor by way of Greece, and not from Constantinople.[5] But the paintings inside these churches were more faithful to the old Byzantine heritage, and a good number of them were the work of Greek masters, anyhow as late as the fourteenth century. It is, indeed, on Serbian soil that many of the finest and most important manifestations of later Byzantine painting have been preserved. But alongside these, other paintings were set up which were of a more purely Slav character, and by the fourteenth century most of the work done in Serbia was becoming almost as distinctively Serb as Russian work had become Russian. Though the country was conquered by the Turks earlier than any other portion of the old Byzantine world,

Serb independence ending with the battle of Kossovo in 1389, Serbia retained under Turkish rule a greater degree of independence than any other part of the Balkans. The eastern and central parts of the country constituted the most important heir of Byzantium in the Balkans under Moslem rule; the western region was linked more closely with Italy, but though its faith was the Catholic and not the Orthodox, something of a Byzantine style affected developments even there until quite a late date.

One further heritor of Byzantium must also be mentioned here, though it is not entirely a Slav one, namely Rumania. The buildings and paintings of the country as a whole were essentially Byzantine in style, even though few of them were set up during the days of Byzantine rule. Patronage was, however, even at this late date, on a more lavish scale than elsewhere in the Balkans, for the country remained independent of Turkish control, and the local rulers and princes were often very prosperous. Numerous monasteries and churches were set up by them. In spite of a great many Western contacts, the architecture, as well as the paintings on the walls and the textiles and other treasures inside the churches, were essentially works of Byzantine type. Little of it was, perhaps, of the very first quality aesthetically speaking, for it belonged to an age of decadence. But nearly all of it was of interest, and it offers an intriguing field for study in view of the comparative completeness and good state of repair of the works that survive.

The actual division between the Byzantine and the Western worlds varied considerably at different periods. Thus in early times the whole of Italy was definitely included in the former, though by the seventh century it was independent, though still closely related; in the eleventh and twelfth centuries, however, parts of Italy, notably Sicily and Venice, had become virtually Byzantine provinces so far as the character of their arts was concerned, even if the rulers of these areas were independent. The rest of Italy at this time was, on the other hand, quite definitely of the West and not of the Byzantine world. In so far as the arts in Italy were purely Byzantine, they do not concern us in this chapter, for they have been dealt with elsewhere in the book. It is, rather, our aim to call attention to the legacy which the art of Byzantium handed on to those of other spheres, and consequently, when we speak of the West, or more narrowly, of Italy, it is to the area of Western and not of Byzantine culture that we refer.

In the period that must be our chief concern here, namely that between the seventh and the twelfth centuries, the West was more or less synonymous first with the Carolingian and then with the Ottonian Empire, that is to say, it comprised southern Germany and parts of France and Italy. But Britain must also be included, for links between Northumbria and the Byzantine world, broadly speaking, were important, and even if the Norse world need hardly be taken into account, Ireland must be noted, for there is evidence to suggest that there were trading contacts between Ireland and parts of the Byzantine Empire, even if they left no very marked impress on the art of the former country.

In addition to these distinctions of locality, a distinction must also be made regarding the character of the contacts between Byzantium and the West, anyhow so far as art is concerned. Thus two main types of connexion may be observed, the one primarily superficial and the other essentially fundamental. In the former, which may be termed the diplomatic type of contact, an exchange of products took place, rich silks or treasures of some sort or another being brought by ambassadors and given to the rulers or ecclesiastical dignitaries of the West as presents. Such things were very often copied, but the copy was a direct one, and the craftsman who made use of the imported model remained a copyist rather than becoming a creator. The influence exercised in this way was superficial, it was unlikely to be lasting, but where it was present it was obvious at first glance. The second type of influence that we distinguish was of a more profound, though sometimes less obvious, character. It was brought about as the result of the penetration of a new and distinct method, outlook, or idea from the Byzantine world, which resulted in a complete change in the nature of the art affected. Though in some ways the results of such influences are less easy to distinguish, they were far more fundamental and more lasting. Connexions of this type were especially marked at two periods, in the eighth century and again in the twelfth, and they are to be observed in the spheres of style, technique, and comprehension, that is to say the understanding or feeling underlying the superficial appearance of the work of art. Relationships of this sort were often of a very subtle character, and they are consequently not always to be discerned at first glance. They are again more important with regard to a mass of material than to single objects, as was the case with regard to the first type that we distinguished. The similarity of approach and outlook that charac-terized most religious painting in East and West alike, and the fact that there was a definite upswelling of a new spirit of creative energy in the art of both areas in the twelfth century, affords a case in point. Before analysing these manifestations further, however, the evidence for contacts between East and West had best be examined in chronological sequence.

Of the fourth and fifth centuries we know but little. There seem to have been a number of Jewish colonies settled in the West, more especially at Arles, and they maintained a definite contact with Palestine and imported from their homeland certain works of art, more especially glass and textiles. Ivories and paintings on panel on a small scale were also doubtless brought from Palestine by Christian pilgrims; the importance of religious pilgrimage even at this early date is clearly shown by the large numbers of flasks to contain holy water which have been found at such shrines as that of St Menas,

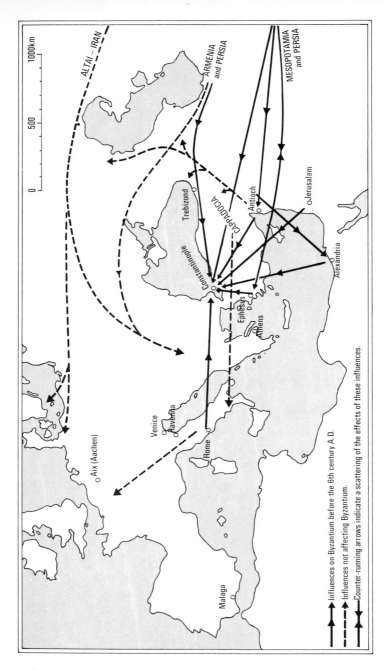

1000km

500

0

ALTAI – IRAN

ARMENIA and PERSIA

MESOPOTAMIA and PERSIA

Trebizond

Antioch

○ Jerusalem

CAPPADOCIA

Constantinople

Alexandria

Ephesus

Athens

Venice

Ravenna

Rome

○ Aix (Aachen)

Malaga

Influences on Byzantium before the 6th century A.D.

Influences not affecting Byzantium.

Counter-running arrows indicate a scattering of the effects of these influences.

536

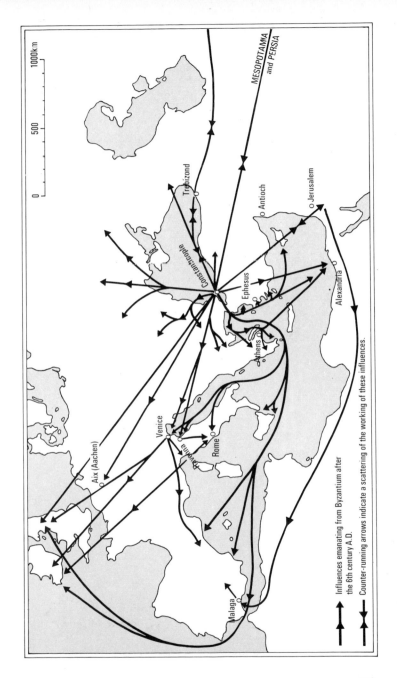

1000 km
500
0

MESOPOTAMIA
and PERSIA

Trebizond

Antioch

Jerusalem

Constantinople

Ephesus

Alexandria

Athens

Venice

Rome

Ravenna

Aix (Aachen)

Malaga

Influences emanating from Byzantium after
the 6th century A.D.

Counter-running arrows indicate a scattering of the working of these influences.

537

not far from Alexandria in Egypt. Considerable numbers of them are now preserved at Monza in Italy. Textiles of linen or wool may also have been brought to the West from Syria, Palestine, and Egypt; the export of silk was retained as a monopoly by Constantinople until the eighth century, but it was not much exported before the sixth century, for until then the secret of its manufacture was known only in the Far East, and all the raw material had to be imported from there, by way of Persia. Before the knowledge of its cultivation was sold to Justinian, the cost of silk must have been prohibitive, and it is unlikely that very much reached the West, even if it was occasionally used in Italy.

In the sixth century relationships between the West and Palestine were maintained, or even increased as a result of pilgrimage. With Constantinople they became rather closer owing to the prosperity of the capital under Justinian's rule. A number of pilgrims passed that way *en route* for the Holy Land, and others made Constantinople the main object of their journey; among these was Réoval, a doctor of Poitiers, who visited the city in order to discourse with the doctors there. In the reign of Justin II (565–78) St Radegonde went to the Byzantine capital, and took back with her relics of the True Cross, as well as a finely bound copy of the Gospels, and shortly after this visit Justin sent her a present of a reliquary, which is probably that still preserved in the Church of St Croix at Poitiers. The same Emperor also sent a large cross to Rome, and Tiberius II (578–82) dispatched presents to Chilperic. Towards the end of the century Gregory the Great was papal envoy at Constantinople before he became pope; by that time most of the more important relics had been assembled there. He apparently made the journey more than once, and on each occasion brought back relics with him. He was very familiar with many parts of the Byzantine Empire, and seems to have travelled extensively in the East. The Byzantine character of work produced in Italy at this time is clearly marked; the Treasurers of the Cathedral at Monza serve as examples.

Quite a number of journeys were also made in an opposite direction, for Greeks often visited the West; there was a whole colony of them for example at Narbonne, and a painting of Christ which was renowned as one of Narbonne's principal treasures was very probably by a Byzantine artist.[1] The Greeks were primarily merchants, and the extent of the trade which these people and similar bodies carried on is indicated by the large numbers of Byzantine coins dating from between about 300 and 650 which have been found in France. The Frankish coinage was subsequently even modelled on these Byzantine prototypes. Similarly Byzantine ivories served as models for Frankish carvings, both on a large and on a small scale, and it is possible that paintings were copied also. A number of Byzantine saints were popular in the West, and a church at Chartres was dedicated to the Greek patrons, SS. Sergius and Bacchus, though later its patron was changed to St Nicholas.

Relationships between East and West in the seventh century must have continued on a similar basis, but Constantinople gradually became more and more important as the destination of the pilgrim traffic, and its importance in this respect was of course accentuated when the holy cities in Palestine fell to the Moslems early in the century, for not only did the holy cities become very difficult of access, but, more important, the True Cross was taken to Constantinople. St Bercaire, abbot of Montier-en-Der, Haute-Marne, did actually get to Palestine, and he brought back carved ivories, but Arculf of Gaul concentrated on Constantinople, and even wrote a guide-book of the city, which served pilgrims for some centuries to come. Colonies of Greeks and Syrians still continued to exist in the West, and trade seems to have been very extensive at this time. The links seem to have been extended as far as England and Ireland, and in the latter place even Chinese objects have been found.[2] St Columbanus is recorded to have lodged with a Syrian family during a visit to Orléans.

With the eighth and ninth centuries relationships between East and West became even more intimate, for the Carolingian rulers, however powerful themselves, and however much they desired to establish a new Rome in the West, nevertheless looked to Byzantium as a model and as a centre of culture and art which could not be disregarded. Numerous embassies were interchanged between the emperors of East and West at this time, and most of those from the East took with them gorgeous presents, many of which are still preserved in Western treasuries. The actual dates at which these embassies were sent are in many cases recorded. Thus Constantine V Copronymus (740–75) sent envoys to Pepin le Bref in 758. Charlemagne received others at Aachen in 812, sent by Michael I, and two years later a further embassy was sent to Louis at the same place. Another followed in 824 to Rouen, another in 833 to Compiègne, and another in 839 to Ingelheim. Costly gifts were sent on each occasion, and it is recorded that Charlemagne's court was all clothed in silks, mostly of Byzantine manufacture. Textiles from the emperor's tomb at Aachen are of Constantinopolitan workmanship; one was probably introduced into the tomb subsequent to the burial. Both Charlemagne and Louis the Pious were familiar with the Greek language,[3] and Greek was read in some of the Western monasteries; it is recorded that the Greek Gospels were admired at Corbie. Louis thus received from Michael II (820-9), in addition to silks, a copy of the writings of Denys the Areopagite. Further evidence as to contacts is afforded by a correspondence between Basil I, the Macedonian (867-86), and Louis II. Charles the Bald appeared in Byzantine dress at the assembly of Ponthieu in 876, and at the Abbey of St Riquier numerous Byzantine treasures were preserved. Presents to ecclesiastics seem to have been almost as numerous as those to emperors; thus Fortunatus, bishop of Grado, brought to France in 803 'two doors of ivory, magnificently carved'; in the Abbey of St Wandrille there was a fine Byzantine text, and at St Denys there were Eastern textiles, with animals, birds, and gryphons as their decoration.

With so much actual Byzantine material in the West, an effect on art which reached fairly deep was not surprising, and its results can be traced in architecture, ivory carving, and to some extent also in miniature painting. And there is reason to believe that the penetration of the influence was accentuated by the arrival of actual artists, who preferred during the Iconoclast period (726–843) to work for Western patrons rather than to adapt their art to non-representational motifs in their own homeland. They were especially numerous in Italy, and without them Italian art would have developed along lines very different from those actually taken. The remarkable paintings at Castelseprio near Milan are perhaps to be accounted for in this way. They also penetrated north of the Alps. Indeed, the marked revival in quality which characterized the period with which we are dealing was in no small degree due to the presence of the Byzantine craftsmen and to the new methods and ideas which they taught the local men. It is recorded, moreover, that people in the West took a great interest in the Iconoclast movement, and special councils were held to discuss it at Gentilly in 767, at Frankfurt in 794, and at Paris in 825.

It would, of course, be wrong to overstress the final influence of all these contacts on the West, for however marked the Byzantine elements may have been, the art of the Western world as a whole was Western art, just as that of the Eastern world was Byzantine, and this became especially noticeable with the dawn of the tenth century, when affairs in the West had been able to settle down and development along native lines had become possible. The results are to be seen most clearly, perhaps, in architecture, where a new and distinct style, which is now usually termed the First Romanesque, had been born.[4] This style was distinguished by the small size of its buildings, by the use of barrel vaults to roof them, and by arcaded or niched ornament to decorate them. It spread over much of France, over northern Spain, and northern Italy, and definitely preceded the development of the more ambitious style which we know as full Romanesque. It was a quite distinctive style, essentially Western in its make-up, but the elements which went to compose it were many of them culled from the Byzantine world, or even from farther to the east, though elements that were ultimately of Persian origin, like blank arcading, probably penetrated to the First Romanesque area by way of the Byzantine region.

In the realm of sculpture somewhat similar developments took place in Britain at a rather earlier date, thanks to contacts with the Mediterranean world. Benedict Biscop thus visited Rome and brought back treasures with him. St Theodore who preached in England in the seventh century was a Greek from Tarsus; his contemporary, Adrian, came from one of the Byzantine provinces. Along with them there appear to have come a number of artisans, for it is recorded that, when Wilfrid decorated St Andrew's at Hexham between 671 and 674, foreign craftsmen assisted in the work. One may conclude that these foreign masters did some of the work themselves, but left the greater part of it to native assistants. The high technical quality of the carving attests the presence of the foreigners, but the individual character of much of the sculpture of this period shows what the pupils were able to give in their turn. Even when the foreign masters were absent, imported prototypes were often followed very closely, as can be seen on the southern face of the Ruthwell cross, where Christ appears as an essentially Byzantine figure. In another scene on the same cross, where Mary Magdalene is shown washing Christ's feet with her hair, our Lord is admirably done, in an essentially Byzantine style, and it is clear that an imported model was closely followed; the Magdalene, on the other hand, is a strange, clumsy figure, lacking all elegance and classical grandeur; here it would seem that the native craftsman was

470 Ruthwell cross. Christ treading on the Asp and Basilisk. Mary washing Christ's feet. *c.* 700

working with no imported model before him, and when he tried to create in this way the results were extremely crude. Similarly the figures of the evangelists in the Lindisfarne Gospels, of much the same date, are basically modelled on Byzantine originals, even to the extent of writing the Greek word for saint, 'Agios', instead of the Latin word, 'Sanctus', though the actual letters are Latin and not Greek. Here the copyist produced rather cruder work than he did in the case of the sculptures, but when he was allowed to follow the native idiom of zoomorphic interlace he produced work of quite extraordinary merit.

This intrusion of the Byzantine style into Northumbria was brought to an end by the Norse invasions of the eighth and ninth centuries, but it continued elsewhere. Thus in Mercia sculptures at

Breedon follow Byzantine models quite obviously, and rather later there are stones in Ireland which attest the influence of East Christian iconography; a cross at Castledermot may be cited.[5] But nowhere was the influence more marked than in Wessex in the tenth and eleventh centuries, where such sculptures as the Bradford-on-Avon angels, the Romsey rood, or a slab with the Crucifixion in St Dunstan's, Stepney, were carved in an essentially Byzantine style. The Byzantine affinities of the York Madonna are again striking, and though less marked, the same is true of the ivories and the miniature paintings done after the Conquest. Professor G. F. Browne thus noted that the art of the beautiful books came to Britain from Byzantium.[6] His conclusions have been subsequently borne out by further researches of a technical as well as a stylistic and iconographic character. Professor A. P. Lawrie, for example, states that the purpurea shell-fish was used for the manufacture of pigment in Ireland, though otherwise it was only known in the Carolingian and Byzantine spheres. Actually, many of these Byzantine elements came to these islands by way of the Continent, especially thanks to Carolingian and Ottonian influence.

The links that bound the Carolingian and the Byzantine cultures have already been noted. They were continued during the Ottonian period in much the same way; indeed, they were probably intensified for, in addition to the exchange of embassies, Otto II (955–83) actually married a Byzantine princess, Theophano. An ivory in the Cluny Museum in Paris, which depicts their coronation, is a direct, if somewhat clumsy, copy of a Byzantine rendering of the subject, where the coronation of Romanos and Eudoxia is shown; there are other Ottonian ivories which are just as Byzantine in style as is this one in iconography. Indeed, it is likely that Theophano brought with her some Byzantine artists in addition to courtiers, and these men must have exercised a considerable influence on the subsequent development of Ottonian art. It is recorded that Otto III (980–1002) consciously modelled the culture of his realm on that of Constantinople.[7]

Farther to the south, the thoroughly Byzantine character of the art and culture of Venice and its neighbourhood exercised a far-reaching effect on the rest of Italy, parts of the country taking on a renewed Byzantine apparel, at times almost as pure as that which they had worn in the old days of Justinian and the exarchate of Ravenna. Even in those parts of Italy which were not so fully

Byzantinized, craftsmen and artists from the Eastern Empire did a good deal of work; its nature has been fully examined by Frothingham, who had also studied the influence exercised by Byzantium on Rome in later medieval times.[8] He shows, for example, that the technique which is usually associated with the name of the Cosmati and which was developed so strikingly in Italy in the thirteenth century was actually derived from the Byzantine technique known as 'opus Alexandrinum'.

Outside the frontiers of Italy in the twelfth century it was probably in France that Byzantine influence was most to the fore. Thus a whole group of buildings in the south-west of that country show marked Byzantine characteristics, more especially in the fact that they are roofed with domes. St Front at Périgueux is the best known of them. It is probable that this church was modelled more or less directly upon St Mark's at Venice, and that the idea of the dome as roof form was also disseminated in the region thanks to the presence of Greek colonies in a number of centres. There is not very much that can be directly attributed to Byzantium in the sculptures of this region, nor even in those of Provence or Burgundy, but the wall paintings of the latter region are often markedly East Christian, notably those in the small Church of Berzé-la-Ville near Cluny and at Le Puy; it has even been suggested that the paintings at Cluny itself, which were preserved until the destruction of the church soon after the French Revolution, were the work of a Greek artist. Indeed, the wall paintings of France in the first half of the eleventh century can be divided into two principal groups, the one essentially native and Romanesque, the other markedly Byzantine in style. It is probable that the Byzantine influence, so far as it affected large-scale painting, penetrated by way of the Abbey of Monte Cassino in Italy,[9] and Abbot Desiderius at Monte Cassino was responsible for bringing Greek craftsmen who worked there and in the Church of Sant'Angelo in Formis near Naples. Byzantine motifs of decoration or forms of ornament which are sometimes to be found in the manuscripts or in architectural sculptures were, on the other hand, more probably copied directly from imported objects, more especially textiles. Eagle capitals, which are quite common, afford the most striking example of such a copying.[10]

The Byzantine influence which is to be seen in early Romanesque painting in France also seems to have penetrated to northern Spain, and work of the interesting Catalan school often appears to be linked with the East Christian world. Paintings in the Leon and Valladolid regions are again óften Byzantine in style. The Eastern elements perhaps in this case penetrated by way of Sicily; Islamic art in Spain and Sicily had been closely linked for a century or more.

In addition to such contacts as these, due to travelling artists, the copying of imported objects, or the movement of monks and the consequent transference of religious ideas, large-scale communication between the West and the Byzantine world was much increased after the eleventh century. Thus the Byzantine Empire and the West united to restore the Holy Sepulchre to Christendom, and in 1099 the First Crusade reached Jerusalem; it was probably almost at exactly the same time that the interior of the third Church of Cluny was being decorated with frescoes, which, as already stated, were in so Byzantine a style that they have been regarded as the work of a Greek craftsman. The majority of the Western troops taking part in the Crusade went thither by way of Constantinople, and a special and more than usually impressive service was held in Sancta Sophia for the benefit of the members of the First Crusade. Pilgrims and travellers followed in the steps of the military and they all brought back treasures and relics with them. Some fifty years later Louis VII, the leader of the Second Crusade, was received by Manuel I (1143–80) at the Blachernae Palace, and was shown most of the churches and treasures of Constantinople; he took back with him a number of treasures, notably silks, and some of his followers seem to have also taken Greek wives. In 1176 the friendly relationships which had been set on foot by this visit were cemented by the marriage of the Byzantine prince imperial Alexios with Louis's daughter, Agnes. She came to the throne as the queen of Alexios II, but survived him and married the next emperor, Andronicos I, whom she also survived, to become finally the wife of a Byzantine nobleman, Theodore Branas.

All these links, which boded so well for future relationships, were, however, rudely shattered by the action of the Fourth Crusade, for instead of attacking the infidel, its members turned their energies towards the sack and looting of Constantinople. The richness of the treasures that were destroyed at this time was inconceivable; it was far more considerable than the very large amount that was stolen and transported to the West, where it has since been preserved in the treasuries of numerous churches and cathedrals, especially in that of St Mark's at Venice.[11] But though the Byzantine loot was prized, it was not copied in the same way that the presents of ivory, metal, and textiles had been copied in the preceding centuries, for each region of the West had by now developed its own art to a stage where copying was no longer called for. And though in 1470 Louis XI sent for Greek and Italian workmen to manufacture silks, the work that they executed was more Western than Eastern. Moreover, with the advance of the Turks into Asia Minor, the wealth, the power, and the influence of the Byzantine world had become much restricted, and from the thirteenth century onwards the Moslem world began to replace the Byzantine as the fabulous home of the most gorgeous materials and the richest and most sumptuous objects.

Even so, however, the role of Byzantium was still not at an end. On the one hand, the writings of the Greek philosophers were brought to the West from Byzantium at this time, to serve as the basis for a new age of philosophical study in the West.[12] On the other, painting was developed along rather new lines, and soon after the middle of the twelfth century the Second Byzantine Renaissance began to exercise an influence on developments in the West, which was finally to some degree responsible for the better-known Italian Renaissance of the fourteenth century. Here once more the influence is to be traced in several distinct ways, notably in iconography, in technique and colouring, and in style and interpretation. Similarities of iconography always constitute the most sure proof of contact, and Millet has examined in the minutest detail all the links from the thirteenth century onwards in his great book on the iconography of the Gospels. The thread leads from the Byzantine world directly to Italy, and the works of Cimabue (1240-1302), Duccio (c. 1260-1339), Cavallini (c. 1269-1344), and Giotto (1276-1337) show very strong Byzantine affinities, as do those of the numerous lesser well-known painters of the same period. And the influence is not only to be discerned in the work of the primitives; it affected also many of the more developed painters of the Quattrocento; Mantegna may be cited as one of the most striking examples.[13]

In addition to the influences exercised on Italian artists, the presence of Greek painters in Italy must also be noted. These men continued to produce more or less purely Byzantine works until the seventeenth century. Their works were, admittedly, not of the first importance, but they were quite often of quality, and their study constitutes a very interesting sideline in the history of art. The most important colony of these artists was at Venice, where they worked mainly for the members of the large Greek colony that was estab-

471 San Francesco, Assisi. The Virgin with Angels and St Francis. Fresco by Cimabue. End of thirteenth century

lished there; many of their works are preserved in the Church of St George of the Greeks in that city, but there are also examples in many of the larger Italian galleries, such as the Uffizi at Florence or the Vatican at Rome. In addition there was quite a flourishing Adriatic school, in the works of which the style of Bellini was curiously mingled with that of later Byzantine painting.

It is highly likely that the Greek painter Domenicos Theotocopoulos came into contact with the Greek artists working in Venice when he came to that city from his native Crete early in the last quarter of the sixteenth century. But there was nothing that he could learn from them, and it was rather towards the work of the great Venetian masters like Titian, Tintoretto, and Bassano that his gaze was directed. But when he had got to Spain he seems to have felt a strange nostalgia for his homeland and its art, and Byzantine

472 Private possession. Panel by Domenicos Theotocopoulos (El Greco).
St Andrew. *c.* 1604–10

elements once more began to come to the fore. Spain and its countryside, eclecticism, and the mystical philosophical speculations of his
day perhaps exercised the most important influence on the development of his style, but the Byzantine basis was never forgotten, and he
may fairly be classed not only as one of the last, but also as one of
the greatest, of Byzantine painters.

Such was, we believe, the Byzantine legacy. The Byzantine tradition was one of the fundamental elements at the basis of Carolingian,

548

of Northumbrian, and of Ottonian art; its influence can be traced throughout medieval Europe and even in Spain and Ireland; it played a very important role in the formation of art in Saxon England and in Germany; it was behind the work of the greatest early painters of Italy, and it was present even in the work of the Italian Renaissance. It was Byzantium that conserved art and culture throughout the Dark Ages; it was Byzantium that made the development of European culture possible; it was Byzantium that served as a bulwark between the West and the rising power of Islam. Most striking of all, however, is perhaps the fact that it is to Byzantium that our gaze now tends to turn for inspiration, enlightenment, and justification, and it is there that are to be found some of the most convincing parallels to the tentative strivings and abstract comprehensions of modern artists. A knowledge of Byzantine art and civilization is thus not only an important study, a delight and an entertainment in itself; it is not only something which is essential towards the full understanding of European culture and history in the past; but it can also help us to sympathize with the aims of artists of our own day and enable us, perhaps, to comprehend more easily the demands and ideas of this troubled age through which we are passing.

Table of Important Dates

The East

Seleucid and kindred dynasties	330 B.C.–200 B.C.
Parthian period	200 B.C.–A.D. 222
Sasanian period	222–650
Arab expansion over Persia, Syria, and Egypt	638–642
The Omayyad dynasty (capital at Damascus)	661–750
The Abbasid dynasty (capital at Baghdad)	750–1258
The Seljuks in Asia Minor	1077–1327
The Ottoman Turks in Asia Minor	1300–1453
The Ottoman Turks at Constantinople	From 1453

The Central Area

Year of creation according to Byzantine reckoning	5508 B.C.
Foundation of Constantinople by Constantine	330
Age of Justinian	527–565
The Iconoclast period	726–843
The Latin domination of Constantinople	1204–1261
The First Bulgarian Empire	679–1018
The Second Bulgarian Empire	1186–1393
The Serbian Empires	1169–1389
Byzantine domination of Sicily	878–909
Norman conquest of Sicily	1071
Conquest of Constantinople by the Turks	1453

Notes

1 Byzantium: the Historical Background

1 She had her own separate emperors, who ruled conjointly with those of the East, till 480.
2 Vasiliev, *Histoire de l'Empire byzantin*, I, p. 222.
3 Rome fell to the Goths in 410, and this warning of the growth of barbarian power was taken in Constantinople.
4 Gaul and the north were already under Frankish control, and it was in this period that they began to grow up as important centres of an independent culture.
5 It was at this date that the cultivation of silk was introduced from the East; see p. 488.
6 The first Islamic dynasty, the Omayyad, ruled at Damascus till 749, when a new house, the Abbasid, transferred the capital to Baghdad. Omayyad art and culture centred in Syria, and was in the main of Byzantine type, whereas those of the Abbasids were essentially Persian in character.
7 The Iconoclast doctrine, supported by the Court and the Army, was most strictly enforced at Constantinople. In more distant places, and more especially in monastic circles, it was never generally accepted.
8 A number of Greek churches were founded in the region of Bari in the tenth century, and there still survive in the same area a large number of rock-cut chapels, the interiors of which are painted in a Byzantine style.
9 For the importance of later Byzantine literature see Vasiliev, *Histoire de l'Empire byzantin*, II, p. 422. He gives a full bibliography of writings which bear upon the subject.

2 The Geographical Basis of Byzantine Culture

1 *L'Ecole grecque dans l'architecture byzantine*, Paris, 1916.

3 The Origins of Byzantine Art

1 The role of Christianity as an essential formative influence will be considered later. It may be noted that many writers, notably Guyer, regard the Christian religion and the character of Byzantine thought resulting from it as far more important than either 'Rome' or 'The East'. See S. Guyer, 'Vom Wesen der

Byzantinischen Kunst', *Münchner Jahrbuch der bildenden Kunst.*, N.F., VIII, 1931, p. 99.

2 See for instance E. H. Swift, *The Roman Sources of Christian Art*, New York, 1951, *passim*. He would assign practically all elements to Rome.

3 The Hittites must have found something in the nature of an established culture when they arrived in Asia Minor between 2000 and 1500 B.C., if we may judge by the difference in character between the monuments which they erected in Asia Minor, such as Boghazköy and Eyuk, and those which they left in northern Syria, most notably at Sencirli and Karkemish.

4 The most characteristic monuments in the style are some tombstones in the Bursa Museum, known as the Altyn Tash stelae. See G. Mendel, *Catalogue du Musée de Brousse*, Athens, 1908, p. 35. See also J. W. Crowfoot, in the *Annual of the British School at Athens*, IV, 1897–8, p. 79.

5 See M. Rostovtzeff, *Caravan Cities*, Oxford, 1932.

6 Parthian art, however, also drew from the old Oriental 'animal art' to which we allude when speaking of the Altai-Iranian element.

7 In his recent book, *The Roman Sources of Christian Art*, Swift attributes the origin of this branch of art to Rome and not to the East, and suggests that it was adopted in Syria as a result of Roman imperialism. This is most unlikely, for the whole style is quite foreign to what may throughout history be regarded as typical of Rome. And in any case, it was in Syria that the style was most fully developed; in such an instance it is the area of full development that counts even more than the area in which an idea was first conceived.

8 See D. Talbot Rice, 'Iranian Elements in Byzantine Art', *Congrès International d'Art et d'Archéologie Iraniens*, Moscow-Leningrad, 1939.

9 The stag from Zoldhalompuszta, now in the Budapest Museum, is one of the finest examples of the art; see Nandor Fetich, *La Trouvaille scythe de Zold-halompuszta*, Budapest, 1928. For a general survey see G. Borovka, *Scythian Art*, London, 1928, and T. Talbot Rice, *The Scythians*, London, 1957.

10 See M. G. Kacarov, 'Notes sur la sculpture rupestre de Madara', in *L'Art byzantin chez les Slaves*, I, i, p. 87.

11 See an extremely interesting article by I. Meschaninov, 'The value of Linguistic Material in the study of Ancient Monuments', in *G.A.I.M.K.*, nos I and 2, Moscow, 1932 (in Russian). Its scientific value is, however, marred by a futile use of the word 'bourgeois' where it is in no sense applicable.

4   The Architectural Background

1 For the walls see Van Millingen, *Constantinople: the Walls of the City and adjoining Historical Sites*, London, 1899, and F. Krischen, *Die Landmauer von Konstantinopel*, Berlin, 1938. For the cisterns and water-supply see Dalman, *Der Valens-Aquadukt in Konstantinopel*, Bamberg, 1933, and Strzygowski and Forchheimer, *Die Byzantinischen Wasserbehälter von Konstantinopel*, Wien, 1893.

2 When further researches come to be made, the arrangement of the courses and the size and shape of the actual bricks will doubtless prove of considerable interest in tracing out the lines of connexion between the various regions where brick was used.

3 Rivoira, *Lombardic Architecture*, London, 1910, II, p. 13.

4 The influence of the synagogue on Christian orientation was also probably important. See Helen Rosenau, *Design and Mediaeval Architecture*, London, 1934, ch. I.

5 G. Millet, *L'Ecole grecque dans l'architecture byzantine*, Paris, 1916.

6 See D. Talbot Rice, 'New Light on the Circular Domed Building', *Seventh International Congress of Byzantine Studies*, Palermo, 1951.

7 The evolution of the plan has been fully studied by K. A. C. Creswell, *Early Muslim Architecture*, Oxford, 1932, I, p. 72.

8 'Preliminary Report on Excavations at Bosra', *Palestine Exploration Fund Quarterly*, 1936.

9 The case for Syria has been admirably put by Creswell, *Early Muslim Architecture*, I.

10 In the shrine of St Menas, to be dated between 400 and 410. See J. B. Ward Perkins, 'The Shrine of St Menas at Maryut', *Papers of the British School at Rome*, XVII, 1949, p. 57.

11 W. M. Ramsay and G. L. Bell, *The Thousand and One Churches*, London, 1909. E. Herzfeld and S. Guyer, 'Meryamlik und Korykos', in *Monumenta Asiae Minoris Antiqua*, III, Manchester, 1930, p. 74.

12 The domed churches of southern France constitute an interesting group. They must have been inspired by Byzantine originals, but the route by which the influence was conveyed is by no means certain.

13 The earliest tall drums occur in Armenia, and even if all that Strzygowski attributes to that land is exaggerated, it is fairly certain that the idea of the tall drum came to the Byzantine world from there.

14 The earliest detached bell tower in the West is probably that at St Martin's at Tours, which is dated 470. There are early-sixth-century examples at Ravenna, but towers were not usual before the ninth century.

15 The great profusion of icons which existed until the Revolution in Russia and survives today in Greece was not attempted in Byzantine times, but there is reason to believe that the artistic quality of those that did appear was outstandingly high.

5 Byzantine Mosaics

1 See E. Kitzinger, in *Dumbarton Oaks Papers*, no. 6, Harvard, 1951. Other floors are, however, of a conservative character and have no Christian connotation. See Doro Levi, *Antioch Mosaic Pavements*, Princeton, 1947, *The Great Palace of the Byzantine Emperors* (Walker Trust Excavations), I, Oxford, 1947, and II, Edinburgh, 1958, and B. Pace, *I Mosaici di Piazza Armerina*, Rome, 1955.

2 See C. R. Morey, *Early Christian Art*, Princeton, 1942, p. 146, who asserts that they are of the same date as the mosaics of the triumphal arch.

3 Benesevic, 'Date de la mosaïque du Mont Sinai', *Byzantion*, I, 1924, p. 145.

4 Traces of another mosaic survive in Cyprus in a small church at Livadia in the Karpass, but no figures are preserved.

5 Similar, though less elaborate, mosaics existed in the Church of the Nativity at Bethlehem; and in the tomb of Beybars, at Damascus, there are some

twelfth-century mosaics which copy those of the Great Mosque; they are much inferior.

6 P. A. Underwood, 'A Preliminary Report on Some Unpublished Mosaics in Hagia Sophia', *American Journal of Archaeology*, *55*, no. 4, 1951, p. 367.

7 For dating see P. A. Underwood and C. Mango in *Dumbarton Oaks Papers*, no. 13, 1959, pp. 235 and 245. For illustrations see T. Schmidt, *Die Koimesis-Kirche von Nikaia*, Berlin and Leipzig, 1927.

8 C. Mango and E. J. Hawkins, 'The Apse Mosaics of St Sophia at Istanbul', in *Dumbarton Oaks Papers*, no. 19, 1965, p. 113.

9 Ainalov assigns these mosaics to the ninth, Muratov to the tenth, and Diehl to the eleventh centuries. Demus, *Byzantine Mosaic Decoration*, London, 1947, p. 53, cites authority for the date 886.

10 T. Whittemore, *The Mosaics of Sophia at Istanbul*, Oxford: First Report, 1933; Second Report, 1936; Third Report, 1942; Fourth Report, 1952; also *Dumbarton Oaks Papers*, no. 13, Oxford, 1961.

11 Schneider, however, suggests that the emperor is Basil I (867–86). See *Istanbuler Forschungen*, VIII, Berlin, 1936, p. 32.

12 *Mediaeval Art*, New York, 1942, p. 107.

13 *The Mosaics of Norman Sicily*, London, 1949. Demus's datings do not always tally with those proposed by Lazarev, 'The Mosaics of Cefalù', *Art Bulletin*, XVII, 1935, p. 134. But Demus's survey is the more thorough.

14 For the St Mark's mosaics, see O. Demus, *The Church of San Marco in Venice*, Dumbarton Oaks, VI, Washington (forthcoming).

15 Diez and Demus, *Byzantine Mosaics in Greece*, Harvard, 1931, p. 116. See also Perdrizet and Chesnay, 'La Métropole de Serres', in *Monuments Piot*, X, 1903.

16 F. Dölger, E. Wiegand, and A. Deindl, *Mönchsland Athos*, Munich, 1942, Abbn. 65, 66, and 67.

17 Noted by Lazarev, *History of Russian Painting*, Moscow, 1947, p. 134. See also his article, 'The Mosaics at Cefalù', *Art Bulletin*, XVII, 1935, p. 213, n. 53, and Figs 26 and 28.

18 They have recently been admirably published; see P. A. Underwood, *The Kariye Djami*, Pantheon Books, 1966.

19 Dölger, Wiegand, and Deindl, *Mönchsland Athos*, Munich, 1942, p. 141.

6 Wall Paintings

1 The most up-to-date account of painting in Italy at this period is that of Anthony, *Romanesque Frescoes*, Princeton, 1951. See also R. van Marle, *The Development of the Italian Schools of Painting*, I, The Hague, 1923.

2 Muratov, *Les Icones russes*, Paris, 1927, Pl. 13.

3 For these paintings see C. Breasted, *Oriental Forerunners of Byzantine Painting*, Yale, 1924.

4 This is stressed by B. V. Baur, *The Christian Church at Dura-Europos*, Yale, 1934, p. 46.

5 See L. E. Browne, *The Eclipse of Christianity in Asia*, Cambridge, 1933.

6 See A. Musil, *Kusejr Amra*, Vienna, 1907.

7   *La Peinture religieuse en Bulgarie*, Paris, 1928, p. 22.

8   Jerphanion, *Les Eglises rupestres de la Cappadoce*, Paris, 1923–42. Four vols of text and three albums of plates. See also N. and M. Thierry, *Nouvelles Eglises rupestres de Cappadoce*, Paris, 1963.

9   T. Wiegand, *Der Latmos*, being vol. iii, part i, of *Milet: Ergebnisse der Ausgrabungen und Untersuchungen*, Berlin, 1913.

10 A. Medea, *Gli Affreschi delle Cripte eremitiche Pugliesi*, Rome, 1949.

11 For the Armenian work as a whole see S. der Nersessian, *Armenia and the Byzantine Empire*, Harvard, 1945.

12 Kurt Weitzmann, *The Fresco Cycle of S. Maria di Castelseprio*, Princeton, 1951, supports a tenth-century date. C. R. Morey, 'Castelseprio and the Byzantine Renaissance', *Art Bulletin*, xxxiv, 1952, favours the seventh century; and others have suggested the eighth.

13 A complete monograph on Nerez, with coloured plates, is still awaited. But there are some good reproductions in Vercors, *L'Art médiéval Yougoslave*, Paris, 1949. The most complete text is that of Okunev, 'La Découverte des anciennes fresques du monastère de Nerez', *Slavia*, vi, Prague, 1927, p. 603. See also D. Talbot Rice and S. Radojćić, *Yugoslav Mediaeval Frescoes*, Unesco, 1951.

14 Kondakov, *Histoire de l'art byzantin*, Paris, 1891.

15 Especially Schmidt and Strzygowski. See 'La Renaissance de la peinture byzantine au XIVme siècle', in *Revue Archéologique*, xx, 1912, ii, p. 127. See also Ainalov, *Byzantine Painting in the Fourteenth Century*, Petrograd, 1917 (in Russian).

16 S. Radojćić, *Mileseva*, Belgrade, 1963.

17 V. J. Djurić, *Sopocani*, Belgrade, 1963.

18 See his chapters in A. Michel, *Histoire de l'art*, i and iii, pt 2, Paris, 1905, and also his *Iconographie de l'Evangile*, Paris, 1916.

19 M. Alpatov, 'Die Fresken der Kachrije-Djami in Konstantinopel', in *Münchner Jahrbücher der bildenden Kunst*, vi, 1929, p. 345.

20 He probably did them soon after 1300. See A. Xyngopoulos, *Manuel Panselinos*, Athens, 1956.

21 Since 1930, when these observations were written, much of the work at and near Trebizond has been destroyed.

22 W. H. Buckler and others, 'The Church of Asinou, Cyprus, and its Frescoes', *Archaeologia*, lxxxiii, 1934, p. 327.

23 For notes on this Western influence see O. M. Dalton and Lord Balcarres, in *Proceedings of the Society of Antiquaries*, London, 1901–3, xix, p. 137.

24 The best edition of *The Painter's Guide* is that of Papadopoulos Keramaeus, in Greek, published at St Petersburg in 1909. A French translation appears in Didron, *Manuel d'iconographie chrétienne*, Paris, 1845, and an English summary in Stokes, *Christian Iconography*, London, 1886, 2 vols.

7   Manuscript Illustrations

1   It was adopted first in the Islamic world and then in the Byzantine. See F. Hirth, *Chinesische Studien*, Munich and Leipzig, 1890, i, p. 259.

2   See K. Weitzmann, *Die armenische Buchmalerei des 10. und beginnenden 11.*

Jahrhunderts, Bamberg, 1933. A sixth-century date was suggested by Strzygowski.

3   M. Rostovtzeff, 'Dura and the problem of Parthian Art', *Yale Classical Studies*, v, 1935, p. 282. He discusses the dissemination of this particular type of stylized tree and notes its presence in the Ashburnham Pentateuch.

4   H. Gerstinger, *Die Wiener Genesis*, Wien, 1931, I, p. 176, favours a sixth-century date.

5   C. R. Morey, *Early Christian Art*, Princeton, 1942, p. 19. *Mediaeval Art*, New York, 1942, p. 50.

6   *The Joshua Roll*, Princeton, 1948.

7   See Doro Levi, *Antioch Mosaic Pavements*, Princeton, 1948. The pavement from the Great Palace at Constantinople is probably to be dated to the later sixth century; see *The Great Palace of the Byzantine Emperors*, I, Oxford, 1947, and II, Edinburgh, 1958.

8   For instance C. R. Morey, *Mediaeval Art*, p. 50. For illustrations see Omont, *Miniatures des manuscrits grecs de la Bibliothèque Nationale*, Paris, 1929.

9   A. Venturi has much of interest to say on differences of style, but he fails to take into account the importance of stylistic differences in the model; see *Storia del Arte*, II, p. 458. The whole manuscript has been reproduced in facsimile; *Il Menologio di Basilio II*, Vatican Codices, VIII, Turin, 1907.

10 See his *Art byzantin*, Paris, 1924, p. 63, and also 'Les Miniatures des Homélies du Moine Jacques et le théâtre religieux à Byzance', in *Monuments Piot*, XXIV, 1921.

11 *L'Influence du drame Christos Paschon sur l'art chrétien d'orient*, Paris, 1931. The subject is also dealt with more generally by her in *Le Théâtre à Byzance*, Paris, 1931, and by Bréhier, in *Journal des Savants*, Aug. and Sept. 1913.

12 See A. M. Friend, 'The Portraits of the Evangelists in Greek and Latin Manuscripts', *Art Studies*, v, 1927, p. 124. Lazarev lists a number of copies of the Gospels which he thinks should be associated with Constantinople in his 'Mosaics of Cefalù', *Art Bulletin*, XVII, 1935, p. 209, n. 47. See also Weitzmann, 'Das Evangelion in Skeuophylakion zu Lavra', *Seminarium Kondakovianum*, VIII, 1936, p. 83.

8   Panel Paintings

1   Pico Cellini, 'Una Madonna molto antica', *Proporzioni*, 1950, No. 3, with coloured plate.

2   G. and M. Sotiriou, *Icones du Mont Sinai*, Athens, 1958.

3   See A. J. Anisimov, *Our Lady of Vladimir*, Prague, 1928. For good illustrations of most of the other icons in Russia see Farbman, *Masterpieces of Russian Painting*, London, 1930.

4   See A. F. Kindersley, in a review of A. K. Coomaraswamy's 'The Transformation of Nature in Art', in *Journal of the Royal Central Asian Society*, XXII, Oct. 1935, p. 672.

5   See L. Bachhofer, 'Chinese Landscape Painting in the Eighth Century', *The Burlington Magazine*, LXVII, Nov. 1935, p. 189.

6 See S. Radojčić, *Icones de Serbie et de Macédoine*, Belgrade, 1961.

7 'Thirteenth Century Crusader Icons on Sinai', *Art Bulletin*, XLV, Sept. 1963.

8 It has thus been suggested that the highlights result from the curious lighting of the Cretan landscape, where the sun produces a similar effect upon the rocks. Actually, however, highlights were used in Roman times, and must have passed to Byzantine painting along with numerous other elements from the old Classical world.

9 *Mélanges Diehl*, Paris, 1930, II, Pls II and III.

10 B. Filow, *L'Ancien Art bulgare*, Paris, 1922, p. 65.

9 Major Sculpture

1 J. L'Orange, *Studien zur Geschichte des spätantiken Portraits*, Oslo, 1933, pp. 17 and 24. See also Haseloff, *Pre-Romanesque Sculpture in Italy*, Florence-Paris, 1930, chs 1 and 3.

2 For other sarcophagi of the type see J. Shapley, in *Art Bulletin*, V, 1922, p. 61.

3 Riegl was the first to suggest the idea of evolution in Rome; the most recent exponent of the thesis is Swift, *Roman Sources of Christian Art*. The protagonist of the Eastern theory was of course Strzygowski.

4 G. Mendel, *Catalogue du Musée de Brousse*, Athens, 1908, p. 35.

5 The two rear columns are usually considered to be medieval copies. Haseloff, however, thinks they are contemporary with the front ones, though by a weaker hand; *Pre-Romanesque Sculpture in Italy*, Florence-Paris, 1930, p. 27. He is probably correct.

6 Achthamar, as an Armenian and not a Byzantine building, is beyond the scope of this book, though it is of very great importance in any comparative study of East Christian sculpture. For illustrations and references see Strzygowski, *Origin of Christian Church Art*, p. 63. For the Trebizond reliefs see D. Talbot Rice, *The Church of Haghia Sophia at Trebizond*, Edinburgh, 1967.

7 See N. J. Giannopoulos and G. Millet, in *Bulletin de Correspondence Hellénique*, VII–IX, 1920, p. 181.

8 Haseloff, *Pre-Romanesque Sculpture in Italy*, p. 18.

10 Minor Sculpture

1 See E. Baldwin Smith, *Early Christian Iconography and the School of Provence*, Princeton, 1918.

2 For a distinction of the four see R. Hinks, *Carolingian Art*, London, 1935, p. 44. For a summary of the arguments for attribution to this or that centre see E. Baldwin Smith, in the *American Journal of Archaeology*, XXI, 1917, p. 22.

3 Especially by Morey, *Early Christian Art*, Princeton, 1942. But he tends to weaken his case by attributing so large a number of ivories to Alexandria.

4 Especially Haseloff, *Pre-Romanesque Sculpture in Italy*, p. 15.

5 *Kleinasien, ein Neuland von Kunstgeschichte*, Leipzig, 1903.

6 The case of a ninth-century date has been admirably set out by K. Weitzmann, *Greek Mythology in Byzantine Art*, Princeton, 1951.

7   *L'Empereur dans l'art byzantin*, Paris, 1936, p. 169.
8   For a study of these see C. Diehl, in *Art Studies*, v, 1927, p. 3.
9   See *Art byzantin chez les Slaves*, II, p. 55.

11   Metal Work

1   L. A. Matzoulevitch, *Die Byzantinische Antike*, Berlin, 1929, and *Une Sépulture d'un roi barbare en Europe orientale*, State publications, Moscow-Leningrad, 1934. Text in Russian with summary in French.
2   All these are illustrated in D. Talbot Rice, *The Art of Byzantium*, Nos 6/7, 75, 28/29, 43 and 69 respectively.
3   On one door was figured St Peter, on the other St Paul. See *Clavijo, Embassy to Tamerlane*, 1403–6, ed. G. Le Strange, Broadway Travellers Series, London, 1928, p. 269.
4   See Creswell, *Early Muslim Architecture*, I, for illustrations and a description of these.

12   Enamels

1   Barany Oberschall, 'The Crown of the Emperor Constantine Monomachos', *Archaeologica Hungarica*, XXII, Budapest, 1937.
2   See Grabar, *L'Empereur dans l'art byzantin*, Strasburg, 1936, Pl. xviii and p. 15.

13   Textiles

1   For an interesting study of the sources of the various techniques see R. Pfister, *Textiles de Palmyre*, Paris, 1934, and a review of the same by J. F. Flanagan, *Burlington Magazine*, LXVII, 1935, p. 92.
2   The Palmyra finds have been fully published by Pfister in a series of volumes. See *Textiles de Palmyre*, Paris, 1934; *Nouveaux textiles de Palmyre*, Paris, 1937. The importance of the role of Antioch has been stressed by P. Ackerman, in her chapter on the textiles in the *Survey of Persian Art*, Oxford, 1939, III.
3   For illustrations of most of these stuffs see Vollbach, Salles, Duthuit, *Art byzantin*, Paris, 1932.
4   *Art byzantin*, I, p. 92 and Pl. 155.
5   Schlumberger, *Epopée byzantine*, I, p. 155.

14   Ceramics and Glass

1   *Art byzantin*, I, Pl. 19.
2   Tolstoy and Kondakov, *Russian Antiquities*, St Petersburg, 1891, IV, p. 32 and Figs 24 and 25. The text is in Russian.
3   Vollbach, Salles, Duthuit, *Art byzantin*, Pl. 42b.
4   For drawings and a full discussion of such lamps, see Grace M. Crowfoot and D. B. Harden, 'Early Byzantine and Later Glass Lamps', *Journal of Egyptian Archaeology*, XVII, Pts iii and iv, 1931, p. 196.
5   They are illustrated by Peirce and Tyler, *Byzantine Art*, London, 1926, Pls. 60, 61, and 62.

6   W. de Grüneisen, *Catalogue de la Collection Grüneisen*, Paris, 1930, No. 151
    Pl. IX.
7   R. Schmidt, *Das Glas*, Berlin, 1922, abb. 18. He favours a Byzantine attribution,
    whereas C. J. Lamm, *Mittelalterliche Gläser* (in F. Sarre, *Forschungen zur
    islamischen Kunst*, vol. v, Berlin, 1929–30), Pl. 34, questions it. See also H. Peirce
    and R. Tyler, *Byzantine Art*, London, 1926, Pl. 94.
8   Pasini, *Il Tesoro di San Marco*, gives plates.
9   *Burlington Magazine*, LXVII, August 1935, p. 66.
10 See A. H. S. Megaw, 'Notes on recent work of the Byzantine Institute in
    Istanbul', *Dumbarton Oaks Papers*, XVII, 1964.
11 O. M. Dalton, *Catalogue of the Early Christian Antiquities in the British
    Museum*, 1901, Pl. xxxiii and p. 159.
12 For a summary of information regarding this group see D. Talbot Rice,
    'Miletus Ware', in *Faenza*, XXXIII, 1947, Fasc. iv–vi, p. 99.

15   Byzantium and the East

1   B. Filow, 'Les Palais vieux-bulgares et les palais sasanides', in *L'Art byzantin
    chez les Slaves*, Paris, 1930, I, p. 80.
2   'Orfèvrerie d'argent de style oriental trouvée en Bulgarie', *Syria*, III, Paris,
    1922, p. 141.
3   See D. Talbot Rice, 'The Leaved Cross', *Byzantinoslavica*, XI, Pt i, Prague,
    1950, p. 72.
4   D. Talbot Rice, 'The Oxford Excavations at Hira', *Antiquity*, VI, Sept. 1932,
    and *Ars Islamica*, I, p. 51, Ann Arbor, 1934.
5   *The Origin of the Plan of the Dome of the Rock*, British School of Archaeology
    in Jerusalem, Supp. Papers, No. 2, 1924.
6   Le Strange, *Baghdad during the Eastern Caliphate*, London, 1900, I, p. 14.
7   Rivoira, *Lombardic Architecture*, London, 1910, I, Fig. 150. One of the most
    important Persian examples is a carpet in the Musée des Arts Décoratifs in
    Paris, which was shown at the Persian Exhibition in London in 1931, No.
    130.

16   Byzantium and the Slavonic World

1   For a full account see G. Schlumberger, *Epopée byzantine*, I, p. 707.
2   The actual plans of the churches show certain variations in detail which were
    perhaps the result of influences from the Chersonese. E. H. Minns, *Scythians
    and Greeks*, Cambridge, 1913, p. 511, gives some small scale drawings of
    buildings in the Chersonese, as well as a full bibliography of writings on that
    region.
3   M. Alpatov, 'Die Fresken der Kachrieh-Djami in Konstantinopel', *Münchner
    Jahrbücher der bildenden Kunst*, 1929, VI, p. 343.
4   The most up-to-date account of Novgorodian art is that of V. Lazarev, *The Art
    of Novgorod*, Moscow, 1947 (in Russian). He stresses the importance of
    Constantinopolitan influence in the earlier wall paintings.
5   *L'Ancien Art serbe; Les Eglises*, Paris, 1919, p. 44.

17 Byzantium and the West

1 Ebersolt, *Orient et Occident*, I, p. 22, gives an entertaining legend about this painting.
2 R. A. S. Macalister, *Archaeology of Ireland*, 1928, p. 344.
3 But see M. L. W. Laisome, *Thought and Letters in Western Europe, 500–900*, 1957, ch. X.
4 See Puig i Cadafalch, *Le Premier Art roman*, Paris, 1928.
5 In Ireland the model belonged to the eastern or Syrian iconographical family, rather than to the Constantinopolitan, and the closest parallels are to be found in Cappadocia. See F. Henry, *La Sculpture irlandaise*, Paris, 1933, especially, pp. 13, 145, 163, 173, 175, and 190.
6 *The Ancient Cross Shafts at Bewcastle and at Ruthwell*, Cambridge, 1916, p. 19, note.
7 Schlumberger, *Epopée byzantine*, I, p. 440.
8 See his articles 'Byzantine Artists in Italy from the Sixth to the Fifteenth Century' and 'Byzantine Art and Culture in Rome and Italy', in *American Journal of Archaeology*, IX, 1894, p. 32, and X, 1895, p. 152. See also Diez and Demus, *Byzantine Mosaics in Greece*, p. 21.
9 R. Gerard, *Sur un Prieuré Bénédictin de la route des Pélerinages*, Paris, 1935, p. 38. See also F. Mercier, *Les Primitifs français*, Paris, 1931, p. 45.
10 See Joan Evans, *Cluniac Art of the Romanesque Period*, Cambridge, 1950, Figs 85–8.
11 Riant, *Des Dépouilles religieuses enlevées à Constantinople au treizième siècle*, Paris, 1865. Mém. de la Soc. des Ants. de la France, 4ème série, Tome VI.
12 Sandys, *A History of Classical Scholarship*, Cambridge, 1921, I, p. 561.
13 See P. Schweinfurth, 'Die Bedeutung der byzantinischen Kunst für die Stilbildung der Renaissance', in *Die Antike*, IX, 1933, Pt 2.

Bibliographies

1 Byzantium: the Historical Background

The best and most recent histories are those of G. Ostrogorsky, *History of the Byzantine State*, Oxford, 1956, and Vasiliev, *Histoire de l'Empire byzantin*, Paris, 1932, 2 vols; the American edition, published two years later, is not as complete. References to further works, and detailed bibliographies of special periods are given there. On a smaller scale S. Runciman's *Byzantine Civilization*, London, 1933, is most useful, and Robert Byron's *The Byzantine Achievement*, London, 1929, is extremely stimulating. The most satisfactory smaller books are Joan Hussey's *The Byzantine World*, London, 1957, and N. Baynes's *The Byzantine Empire*, in the Home University Library Series. There is also a useful outline in *The Cambridge Mediaeval History*, IV, 1966. *Byzantium*, Oxford, 1948, edited by Baynes and Moss, contains a short historical survey, as well as useful chapters on Orthodox Christianity, Monasticism, and kindred subjects.

2 The Geographical Basis of Byzantine Culture

The best and fullest work on the build of the land, its character and its climate, is still D. G. Hogarth's *The Nearer East*, London, 1920. For routes of communication see W. M. Ramsay, *The Historical Geography of Asia Minor*, London, 1890. An 'art-geography' of the Nearer East remains to be written.

3 The Origins of Byzantine Art

The problems are dealt with as a whole in all the great monographs on Byzantine art, notably O. M. Dalton, *Byzantine Art and Archaeology*, Oxford, 1911 (essentially a textbook), and *East Christian Art*, Oxford, 1925 (an essentially readable survey); C. Diehl, *Manuel d'art byzantin*, Paris, 1925; O. Wulff, *Altchristliche und Byzantinische Kunst*, Berlin, 1914.

The most convenient summaries of particular points of view will be found in J. Strzygowski, *Origin of Christian Church Art*, Oxford, 1923; C. Morey, *Early Christian Art*, Princeton, 1942; and E. H. Swift, *The Roman Sources of Christian Art*, New York, 1951. The best plates are to be found in H. Peirce and R. Tyler, *Art byzantin*, W. F. Volbach, *Frühchristliche Kunst*, Munich, 1958, and D. Talbot Rice, *The Art of Byzantium*, London, 1959.

563

4 The Architectural Background

Résumés of the subject are given in most architectural histories. More complete, however, is the survey in the first chapter of Dalton's *East Christian Art*, Oxford, 1925. See also J. A. Hamilton, *Byzantine Architecture and Decoration*, London, 1934, revised ed. 1956, and Simpson's *History of Architectural Development*, vol. II, *Early Christian Byzantine and Romanesque Architecture*, by Cecil Stewart, London, 1954. For the fundamental problems of origins it is necessary to consult the works of the original authorities. Strzygowski's theories are summarized in his *Origin of Christian Church Art*, Oxford, 1923; Rivoira's in *Lombardic Architecture*, 2nd ed., Oxford, 1933, and his *Moslem Architecture*, Oxford, 1918. The case for Syria is probably most fully put by Creswell in his *Early Muslim Architecture*, Oxford, 1932. More recently the problem has been surveyed by E. H. Swift, *The Roman Sources of Christian Art*, New York, 1951, though his conclusions are at times biased. Sounder, though shorter, is J. B. Ward Perkins's paper, 'The Italian element in late Roman and early Mediaeval Architecture', *Proceedings of the British Academy*, XXXIII, 1947.

The numerous more particular studies of regions or special groups are cited in the manuals, but a few of special importance may be noted here, namely G. Millet, *L'Ecole grecque dans l'architecture byzantine*, Paris, 1916; Lethaby and Swainson, *Santa Sophia*, London, 1894; and E. van Millingen, *Byzantine Churches in Constantinople*, London, 1912.

5 Byzantine Mosaics

Mosaics are fully dealt with in the principal manuals on Byzantine art already cited, namely those of Dalton, Diehl, and Wulff. In addition the most useful general work is probably that of M. Van Berchem and E. Clouzot, *Mosaïques chrétiennes*, Geneva, 1924. There are numerous monographs on particular buildings or areas, most important of which are: for Italy: E. Wilpert, *Die römischen Mosaiken und Malereien der kirchlichen Bauten vom 4. bis 13. Jahrhundert*, 1917; and C. Errard, *L'Art byzantin d'après les monuments de l'Italie, de l'Istrie et de la Dalmatie*, Paris, c. 1910, and also several more recent works by G. Bovini. For Greece: E. Diez and O. Demus, *Byzantine Mosaics in Greece*, Harvard, 1931; and Diehl, Saladin, and Le Tourneau, *Les Monuments chrétiens de Salonique*, Paris, 1918. For Nicaea: O. Wulff, *Die Koimesiskirche in Nicaia*, Strasburg, 1903; and T. Schmidt, *Die Koimesis-Kirche von Nikaia*, Berlin and Leipzig, 1927. For Constantinople: P. Underwood, *The Kariye Djami*, Pantheon Books, 1966, for the fullest account of Kariye Camii, and *The Mosaics of Haghia Sophia at Istanbul*, by T. Whittemore, Oxford, 1933, 1936, 1942, and 1952. For Sicily: O. Demus, *The Mosaics of Norman Sicily*, London, 1949, and E. Kitzinger, *The Mosaics of Monreale*, Palermo, 1961.

For miniature mosaics, in addition to the Manuals, see D. Talbot Rice, 'New Lights on Byzantine Portative Mosaics', in *Apollo*, XVIII, 1933, p. 265, and O. Demus, 'Byzantinische Mosaikminiaturen', in *Phaidros*, Folge 3, Wien, 1947.

564

A most important volume, with superb plates in colour, was published in 1953 by Skira, with text by A. Grabar, under the title *Byzantine Painting*. See also D. Talbot Rice, *The Art of Byzantium*, London, 1959.

6 Wall Paintings

Full bibliographies are given in the manuals cited, namely Dalton, Diehl, and Wulff. See also Muratov, *La Peinture byzantine*, Paris, 1928, and Diehl, *La Peinture byzantine*, Paris, 1932, for general summaries, and for the Renaissance Millet, *Iconographie de l'Evangile*, Paris, 1916. Millet's chapters in Michel, *Histoire de l'art*, I, Paris, 1905, are also important. A novel aspect of Byzantine painting, which throws light on the Byzantine theatre, is brought out in Madame Cottas's book, *L'Influence du drame Christos Paschon sur l'art chrétien d'Orient*, Paris, 1931. See R. Byron and D. Talbot Rice, *The Birth of Western Painting*, London, 1930, for a critical appreciation, and Grabar, *Byzantine Painting*, Skira, 1953, for illustrations in colour. The best coloured reproductions, however, are to be found in the large Unesco volumes on Yugoslavia, Bulgaria, Rumania, and Cyprus.

The following are the more important works dealing with special regions. All these contain fuller bibliographies.

Italy

    R. van Marle, *The Development of the Italian Schools of Painting*, I, The Hague, 1923. E. Bertaux, *L'art dans l'Italie méridionale*, Paris, 1904. Anthony, *Romanesque Frescoes*, Princeton, 1951.

Syria

    C. Breasted, *Oriental Forerunners of Byzantine Painting*, Yale, 1924. C. R. Morey, *Mediaeval Art*, New York, 1942. Rostovtzev, *Dura-Europos and its Art*, Oxford, 1938.

Egypt

    W. de Gruneisen, *Les Caractéristiques de l'art copte*, Florence, 1922.

Asia Minor

    G. de Jerphanion, *Les Eglises rupestres de la Cappadoce*, Paris, 1923–42. N. and M. Thierry, *Nouvelles Eglises rupestres de Cappadoce*, Paris, 1963. D. Talbot Rice, *The Church of Haghia Sophia at Trebizond*, Edinburgh, 1968.

Bulgaria

    A. Grabar, *La Peinture religieuse en Bulgarie*, Paris, 1928. B. Filow, *L'Ancien Art bulgare*, Berne, 1919. A smaller edition was published in Paris in 1922, and in Germany in 1932.

Yugoslavia

    V. R. Petković, *La Peinture serbe du Moyen Age*, Belgrade, 1930. N. Okunev, *Monumenta Artis Serbicae*, 4 albums, 1928–32. An exhibition of facsimiles which was held in Paris in 1949. See *L'Art byzantin chez les Slaves*, ed. by G. Millet, Paris, 1932, S. Radojčić, *Mileševa*, Belgrade, 1963, and V. J. Djurić, *Sopoćani*, Belgrade, 1963.

Rumania

    Iorga and Bals, *L'Art roumain*, Paris, 1922. Henri, *Les Eglises de la Moldavia du Nord*, Paris, 1931. Stefanescu, *L'Evolution de la peinture religieuse en Bucovine et en Moldavie*, Paris, 1928, and other works.

Constantinople

See preliminary reports by P. A. Underwood, in *Dumbarton Oaks Papers*, nos 9ff., and also *The Kariye Djami*, 1966.

Mistra

Millet, *Monuments byzantins de Mistra*, Paris, 1910.

Athos

Millet, *Monuments de l'Athos*, Paris, 1927. F. Dölger, E. Wiegand, and A. Deindl, *Mönchsland Athos*, Munich, 1945.

Cyprus

G. Sotiriou, *Byzantine Monuments of Cyprus*, Athens, 1935 (in Greek). So far only vol. II, the plates, has appeared.

Trebizond

G. Millet and D. Talbot Rice, *Byzantine Painting at Trebizond*, London, 1936.

7 Manuscript Illustrations

Chapters on the manuscripts appear in the various manuals, where references to earlier specialized works are given. In addition the following may be cited, either because of their importance as general works or because of their fairly recent publication. Ebersolt, *La Miniature byzantine*, Paris, 1926; Gerstinger, *Die griechische Buchmalerei*, Wien, 1926; and K. Weitzmann, *Die byzantinische Buchmalerei des 9. und 10. Jahrhunderts*, Berlin, 1935, are the most important general works. Relevant chapters in J. A. Herbert's *Illuminated Manuscripts*, London, 1911, though in some ways out of date, are useful. K. Weitzmann's books on the ninth century, though they raise a number of very contentious problems, are also of outstanding importance. They comprise *Illustrations in Roll and Codex*, Princeton, 1947; *The Joshua Roll*, Princeton, 1948; and *Greek Mythology in Byzantine Art*, Princeton, 1951. J. J. Tikkanen's *Studien über die Farbengebung in der mittelalterlichen Buchmalerei*, edited by Tancred Borenius, Helsingfors, 1933, is also useful. Of outstanding importance, of course, are the various volumes of facsimiles issued by the great libraries, notably Omont, *Miniatures des manuscrits grecs de la Bibliothèque Nationale*, Paris, 1929. For Armenian manuscripts see especially S. der Nersessian, *Armenia and the Byzantine Empire*, Harvard, 1945, where references to more extensive researches by herself and Macler are given. There are excellent colour plates in L. A. Dournovo, *Armenian Miniatures*, London, 1961.

8 Panel Paintings

The most important general study of the subject is that of Wulff and Alpatov, *Denkmäler der Ikonmalerei*, Dresden, 1925. For an outline in which Greece is considered as well as Russia, see N. P. Kondalov, *The Russian Icon*, translated and edited by E. H. Minns, Oxford, 1927. The Prague edition of the same work is more fully illustrated with a magnificent series of plates, but is in Russian.

There is no single book on Greek icons, though articles on individual panels or groups of paintings are numerous. Xyngopoulos's *Catalogue of the Icons*, Benaki Museum, 1936 (in Greek), is probably the most important. Sotiriou's

Guide du Musée byzantin d'Athènes may also be noted. See also D. Talbot Rice, *Byzantine Icons*, London, 1959, and G. and M. Sotiriou, *Icones du Mont Sinai*, Athens, 1958.

Books on Russian icons are comparatively numerous. For a short summary, with illustrations in colour, see the writer's King Penguin, *Russian Icons*, London, 1947. For a fuller study see Kondakov, as above, and M. Farbman, *Masterpieces of Russian Painting*, London, 1930. The most recent material has been collected by Lazarev and is incorporated in his important *History of Byzantine Painting*, Moscow, 1947 (in Russian). See also T. Talbot Rice, *Russian Icons*, London, 1963, and K. Onasch, *Icons*, London, 1962.

Cyprus has been dealt with as a whole by the writer and others in *The Icons of Cyprus*, London, 1937.

9 Major Sculpture

Apart from chapters in the manuals, the most useful general works are Bréhier's *La Sculpture et les arts mineurs*, Paris, 1936, and an article on sculpture in the Italian *Encyclopedia of Art*, Rome and New York, 1959 ff. For the early period there are admirable illustrations and most useful notes upon them in Peirce and Tyler, *Art byzantin*, Paris, 1932 and 1934. The material found in Constantinople is mostly dealt with in G. Mendel, *Catalogue des Sculptures du Musée Ottoman*, Constantinople, 1912–14; for finds made subsequently see Arif Mufid, in *Archaeologischer Anzeiger*, 1931. For material at Athens see G. Sotiriou, *Guide du Musée byzantin d'Athènes*, 1932. The most important work on later Byzantine sculpture is that of Bréhier, published as two articles, firstly 'Étude sur la sculpture byzantine', in *Nouvelles Archives des Missions scientifiques*, n.s., fasc. 3, xx, 1911, and secondly, 'Nouvelles recherches', in xxi, fasc. 3, 1916, of the same periodical. For illustrations see also D. Talbot Rice, *The Art of Byzantium*, London, 1959.

10 Minor Sculpture

In addition to chapters in the manuals and Moray's important *Early Christian Art*, Princeton, 1942, the most important work on the earlier ivories is Delbrueck's *Die Consulardiptychen*, Berlin and Leipzig, 1929. There are also admirable plates and useful descriptions and discussions in Peirce and Tyler, *L'Art byzantin*, I and II, Paris, 1932 and 1934. The most useful work on a smaller scale is W. F. Volbach, *Elfenbeinarbeiten der Spätantike und des frühen Mittelalters*, Mainz, 1952. For the ivories of the middle and later periods the standard work is Goldschmidt and Weitzmann, *Die byzantinischen Elfenbein-skulpturen des 10. bis 13. Jahrhunderts*, Berlin, 1913. Miss Longhurst's *Catalogue of Carvings in Ivory in the Victoria and Albert Museum*, Part I, 1927, also contains a great deal of useful information. Large numbers of ivories and steatites are illustrated in Schlumberger's *Epopée byzantine*, though the book is primarily a history, and there are useful plates also in Vollbach, Salles, and Duthuit, *Art byzantin*, Paris, c. 1932, and in D. Talbot Rice, *The Art of Byzantium*, London, 1959.

11 Metal Work

For the early silver plate see especially O. M. Dalton, *Catalogue of the Early Christian Antiquities in the British Museum*, 1901; Ebersolt, 'Le Trésor de Struma', in *Revue Archéologique*, XVII, 1911, ii, p. 407; and Bréhier, 'Les Trésors d'argenterie syrienne et l'école artistique d'Antioch', in *Gazette des Beaux Arts*, 1920. Excellent illustrations of the earlier metal work appear in Peirce and Tyler, *L'Art byzantin*, vols I and II. See also D. Talbot Rice, *The Art of Byzantium*, London, 1959, and E. Cruikshank-Dodd, *Byzantine Silver Stamps*, Dumbarton Oaks Studies, No. 7, Harvard, 1961.

For the middle period, apart from the manuals, the most important book is certainly Ebersolt's *Les Arts somptuaires de Byzance*, Paris, 1923; see also his *Les Sanctuaires de Byzance*, Paris, 1921. There are also good plates in Vollbach, Salles, and Duthuit, *Art byzantin*, Paris, 1932. For the treasury of St Mark's see Pasini, *Il Tesoro di San Marco*, Venice, 1185–7.

The fullest publication on coins is Wroth, *Catalogue of Imperial Byzantine Coins in the British Museum*. Sabatier's *Description générale des monnaies byzantines*, 1862, is of first importance, but is practically unprocurable. On a smaller scale, but extremely useful, is H. Goodacre's *Handbook of the Coinage of the Byzantine Empire*, published by Spink and Son, London, 1933.

The standard work on the seals is Schlumberger, *Sigillographie byzantine*. C. H. Constantinopoulos, *Byzantine Lead Seals*, Athens, 1930, is more up to date, but it is in modern Greek.

12 Enamels

N. P. Kondakov's *Histoire et monuments des émaux byzantins*, St Petersburg, 1892, is the standard work, but it includes a number of examples which have since been shown to be forgeries, so that the chapters in the manuals are now probably more useful. See also J. Ebersolt's *Les Arts somptuaires de Byzance*, Paris, 1923. Though they deal only with particular examples, Dalton's publication of the Pierpont Morgan enamels, *Burlington Magazine*, XXI, 1912, pp. 3, 65, 127, 219, and 290, and that of the Budapest crown by Barany Oberschall, 'The Crown of the Emperor Constantine Monomachos', *Archaeologica Hungarica*, XXII, Budapest, 1937, are both of general importance. C. Amiranashvili, *Les Emaux de Géorgie*, Paris, 1964.

13 Textiles

No monograph on Byzantine textiles exists, and it is to be doubted if enough material is as yet available to furnish any more than the illustrations. There are, however, admirable plates of the earlier stuffs in Peirce and Tyler's *Art byzantin*, and of the later ones in the book with the same title by Vollbach, Salles and Duthuit. Von Falke's great book, *Kunstgeschichte der Seidenweberei*, first published in two volumes in 1913, but reissued in a single volume in 1921, also contains valuable plates, and its text is of primary importance, even if many of his identifications can no longer be relied upon. Ebersolt's *Les Arts somptuaires de Byzance*, Paris, 1923, also contains valuable material, and Chartraire's 'Tissus anciens du Trésor de la Cathédrale de Sens', in *Revue de l'art chrétien*, 1911, p. 277, should also be consulted. The question of centres of manufacture for the Orientalizing stuffs is also fully discussed by P. Ackerman, in the chapter on textiles in the *Survey of Persian Art*, Oxford, 1939, III. For Egypt the bibliography is fuller; the most important works are probably Vollbach and Kuehnel, *Late Antique, Coptic and Islamic Textiles of Egypt in the German State Museum*, Berlin, 1920, and the four volumes of the *Victoria and Albert Museum Catalogue*, by A. F. Kendrick. R. Pfister's works on the textiles of Palmyra are also important, especially his *Textiles de Palmyre*, Paris, 1934, and his *Nouveaux Textiles de Palmyre*, Paris, 1937. For the later embroideries see G. Millet *Broderies religieuses de style byzantin*, Paris, 1947.

14   Ceramics and Glass

For Byzantine glass it is necessary to turn to works which deal with glass as a whole, such as R. Schmidt, *Das Glas*, Berlin, 1922, rather than to manuals on Byzantine art, which, except for material on the *fonde d'oro*, are by no means up to date. The most complete work on the pottery as a whole is the writer's *Byzantine Glazed Pottery*, Oxford, 1930, where a full bibliography is given. The material there included has been brought up to date so far as the polychrome ware is concerned in an article by the writer, 'Byzantine Polychrome Pottery; a Survey of Recent Discoveries', in *Cahiers Archéologiques*, VII, Paris, 1954. See also R. B. Stevenson, in *The Great Palace of the Byzantine Emperors*, Oxford, 1945. See also D. Talbot Rice, 'The Pottery of Byzantium and the Islamic World', in *Studies in Islamic Art and Architecture in Honour of Professor K. A. C. Creswell*, American University of Cairo, 1965.

15   Byzantium and the East

For the history of the Omayyad period the most important works from our point of view are those of Père Lammens, the more outstanding of which are collected in his *Etudes sur le siècle des Omayyades*, Beyrouth, 1930. For that of the Abassid period see Vasiliev, *Byzantines and Arabs*, originally published in Russian in St Petersburg in 1902, but reissued, partly in French and partly in German, in Brussels in 1935. A useful bibliography under the title 'Bollettino byzantoarabico' was published by M. Guidi in *Byzantion*, VII, fasc. 2, 1931, p. 396.

For information regarding artistic links see the chapter, 'Byzantium and Persia', by the writer, in *The Legacy of Persia*, Oxford, 1953, and also his 'Iranian elements in Byzantine Art', *Troisième Congrès international d'art et d'archéologie Iraniens*, 1935, Moscow-Leningrad, 1939.

16   Byzantium and the Slavonic World

Literature on Russia in Russian is extensive; of works in Western languages the most useful are L. Réau, *L'Art russe*, I, Paris, 1921, M. Alpatov and N. Brunov,

Geschichte der altrussischen Kunst, Augsburg, 1932, and T. Talbot Rice, *Russian Art*, London (Penguin Books), 1949, and *Concise History of Russian Art*, London, 1963.

For Bulgaria see B. Filow, *Geschichte der altbulgarischen Kunst*, Berlin and Leipzig, 1933. Serbian architecture is dealt with by G. Millet in his *L'Ancien Art serbe; Les Eglises*, Paris, 1919; the fullest work on the paintings is Petkovic's *La Peinture serbe du moyen âge*, Belgrade, 1930, but a clearer impression of the quality of the work is given by the coloured plates of the Unesco volume on Yugoslav art, with introduction by S. Radojčić and preface by D. Talbot Rice. See also Vercors, *L'Art médiéval yougoslave*, Paris, 1950. The Rumanian paintings have been fully published, notably by I. D. Stefanescu, in a series of volumes published in Paris. See also Iorga and Bals, *L'Art roumain*, Paris, 1922. See also the Unesco volume by A. Grabar and G. Oprescu.

For articles on various branches of art in the Balkans and in Russia see *L'Art byzantin chez les Slaves*, ed. G. Millet, Paris, 1930.

17   Byzantium and the West

One of the first to appreciate the immensity of the debt of the West to Byzantium was Lethaby: see his *Mediaeval Art*, originally published in 1904, but reissued, edited by the present writer, in 1949, and W. Oakeshott, *Classical Inspiration in Mediaeval Art*, London, 1959. For the historical links, the most useful general work is probably C. Dawson's *The Making of Europe*, London, 1932; and for a summary of the artistic ones J. Ebersolt's *Orient et Occident*, I, Paris, 1928, and II, Paris, 1929, has not been bettered. For the later period see R. Byron and D. Talbot Rice, *The Birth of Western Painting*, London, 1930.

In addition to these more general works, particular aspects of the question have been dealt with in various specialized articles in periodicals. The following are some of the more important: Halpen, 'La cour d'Otton III à Rome', *Ecole française de Rome, Mélanges d'archéologie*, XXVI, 1905; J. Gay, 'L'abbaye de Cluny et Byzance du début du XIIme siècle', *Echos d'Orient*, XXX, 1931, No. 161; Gasquet, *L'Empire byzantin et la monarchie franque*, Paris, 1888. For links with Saxon England see the writer's *English Art, 871–1100*, Oxford, 1952, and for general information C. R. Morey, *Mediaeval Art*, New York, 1942, *passim*.

Index

More about Penguins and Pelicans

Penguin Book News, an attractively illustrated magazine which appears every month, contains details of all the new books issued by Penguins as they are published. Every four months it is supplemented by *Penguins in Print*, which is a complete list of all books published by Penguins which are still available. (There are well over two thousand of these.)

A specimen copy of *Penguin Book News* can be sent to you free on request, and you can become a regular subscriber at 3s for twelve issues (with the complete lists). Just write to Dept EP, Penguin Books Ltd, Harmondsworth, Middlesex, enclosing a cheque or postal order, and your name will be added to the mailing list.

Some other books published by Penguins are described on the following pages.

Note: *Penguin Book News* and *Penguins in Print* are not available in the U.S.A. or Canada

Early Christian and Byzantine Architecture

Richard Krautheimer

This volume of the Pelican History of Art, written by the
foremost authority in the world, presents Early Christian
and Byzantine architecture not merely as a prelude, or a
counterpart, to Western medieval building, but primarily
as an outgrowth of Roman architecture in its different
aspects and as determined by changing liturgical require-
ments. Roman civic architecture survives in the Early
Christian basilica throughout the Empire from Constantine
to Justinian. Simultaneously the principles of vaulted
architecture of the Late Empire survive and increasingly
determine the character of church building in Byzantium
and throughout the East from Justinian until the fall of
Constantinople and beyond. The demands of the liturgy
modify the basic types. Combined with changing aesthetic
concepts they lead to the wealth of architectural designs
in the various provinces of the Roman-Christian and
Byzantine world. Text and illustrations introduce the
reader to some of the most moving buildings ever erected.

Fourteen Byzantine Rulers

Michael Psellus

Translated by E. R. A. Sewter

Fourteen Byzantine Rulers is a new translation of the
Chronographia, which forms the principal source of the
history of the Eastern Empire during the period (A.D.
976–1078) when Byzantium declined from a military power
to an effete bureaucracy. The Christian scholar Psellus,
who was adviser, friend, and tutor to successive emperors,
used his first-hand acquaintance with the politics of the
imperial court to write a memoir of his own times. A keen
student of Plato and the Greeks, he turned his account into
a work of art which vividly illustrates the Byzantine
way of life.

Chronicles of the Crusades

Villehardouin and Joinville

Translated by Margaret R. B. Shaw
This volume contains two famous French chronicles.
Villehardouin's *Conquest of Constantinople* presents a
reasonably objective history of the Fourth Crusade, which
ironically turned into an assault on the Christians of the
Orthodox Church. Joinville's *Life of Saint Louis*, on the
other hand, is more like a travel book than a biography
in its simple and human wonder at the courage of men
and all the curiosities which the author witnessed during
the Seventh Crusade.

The colloquial modern English of these new translations,
by Margaret Shaw, brings the thirteenth century very
close to our times.

A History of the Crusades
(*in three volumes*)

Steven Runciman

'*The best history of the Crusades in English*'

'Whether we regard the Crusades as the most tremendous
and most romantic of Christian adventures, or as the last
of the barbarian invasions, they form a central fact in
medieval history. Before their inception the centre of our
civilization was placed in Byzantium and in the lands of
the Arab caliphate. Before they faded out the hegemony
in civilization had passed to Western Europe. Out of this
transformation Modern History was born. . . .'

In chronicling this transformation Sir Steven Runciman
has written a book which, from beginning to end, enthrals
the layman as completely as it satisfies the historian. The
excitement of battle, the horror of senseless massacre,
the interplay of personalities and ambitions, the effect on
the whole development of European history – these are
his themes. As he rightly states: 'The whole tale is one
of faith and folly, courage and greed, hope and disillusion.'

Vol. 1: *The First Crusade*
Vol. 2: *The Kingdom of Jerusalem*
Vol. 3: *The Kingdom of Acre*

European Painting and Sculpture

Eric Newton

The object of this book, which has been completely
revised, is to provide a short account of the development
of the fine arts, and in particular of painting, in Europe
from the earliest times to the present day. The author's
aims have been three – brevity, continuity, and a sense of
proportion. Each artist or group of artists is treated not
as an isolated phenomenon but as a link in the chain
of tradition, with the emphasis rather on the strength, the
shape, and the direction of the chain at each point in its
evolution than on the individual link. The author's
personal sense of what is important, on which a sense of
proportion must depend, is clearly conveyed; nevertheless
the reader who does not share his tastes will not find the
book invalidated on this account. In order to achieve
brevity and avoid restating fundamental principles
throughout the book, the opening chapters contain a brief
exposition of the author's attitude to works of art in
general and an explanation of the characteristics of
European art as a whole.

This book contains 32 pages of plates.

An Outline of European Architecture

Nikolaus Pevsner

This seventh revised edition of Nikolaus Pevsner's classic
history is presented in an entirely new and attractive style.
The format has been enlarged and the illustrations appear
next to the passages to which they refer. Their numbers
have swelled to nearly 300, including drawings, plans, and
photographs. The final chapter of the Penguin Jubilee
edition (published in 1960 and still available at £7 7s) has
been incorporated, carrying the story from 1914 to the present
day, and there are substantial additions on the sixteenth to
eighteenth centuries in France as well as many minor
revisions. The book tells the story of architecture by
concentrating on outstanding buildings, and reads
exceedingly well in its concentration and its combination
of warmth and scholarship.

Style and Civilization

This series interprets the important styles in European
art in the broadest context of the civilization and thought
of their times. It aims, in this way, to achieve a deeper
understanding of their character and motivation.

PRE-CLASSICAL

John Boardman

The power and personality of King Minos or Agamemnon
are shrouded in legend. But from the art and artefacts
that have survived we can begin to draw pictures of the
real quality of life in the Bronze Age palaces of Crete or
Mycenae, or in the world of Archaic Greece after the
Dark Ages. This book portrays through the forms and
subjects of their art the civilizations that stand at the
beginnings of the Western tradition.

GOTHIC

George Henderson

Notre Dame or Canterbury, exquisite illumination, stern
sculpture or the stained glass of Chartres – the rich and
complex nature of Gothic art has always fascinated us.
Every age has held its own vision of the Gothic world – a
world of barbarism, or of chivalry, or of piety. Here is
an attempt to reach a deeper understanding of the Gothic
style by examining its many forms in the context of contemporary religious or philosophical attitudes, and against
the background of the social and political order of the
Middle Ages.

EARLY RENAISSANCE

Michael Levey

Humanity and the human form dominate Early Renaissance art – from the intensely realistic figures sculpted by Donatello and portrayed by Van Eyck to the sophisticated beings created by Dürer or Leonardo. New techniques, discovery of visual perspective, fresh interest in the antique past, all combined to make art a fully rational activity, incorporating truths of human nature and the universe. In place of Gothic mystery came clarity – reflected in the calmly ordered space of Renaissance buildings. This book emphasizes that persistent preference for sober, logical, harmonious art – true to experience and yet optimistic – which characterizes the Early Renaissance.

MANNERISM

John Shearman

The refinement of Benvenuto Cellini's golden salt cellar or the monstrous fantasies of the Boboli Gardens in Florence – both are characteristic of Mannerism, a virtuoso style of life and art that intervened between Renaissance and Baroque in the sixteenth century. Mannerism was perhaps the most self-consciously 'stylish' of all styles – in literature, music and the visual arts alike. In the way that we have once again come to appreciate *art nouveau* so it is again possible for us to understand the spirit and beauty of Mannerist art.

The Architect and Society

The aim of this series, specially written for Penguin
Books, is to present the great architects of the world in
their social and cultural environments.

PALLADIO

James S. Ackerman

Palladio is the most imitated architect in history. His
buildings have been copied all over the Western world –
from Leningrad to Philadelphia – and his ideas on
proportion are still current nearly four hundred years after
his death. In this, the first full account of his career to be
published in English, Professor James Ackerman investi-
gates the reasons for his enormous and enduring success.
He presents him in his historical setting as the contemporary of Titian, Tintoretto, and Veronese, but is constantly
alert to his relevance for us today.

INIGO JONES

John Summerson

Inigo Jones was the first English classical architect, famous
in his own time (he was nine years junior to Shakespeare)
and the posthumous sponsor of the Palladianism of the
eighteenth century.

In this revolutionary book Sir John Summerson
clears away a mass of legend in order to direct attention to
the essential Inigo, basing a new assessment of his genius
on the evidence of buildings and designs of undoubted
authenticity. While the Queen's House at Greenwich and
the famous Whitehall Banqueting House receive due
acknowledgement, such long lost works as the Covent
Garden *piazza* and the transformation of old St Paul's are
shown, after rigorous examination of the records, to be
even more eloquent of their architect's philosophy. Inigo
Jones emerges as a unique figure in the Europe of his time
and an architect of fundamental importance.